ARGENTINA

A Tale of Two Utopias

Anarchism, Soccer, Neoliberalism

Tomas Rothaus

PM

Argentina, a Tale of Two Utopias: Anarchism, Soccer, Neoliberalism
© 2026 Tomas Rothaus
This edition © 2026 PM Press

ISBN: 979–8–88744–147–4 (paperback)
ISBN: 979–8–88744–148–1 (ebook)
Library of Congress Control Number: 2025935754

Interior design by briandesign

10 9 8 7 6 5 4 3 2 1

PM Press
PO Box 23912
Oakland, CA 94623
www.pmpress.org

Printed in the USA.

Praise for *Argentina, a Tale of Two Utopias*

"*Argentina, a Tale of Two Utopias* weaves complicated histories of anarchism, football, resistance, and everyday life in Buenos Aires into an artful narrative of youthful exuberance and political turmoil. As opposition boils up again today in Argentina, this riveting snapshot of popular outrage from below presents readers with a fascinating point of inflection to connect general strikes and dreams of revolution, past and present."
—Mark Bray, author of *Antifa: The Anti-Fascist Handbook*

"In this beautifully narrated book, Rothaus lovingly historicizes the development and violent suppression of anarchist movements, spaces, and traditions (from the names of pastries to storied prison breaks), the history of numerous football clubs and antifascist ultras who continue to keep those traditions alive, and the author's own story of discovering radical politics. The histories of anarchist presses, social centers, and uprisings are told alongside the foundation of anarchist sports clubs like Club Atlético Libertad, El Porvenir, and (the GOAT) Diego Maradona's first club, Argentinos Juniors of La Paternal. From syndicalism to the touchline and back again."
—Andreas Petrossiants, Stop Cop City United
and coauthor of *Diversity of Aesthetics*

"*A Tale of Two Utopias* is a gripping, firsthand chronicle of resistance, rebellion, and the enduring influence of anarchist ideals in Argentina. Blending the fervor of urban battles with the collective, almost psychedelic ecstasy of football triumph, this book unfurls the downtrodden radical history that shaped a nation's struggles and dreams. With vivid storytelling and acerbic political insight, it offers a crucial lens on the 2001 uprising—an event that continues to echo in today's fight against neoliberalism and its proto-fascist offspring. A must-read for anyone seeking to understand how the passions of the past inform the revolutions of the future."
—Oli Mould, author of *Against Creativity* and
Seven Ethics Against Capitalism

"Nothing excites stronger feelings than sports and politics. If you are passionate about one of them, read this book: It will help you understand why people are so passionate about the other."
—CrimethInc. Writers' Bloc

dedicado a quienes fueron la chispa de la rebelión
para juntxs ser el fuego
deseando que sus llamas arrasen todo a su alrededor
al calor de la venganza y la liberación
para sobre la tierra arrasada construir el mundo nuevo

dedicado a quienes fueron, son, y serán
la dignidad rebelde

a todxs nuestrxs combatientes

★

dedicated to those who were the spark of rebellion
who found each other to become fire
so that its flames sweep away everything in their path
in the heat of revenge and liberation
to build atop the scorched earth the new world

dedicated to those who were, are, and will be
the dignity of rebellion

to all our combatants

Contents

Foreword

Gabriel Kuhn

In the summer of 2023, a friend and I interviewed a number of left-wing radicals who had come to Sweden in the 1970s fleeing the military dictatorships of Chile, Uruguay, and Argentina. When we interviewed a former ERP militant (you'll learn more about this Trotskyite guerrilla group in the book at hand), we asked her whether there was a lot of talk about politics in her family when she was growing up. She looked bewildered. "Don't you know that Argentinean families talk about two things only? Politics and football!"

You'll get to read a lot about football in this book. Yet, as the anecdote above was meant to clarify, it's not a random pet interest of the author that you have to accept if you want to know what he has to say about Argentina. It's an *inherent part* of what he has to say about Argentina—and what a lot of people would have to say about the country.

It also means that you don't have to like football (although it probably helps) to learn something (a lot!) from this book. All you need is an interest in Argentina and politics, particularly radical politics.

At the heart of this publication is the Argentinean uprising of December 2001, which toppled the government and was the apex of months of civil unrest. It was an ecstatic moment for the author, as it was for thousands (millions?) of others, despite the tragic losses it implied, and it's worth recalling the event just to remember, "No, we don't always lose!"

However, this book is about much more than the December 2001 uprising. It tells the story of a country with such a rich political history that, for better or worse, it often serves as a microcosm of geopolitical developments. Tomas chronicles the fascinating history of Argentina's anarchist movement and reflects on its revolutionary potential and relationship to the broader left. He also traces the history of the countercurrent, the fascist forces that have seized power in the country all too often.

Sadly, the latter is a reality far from over. Far-right libertarian Javier Milei—part goofball, part lunatic—winning the presidential election in Argentina in November 2023 was a brutal reminder of it. Tomas has dedicated two appendixes to this development, which, once again, shows the pivotal role that a Latin American country can play for political developments the world over. The 1973 coup in Chile, when the military, backed by the US, ousted and caused the death of the democratically elected socialist president Salvador Allende, was an event with tremendous international ripple effects. The regime that followed, led by General Augusto Pinochet, served as a test laboratory for the neoliberalism that has had an almost uninterrupted run of success around the globe since then. Are we about to witness something similar again?

A mere eight years ago, I translated a book about the extreme right in the US, authored by Matthew N. Lyons from the *Three Way Fight* blog, into German. Lyons, who later expanded the book into the volume *Insurgent Supremacists: The U.S. Far Right's Challenge to State and Empire* (2018), dedicated a chapter to national and free-market anarchists. I am ready to admit that I thought it unnecessary to include such obscure tendencies, since, clearly, they were a fringe phenomenon with no prospect of any long-lasting political significance. When Lyons wrote that they could serve "as a bridge to bring together different right (and even non-right) tendencies," I believed he was exaggerating. I was wrong. He wasn't exaggerating, he was dead on the money. Javier Milei brings together tropes that right-wingers in Europe are still struggling to combine: gung-ho libertarian economic policies and traditional nationalist, chauvinist, and fascist convictions. If this is an image of the future, it is terrifying.

Argentina, a Tale of Two Utopias makes the dangers we are facing perfectly clear. But it also illustrates what is needed for the future to look much brighter. Written in a way so engaging that it causes jealousy in anyone putting pen to paper themselves, this book entertains, educates, and inspires.

With all that said, I don't agree with everything. Water polo is, in fact, a pretty good sport—even if, in this case, Argentina isn't a contender for the world championship crown.

Racing Club vs. Vélez Sarsfield

Amalfitani Stadium, Liniers, Buenos Aires, December 27, 2001, Early Afternoon

La locura me hizo entrar en tu camino	*Madness put me down your path*
la distancia no me puede importar	*distances can't matter*
es que sin vos, a mi canción le falta el alma	*without you, my song has no soul*

—El Bordo, "La banda"

On Thursday, December 27, 2001, the country was on fire. Now-former President Fernando de la Rúa had fled the presidential palace in a helicopter only a few days earlier, and the memory of the 38 deaths at the hands of the repression against the social uprising was fresh. Nonetheless, in the midst of that chaotic scene, the ball rolled on.

—*Clarín* newspaper, December 27, 2016

The sky has turned a menacingly dark shade of gray inside of a few short minutes. Before we know it, it's pouring pebble-sized hail down on the visitors' section of the Estadio José Amalfitani on Buenos Aires's west side and onto the heads of the fifteen thousand or so of us who have managed to get our hands on the golden ticket to be here this December 27 in the afternoon, turning our section of the stadium into a sea of light-blue-and-white flags and banners, fireworks, and balloons. Another forty thousand, those unable to secure tickets to witness this historic match in person, have converged on Racing Club's stadium in Avellaneda to watch the match on a giant screen. History has already

DEPORTIVO

ClarínX · BUENOS AIRES, JUEVES 27 DE DICIEMBRE DE 2001

LA ENCUESTA DE LA SEMANA
¿Quién debe ser el arquero titular de la Selección de fútbol que jugará el Mundial de Corea-Japón?

A) Burgos B) Cavallero C) Bonano D) Saja E) Campagnuolo F) Roa G) Comizzo H) Otros. Envía tus votos a **www.clarin.com** o al teléfono **5555-7222**. Los votos se recibirán hasta hoy a las 11. Entre los participantes se sorteará una camiseta de su equipo favorito.

A PLENO EN CELESTE Y BLANCO. EL GRAN CHOQUE ENTRE RACING Y VELEZ EN LINIERS, SE JUGARA A ESTADIO LLENO. AYER SE VENDIERON CASI TODAS LAS PLATEAS: SOLO QUEDAN 800 DE 80 PESOS.

El día del
gran sueño

Racing va en busca del título después de 35 años. Lleva tres puntos de ventaja. Y enfrenta a Vélez en Liniers a las 17.10. River recibe a Central, necesita ganar y que Racing pierda para disputar un partido de desempate.

Clarín, December 27, 2001: "The day of the great dream."

LA NACION [ ] **RACING CAMPEON**   *Viernes 28 de diciembre de 2001*

Una alegría increíble

La bandera que ayer estrenaron los hinchas de Racing y que desplegaron en la popular visitante: "Vamos por la gloria", pedía la frase debajo del escudo de la Academia

Abrazos, lágrimas, locura, en una tarde para el recuerdo

La Nación, December 28, 2001: "Hugs, tears, and insanity in an afternoon to remember."

been made once this week, and it seems even nature is aware of the history that could be made today and is determined to provide us with an appropriately dramatic backdrop.

I remember absolutely nothing about the game itself, except that we score a goal and the result obtained, a 1–1 draw, is the one we need to end our club's thirty-five-year championship drought.[1] José, Carlos, and I hug each other and weep like lost children. All around us is one never-ending mass of humanity, of old men embracing their grand-children as both cry tears of joy, of avalanches of people pressing down against the chain-link fence, trying feverishly to dismantle it and join the celebrations on the field as police officers spray pepper spray at them from the other side. Failing at dismantling the fence, they plead with the officers for a chunk of the grass to take home as a reminder of the long-awaited day. Never before in my life, nor after, have I seen so many grown adults weep so openly and intensely. In the midst of it all, as we sing together through tears of joy, I think of everything that has happened this past week, and I am overcome with emotion. It's all too much for a young heart.

★

That day my club, a historic giant of Argentine football that not three years earlier had been declared bankrupt, ceased to exist, and was then privatized, was putting an end to the decades-long championship drought. And one week before the game, I had stood on the streets of downtown Buenos Aires, shoulder to shoulder with my comrades, fighting on the barricades as popular fury forced the president of Argentina to flee the presidential palace from a rooftop helicopter while red flags fluttered in the wind not two hundred meters away.

In the span of seven days, the twin impossible utopias, the unreachable horizons in my life to be walked toward but never reached, were both either in our hands or within tantalizingly close reach.

For a week, a day, an hour, a moment, we became the terror of tyrants and the masters of our destinies. For all we knew, we might still topple a system, but at the tragic cost of thirty-eight lives, we had already toppled a government. In those hours, and in the days and months that followed, with the state seemingly dissolving around us— reappearing only sporadically in the form of murderous repression—we got a glimpse of the new world. The other world, the one we are always looking for and building. For a fleeting moment in time, we pulled back the curtain of the old world and saw it exists right here. It's an endless array of possibilities, hiding in plain sight on the same streets you've walked a thousand times, coming to life when ordinary people come together and dare to change everything.

When you least expect it, everything is possible.

Anarchists set fire to a Greek flag outside the gates of the Athens Polytechnic on November 17, 1995.

The Twin Utopias

La riqueza de este viaje es el cambio a esta realidad, porque si me muero es por luchar	*The richness of this journey is how we change reality, because if I die it'll be in struggle*

—Callejeros,[1] "El nudo"

This is my story of those days, and to the best of my abilities at least a superficial sketch of the conditions that created them. It is a largely narrative account attempting to capture the spirit of the moment—the calculating analysis I'll leave to the academics. It is only the story of those days as seen through my own personal and wholly subjective experience, nothing more. But also nothing less. It's the story of forty-eight hours that are probably responsible for cementing my anarchism for a lifetime.

Some of the chance encounters of my youth during the mid-1990s had already bred in me an understanding of anarchist ideas that placed itself squarely in a century-long tradition of struggle, rather than youthful subcultural rebellion. I lived most of my adolescence alternately between the cities of Paris, Athens, and Buenos Aires. In Athens, when my teenage rebellion was still not much more than liking the then-fashionable punk rock of Green Day and the Offspring, somebody recommended I listen to the Sex Pistols' "Anarchy in the UK." The song was good, but I didn't know what the word meant. This being the prehistoric world before the internet and I a curious mind, I wandered into my school's library and opened the corresponding entry in the *Encyclopaedia Britannica*, written by none other than Peter Kropotkin. The first two paragraphs read:

ANARCHISM (from the Gr. ἀν– and ἀρχή, contrary to authority), the name given to a principle or theory of life and conduct under which society is conceived without government—harmony in such a society being obtained, not by submission to law, or by obedience to any authority, but by free agreements concluded between the various groups, territorial and professional, freely constituted for the sake of production and consumption, as also for the satisfaction of the infinite variety of needs and aspirations of a civilized being. In a society developed on these lines, the voluntary associations which already now begin to cover all the fields of human activity would take a still greater extension so as to substitute themselves for the state in all its functions....

If ... society were organized on these principles, man would not be limited in the free exercise of his powers in productive work by a capitalist monopoly, maintained by the state; nor would he be limited in the exercise of his will by a fear of punishment, or by obedience towards individuals or metaphysical entities, which both lead to depression of initiative and servility of mind. He would be guided in his actions by his own understanding, which necessarily would bear the impression of a free action and reaction between his own self and the ethical conceptions of his surroundings. Man would thus be enabled to obtain the full development of all his faculties, intellectual, artistic and moral, without being hampered by overwork for the monopolists, or by the servility and inertia of mind of the great number.[2]

These paragraphs and the rest of the entry spoke to what I instinctively believed in my rebellion against the world of capitalism and the state that I couldn't articulate for myself back then but can now:

That humans are naturally social creatures (if you don't believe so, see how many humans flourish in healthy societies versus how quickly humans go crazy, get depressed, and are even driven to suicide in isolation) and that a system based on competition rather than cooperation is a vestige from a primitive past. Capitalism, and the modern state its industrialization has generated, may have represented progress from feudalism, but it is long past time for human progress to wipe them both from the face of the earth.

That misery and needless suffering in a modern world in which scientific and technological advances have generated more abundance, wealth, and material goods than at any time before in human history are grotesque crimes against humanity, which we have normalized in the name of private property and the "right" of those who already have it to accumulate more capital—an atrocity similar to the one nationalism exposes us to on a daily basis, with its wars and its massacre of thousands on the borders of Fortress Europe and the US (to name the most infamous).

That letting a human being drown in an ocean because they lack a piece of paper is an act of barbarism, just as forcing another to waste away their existence working just for the right to exist in society and have access to its benefits is a crime.

That it is imperative to be outraged by these everyday horrors of the state and class society. To stand defiantly against those who seek to perpetuate them. To always remember that when police, capitalists, and the state point to the urban jungles we live in, so often bursting with crime, poverty, and violence, as arguments for their necessity and inevitability, they are purposefully neglecting to point out that it is they who generate the conditions that breed the crime, the poverty, and the violence.

Most of all, that we need to work tirelessly to replace them with something less brutal and more sane: a society that recognizes that because we are social beings, because our lives are inexorably intertwined and the wealth of society is created by the whole of society, this same wealth should be held commonly, and the means that create that wealth in turn should be run by those essential in its creation. A society in which there is democracy in the workplace, a workplace organized for the benefit of society, and a society where work is not the central element of one's existence. A society structured around mutual aid and the common good—guided by the principle of "from each according to his ability, to each according to his needs," and likewise a society respectful of the individual and their freedoms.[3]

That it was clear that the original Bakuninist axiom that "freedom without Socialism is privilege and injustice, and that Socialism without freedom is slavery and brutality" had been proven correct by the experiences in both the Eastern and Western blocs during the course of the twentieth century.[4]

Fascinated by Kropotkin's writing, my youthful introduction to anarchism would be completed thanks to a combination of curiosity and circumstance. First, I looked for books explicitly about anarchism, and I found nothing less than Paul Avrich's *The Haymarket Tragedy*. This book provided me not only with insight into the ideas and motivations held by the anarchists of the time, but also with an understanding of what the attempt to put those ideas into practice could entail in terms of commitment and sacrifice—as well as the extent to which the pursuit of anarchist ideas had once shaped the struggles of the working class.

The final piece of the puzzle fell into place on November 17, 1995—the anniversary of the 1973 Athens Polytechnic uprising, a university occupation by students in opposition to the military junta that culminated with the Greek military raiding the campus and killing approximately forty protesters. Fast-forward to the '90s and it was now the anarchists who were routinely occupying the campus of the Athens Polytechnic in order to articulate their rejection of the state and use its gates as a launchpad for attacks against the cops.

I was still unaware of this context, though, as I sat there watching the clashes in front of the Polytechnic unfold on live TV throughout the course of the evening and into the night. The journalists spoke only of vandals and hooligans who had infiltrated otherwise peaceful demonstrations, stripping them of any political agency or motivation.

As the night wore on and an apparently endless stream of Molotov cocktails flew toward the police lines, I began to decipher, despite my limited Greek, some of what the masked "vandals and hooligans" were chanting. I clearly made out "freedom" and "against nationalism." Soon after, Greek flags began to emerge from the campus, only to be promptly set on fire. The walls read "Neither Fascism nor Democracy" and "Long Live Anarchism!"

It didn't take long for me to realize that anarchism was not a long-lost and forgotten ideology of the nineteenth century, but rather that I was observing an unbroken line stretching from the words of Kropotkin in that encyclopedia, to the anarchists of Chicago so lovingly depicted in Avrich's book, to the masked anarchists of the present facing off with police on the streets of Athens—expressing the language of modern anarchism and antiauthoritarianism in their banners, graffiti, chants, and even the forms of action and targets.

Soon after, I found myself in Paris, with its thriving anarchist ecosystem: an anarchist FM radio station by the name of Radio Libertaire, several anarchist bookstores and infoshops, social centers, squats, a mass-produced and widely distributed weekly periodical in *Le Monde Libertaire* as well as numerous monthly publications, the strong countrywide antifascist and antiracist network SCALP (Section Carrément Anti–Le Pen, or "Absolutely Anti–Le Pen Group"), and most importantly the anarcho-syndicalist CNT (Confédération Nationale du Travail)— fresh off the successful general strike of 1995 and in a period of rapid expansion. I was quickly introduced there to a combative anarchism that not only was implanted in the social struggles of the day, but most importantly an anarchism that while also subcultural was most definitely not exclusively so. It was an anarchist universe blending workers with students, the subcultural punk or skinhead mixing with people who didn't wear their ideas on their outfits, young and old. And the "olds" were none other than the veterans of the Spanish Civil War, who had founded the CNT and still had their offices within the CNT's Paris headquarters—and enthusiastically took in a young Spanish-speaking anarchist who enjoyed nothing more than to visit them after school and listen to them talk of social revolution, the Spanish Civil War, and the enduring relevance of the ideas of libertarian socialism.

In 1997, I moved back to Buenos Aires for a year, before returning to Paris, where I spent 1998 and 1999, at that point returning again to Buenos Aires for another year—which I left again toward the middle of 2000. Anarchism in Buenos Aires was neither as spectacular as its contemporary in Athens nor nearly anywhere as deeply implanted and large as it was in Paris. But in Buenos Aires I quickly landed in the small but tight-knit and committed community around the Biblioteca Popular José Ingenieros, founded in 1935. Finally being able to participate in discussions, debates, and fireside chats at anarchist camps in the Buenos Aires suburbs in my native language allowed me to exchange my ideas and hone my anarchism.

But while all these experiences certainly cemented me as an anarchist ideologically and provided me with sympathy, affection, and identification with the deep and varying traditions of anarchist ideas, militance, and struggle, we weren't exactly on the verge of revolution, and if history had played out differently, I will never know to what extent my anarchist convictions might or might not have persevered over the years and decades to come.

I firmly believe that I have these days in the Buenos Aires of December 2001 to thank for that. Two days taught me that apparently anything is possible at any moment. That hope and change, not of the Barack Obama variety but of the glorious social revolution variety, might be waiting around the least expected corner. How can you stop believing in something that is evidently so powerful that it can, even in the darkest of times and under the least auspicious of circumstances, suddenly reemerge with such power and fury?

The previous twenty-five or so years leading up to 2001 had not been kind to revolutionaries in Argentina. In the 1970s, the proverbial and collective "we" of the revolutionary left took up arms by the thousands and confronted the state head-on. What followed was not only defeat but a military dictatorship and Dirty War that left tens of thousands dead and disappeared, as well as what is an undetermined but feasibly six-figure number exiled. The 1980s marked the return to Argentina of capitalist democracy, but not before the generals plunged the country into war with the United Kingdom over the Islas Malvinas (referred to as the "Falkland Islands" by the British) and took another thousand lives in a desperate attempt to retain power by ginning up nationalist sentiment. The remainder of the decade was marked by chronic political instability, a failed coup attempt or two, and out-of-control hyperinflation that converged into the wave of neoliberalism that spread across the world in the wake of the fall of the Eastern bloc, the final victory of capitalism, and the "end of history" of the early 1990s.

The practical consequences of the end of history for the Argentina of the '90s were swift, and brutally experienced by the working class of the country. The national currency's conversion rate was tied at one-to-one to the US dollar in a policy called "convertibility." While this allowed Argentina's wealthier classes to feel like part of the First World and travel the globe, the immediate spike in production costs had devastating effects on Argentine industry and workers—as factories, no longer able to compete internationally, were forced to shutter. Parallel to this, and again in line with the fashionable worldview of the era of unfettered capitalism, the government launched a wave of privatization of strategic enterprises in the fields of energy and transportation, which rapidly led to waves of firings, price hikes, and decreased quality as foreign

Clarín, April 13, 1997: The emergence on the national stage of the *piquetero* movement of unemployed workers.

"Serious disturbances in Neuquén: One dead."

companies failed to deliver on promised investments and upgrades to critical infrastructure.

Standing in the face of this was a broad spectrum of the left that was still widely in disarray from the experiences and traumas of the last few decades. Anarchism and anarchists were a small and marginal political phenomenon, while the authoritarian left had splintered into an alphabet soup of small and often feuding parties and organizations, all of which put together were anyways incapable of reaching even a 3 percent mark in national elections. A lot of the energy and activity of the era was concentrated around campaigns to expose and denounce the many mass murderers and torturers of the dictatorship era who walked freely among us, having benefited from amnesty laws passed after the return to democracy. It was, and in some cases still is, essential, emotional, and often dangerous work, but it was clearly not the stuff of impending revolutions or uprisings.

So while the late '90s did see some promising developments as far as collective resistance to the nightmare of unhinged neoliberalism, with the growth of workers' and unemployed autonomous organizations and localized uprisings such as the one in Cutral Có, in the province of Neuquén in 1997, there was no reason to suspect that a massive and radical rejection of the entirety of the existing order was on the immediate horizon. On the contrary, the escape valve that appeared to release some of the pressure put on society by a decade of neoliberalism, and provide a prospect of hope to release pent-up frustrations, was the election of the mild and moderately center-left coalition Alianza in late 1999, bringing Fernando de la Rúa to the presidency on December 10, 1999.

Few could have predicted that exactly two years and ten days later that same president would be forced to hurriedly flee the Casa Rosada (Pink House), Argentina's presidential palace, on a rooftop helicopter while police below fought pitched battles with tens of thousands of demonstrators trying to storm the building. And right there, during the tumultuous days of Argentina around December 20, 2001, is where our story begins.

I still have difficulty writing properly about those days. Sometimes I start writing and promptly begin crying, two decades still not providing enough distance from the events to dim the memory of just how momentous and inspiring they were. In 2002, I gave several talks about the uprising in Boston, New York, and San Francisco, and I remember having to gather myself to make sure I would not tear up at some point in the narration. I am also constantly intimidated by writing about those days, thinking that I can't possibly do justice to something so historic, to a moment in time so unique that it changed thousands of lives forever. And sometimes I feel a tinge of sadness at the idea that maybe the greatest days of my life were already behind me before I was even out of my teens, because how could anything possibly ever surpass this?

To that point, my life had always been dominated by what I jokingly referred to as "the twin utopias." If at any given waking moment of my existence you were to ask me what was on my mind, it was always one of these two ideas (maybe with the occasional exception of a romantic entanglement or two that might have been weighing on my mind). Both represented equally remote points on the horizon, impossibly far away, almost absurd to think I might experience them in my lifetime, much less anytime soon. Objectives still to be fought for and aspired to, as matters of personal conviction and principle absolutely, but the prospect of seeing them actually realized was spoken about only in hushed tones and wild daydreams.

One, of course, is the social revolution: the ushering in of a glorious red (and black) dawn, *le grand soir*, and a new era for humanity. A

Clarín, December 28, 2001: "Shine." A snapshot of the week the impossible became reality.

world free of oppression, free of patriarchy, free of sexism and racism, and where the state and capital have finally been assigned to their proper place in the dustbin of history, replaced with voluntary association, mutual aid, and the international brotherhood and sisterhood of humanity. Despite my secular upbringing, I at least subconsciously found myself drawn—probably in the tradition of a lot of Jewish anarchists—to the concept of a new dawn, a new humanity, and a new world that would arise on one glorious day following centuries of struggle.

The other utopia was just as important to me, and it is no exaggeration to say that for most of my youth, it seemed as equally, if not even more so, unattainable as the first one: to see my club, Racing Club de Avellaneda, finally win an Argentine football championship, something we had not achieved since 1966, a span of thirty-five long and painful years.

I'm sure the plot twist of "Why in hell does a seemingly at least moderately intelligent anarchist with a clear understanding as to the negative roles of all the different opiates of the masses, be they religion, drugs, or soccer, care so deeply about a group of eleven millionaires pushing a ball across a white line?" requires explaining. To do so, I will try now, apparently, to explain passion. To bring Argentine anarchist history and context to the table in order to provide arguments of logic and reason for a question that is, in the end, purely of the heart and probably inexplicable by definition. It sounds difficult, impossible, possibly utopian. And so, true to anarchist tradition, let us dive right in.

1

The Tides of Anarchy: The Anarchist Mass Movement of Late Nineteenth-Century Argentina

Oíd, mortales, el grito sagrado,
de Anarquía y solidaridad,
oíd el ruido de bombas que
estallan, en defensa de la
libertad.
El obrero que sufre proclama la
anarquía del mundo a través
coronada su sien de laureles,
y a sus plantas rendido el
burgués

Listen, mortals, to the sacred
cry, of Anarchy and solidarity,
listen to the sound of bombs
exploding, in defense of liberty.
The suffering worker proclaims
anarchy across the globe
His head crowned with laurels,
and at his feet, surrendered,
the bourgeois

—Anarchist folk adaptation of the national anthem of Argentina

On any given day in Argentina, if someone were to wander into a bakery and ask for any one of their favorite treats to go enjoy with their friends while drinking maté at the park, their order might sound something like, "I'll take a cream of milk cannon, half a dozen cream bombs, a few friar's balls, some nun's moans, and a vigilante, please." It's an exceedingly peculiar testament to anarchist influence in Argentine society at the turn of the nineteenth century—in this case in the labor movement and more specifically in the bakers' union, a union completely dominated by anarchist bakers who ironically baptized pastries alternately to exalt the symbols of anarchist militance or to poke fun at police and religion.

A piece of history largely lost to most, and that even comes as a surprise to most Argentines today, is that though precious little knowledge of it has survived outside of very political or academic circles,

Simón Radowitzky, whose bomb killed the infamous Colonel Ramón Falcón, who was responsible for the repression on May 1, 1909, that took the life of eight anarchist workers. Art by PRBLMTKX.

Workers hold up an edition of the anarchist daily *La Protesta* during an anarchist-led union assembly in 1904. *La Protesta*, at times an organ of the FORA, reached a peak daily circulation of one hundred thousand copies.

one of the strongest and most deeply embedded political currents in Argentina for several decades from the late nineteenth century onward was anarchism. This was true for large swaths of the Argentine working class, and especially so among European immigrants to Argentina, leading the Argentine ruling class to run anarchist scare campaigns similar to those seen in the United States during the same period in history: "a foreign ideology imposed on our country by European brutes." This was eventually the pretext used in 1902 to pass the Residency Law (Ley de Residencia), allowing the deportation of foreigners "whose conduct endangers national security or disturbs the public order," a law subsequently used to deport numerous anarchists.[1] But whatever the ruling class may have thought of it, the reality was that by the start of the twentieth century, anarchism—a "social pathology," as the police chief of Buenos Aires described it—was deeply implanted in Argentina.[2]

Those who are familiar with the history of Argentine anarchism are likely to be most aware of its heroic, often tragic, history of struggle on the labor front against capital and the state. By 1903, anarchists had gained control of the FORA (Federación Obrera Regional Argentina, or "Argentina Regional Workers' Federation"), which would go on to become one of the world's largest anarcho-syndicalist organizations—an organization that in its 1904 congress took an explicitly anarcho-communist

A FORA mobilization in Buenos Aires, year unknown.

position, instructing "all its adherents the broadest propaganda and illustration, with the objective of inculcating workers with the economic and philosophical principles of anarchist communism" through which workers would achieve "total emancipation," bringing about the "social evolution" of society.[3]

Said to have over one hundred thousand adherents at its peak during the first decade of the twentieth century, and a peak of 105 affiliated unions in the year 1906, the FORA was at the forefront of worker and anarchist combativeness during that time.[4] Aside from "their immense May Day mobilizations" and "the momentum and leadership which they provided to numerous labor conflicts," there were "seven anarchist-led general strikes" during a decade that saw anarchists mobilize "a large percentage of Buenos Aires workers—port workers, cart drivers, coachmen, sailors, stokers, mechanics, painters, bricklayers, plasterers, bakers, and laborers."[5]

Independent of the FORA, which despite its explicit anarchism was a mass organization, there were also six thousand anarchist activists in the country in 1902, according to estimates from the Argentine police, and two years later "the Interior Minister calculated that there were 'more than 4,000' anarchist activists in the Federal Capital alone."[6] While not necessarily a huge quantity of activists, their influence was significantly magnified not only by the mass of anarchist sympathizers around them but also by how they viewed themselves and their role within social and labor struggles: "The anarchists saw themselves as the spark that would ignite the revolutionary bonfire and did their best to turn each clash into a revolution. And it was only from this vanguardist perspective that they were interested in organizing the workers' movement." Needless to say, this distinctively Bakuninist perception of revolution "presumes that individuals (the people) have a natural, irresistible instance for justice that will lead them to spontaneously destroy authority during periods of social convulsion." It's a sentiment that was echoed by Errico Malatesta when he argued that "anarchists only needed to organize a small minority and that the majority is inherently apathetic and hostile to transformation."[7] His assertion was that it was sufficient, even beneficial, and maybe even unavoidable and necessary for a minority to be the hand that guides the masses toward revolution: "Humanity has always advanced through the initiative and efforts of individuals and minorities, whereas the majority, by its very nature, is slow, conservative, submissive to superior force and to established privileges."[8]

This was, unsurprisingly, by no means a unanimously held opinion among the anarchist movement and was indeed vociferously resisted, as it was seen as relegating class struggle to a mere means to an end by more workerist elements. But it was certainly determinant enough that every conflict had the latent potential to become an explosive clash, since anarchist elements were determined to turn every labor dispute into a potential revolutionary general strike and every clash with the state into a symbolic or practical act of open defiance against it.

Of the seven anarchist-led general strikes of the first decade of the twentieth century, when the movement was at its peak, the high point of generalized open conflict between the anarchist-led workers' movement and the state was the so-called Red Week (Semana Roja) of May 1909. On the first of May, Colonel Ramón Falcón, infamous for his anti-anarchist zeal, ordered the repression of anarchist workers, seventy thousand strong, attending a rally organized by the FORA in commemoration of the Haymarket martyrs. As Osvaldo Bayer, renowned historian of

A street named after Colonel Ramón Falcón, in the district of Lomas de Zamora, southern Buenos Aires.

anarchism in Argentina, puts it, "It was a ferocious and cowardly attack as, without prior warning, the colonel ordered the police firing squad to open fire on the workers' columns."[9]

Following an hour of pitched battle, eight anarchists lay dead and forty wounded. Falcón then proceeded to order the closing of all offices and structures of the FORA and launched a brutal wave of repression, which the workers and anarchist movement responded to with a general strike, paralyzing the country for a week, while three hundred thousand people accompanied the funeral procession of the slain anarchists. The general strike was so powerful that on May 14 the government sat down to negotiate with a strikers' committee, a first-ever at that point.

"The anarchists were not men who shied away from conflict or kept silent," and they were determined that "the tyrant would pay for his cowardice with his life."[10] And so it was that on November 14 of that same year, a young Jewish anarchist from Russia (present-day Ukraine) by the name of Simón Radowitzky would avenge the fallen comrades by hurling a homemade explosive into the carriage transporting Colonel Falcón, killing him instantly. Radowitzky would go on to be arrested later that same day to the cry of "Long live anarchy!"[11]

Radowitzky's act would become the most well known of anarchist acts of propaganda by the deed, although a few attempts on the lives of Argentine presidents had taken place in the years preceding. On a rainy night in 1905, President Manuel Quintana's life was spared only thanks to the "poor quality of the bullets used by the Catalan anarchist Salvador E.J. Planas y Virell."[12] Forensic analysis eventually "determined that the cartridge was 'not in a condition to fire.'"[13]

Three years later, on February 28, 1908, it was President José Figueroa Alcorta who narrowly escaped death at the hands of an anarchist assassin, when the bomb thrown at him by Francisco Solano Regis began to smoke but failed to explode. The anarchist periodical *La Protesta* would declare only a few short days later that "one more time vindictive violence springs as a consequence of bourgeois violence.... We understand and justify it; one is the immediate consequence of the other."[14] Solano Regis would go on to declare following his arrest his belief that "by killing the president of the Republic I would be performing a good deed for humanity."[15] Sentenced to twenty years in prison, in January 1911 he and other anarchist comrades escaped from the Las Heras prison in Buenos Aires, in what the well-known circular *Caras y Caretas* called "an escape without precedent in the history of urban prison breaks."[16] He is rumored to have fled to Uruguay, never to be found again.

In 1910, as the preparations for the state-sanctioned festivities commemorating the centennial of Argentina's independence intensified, the Argentine government launched an unprecedented wave of repression against the whole of the anarchist movement. The anarchists were unsurprisingly critical of the nationalism and patriotic fervor surrounding the Centenary, and the state was determined not to allow anarchist influence to disrupt the festivities.

In early May, just a few weeks before the May 25 date of the Centenary anniversary, anarchists and socialists launched a general strike, which the state responded to on May 14 by declaring a state of emergency:

> It correctly believed that a crackdown would enable it to pull off the pageantry of the approaching Centenary, with all its symbolic

weight. And the repression was exceedingly effective. The new Social Defense Law and the imposition of martial law provided the legal framework for closing public offices, muzzling the press, imprisoning dozens of activists, and deporting others.... But what made the repression around the Centenary so unique was its unprecedented duration and the draconian violations of individual and press freedoms that it entailed, which set a precedent for the repeated human rights violations that would take place later.[17]

The April 1, 1911, edition of *The Libertarian* reported:

Innocents are imprisoned ..., women are attacked ..., workers are deported, clothes and money are stolen from children, the elderly, and homemakers ..., peaceful strikers are persecuted and treated like they are rabid dogs, workers' institutions are raided and shut down, the circulation and sale of our press is undermined, armed patrols go to cafes and homes and search them in ways that offend elemental standards of freedom and decency.[18]

Unique and novel were not only the scope, intensity, and breadth of the repression but also the "civilian participation in the attacks on socialists, anarchists, foreigners, and particularly Jews, all of which the government not only permitted but also encouraged."[19] Patriotic mobs organized antiworker demonstrations, attacking anarchist, socialist, and union spaces. Although the workers responded, and clashes left several dead and wounded in both camps, the anarchists were no match for the blend of government repression and state-sanctioned right-wing violence. Nationalist organizations, embryonic of what would a few years later become the virulently far-right, xenophobic, and anti-Semitic paramilitary organization Liga Patriótica Argentina (Argentine Patriotic League), "attacked workers centers, torched the editorial offices and printing machines of *La Protesta*, The Battle, and *La Vanguardia*, stormed bookstores, cafes, brothels, shops in the Jewish neighborhood Once, and physically assaulted activists and people suspected of being foreigners."[20]

The tide was clearly turning, and as is made clear above, the effects of the government crackdown extended to the entirety of the anarchist movement, its ecosystem, and even its sympathizers—not just its most

A mural in remembrance of the events of the Semana Trágica in Plaza Martín Fierro, where the Vasena steelworks were once located. Today it is the location of the San Cristóbal neighborhood of Buenos Aires.

combative and militant elements. The broad and varied network of periodicals, study circles, social centers, organizations, and anarchist cultural and social life were essentially decimated and took several years to regenerate. Anarchism in Argentina, however, most certainly did not die with the Centenary repression and would remain a prominent force for over twenty more years. Indeed, some of its most momentous, and likewise tragic, conflicts with the state were still ahead—conflicts in which the relatively new phenomenon of armed right-wing nationalist organizations acting in unison with state actors would take an ever broader and significantly more tragic dimension.

Most notorious is the Semana Trágica (Tragic Week) of 1919, a vicious union battle that began with an anarchist-led steelworkers' strike and escalated into a pitched conflict that pitted striking workers, their community, and other workers in solidarity against strikebreakers, police forces, and right-wing nationalist vigilantes whose antiworker and anti-Semitic pogroms eventually claimed thousands of lives. What had begun as sporadic clashes between strikers and scabs (aided by

The forces of "order" arrayed against anarchists and strikers, ca. 1919.

armed right-wing civilian shock troops from the Argentine Rural Society) at the Vasena steelworks began to escalate on December 30 of the preceding year with the murder of Domingo Castro, as he was headed to an anarchist union space, by a police officer by the name of Oscar Ropts. On January 3 and 4, massive confrontations with live ammunition from both sides erupted outside the union offices, during which the neighborhood residents and striking workers erected barricades and eventually forced the police and strikebreakers to retreat, mortally wounding police officer Vicente Chávez in the process. While the bourgeois press screamed "Bloody Strike," the anarchist press, by way of *La Protesta*, celebrated: "The people stand with the strikers. The motto is victory or death! Always like this, comrades. Bullets for the cossacks! Hurrah for those who know when to take action!"[21]

Three days later, outside the union offices, the first massacre of what was to become the Semana Trágica would take place, as "at approximately 3:30 p.m. over one hundred police officers and firefighters armed with Mauser rifles, supported by strikebreakers with rifles and Winchester carbines, opened fire against the wooden houses, the strikers, and the neighbors. During the course of over two hours they

An immense funeral procession on its way to Chacarita Cemetery, January 9, 1919.

shot more than two thousand bullets."[22] The bullets pierced through the wooden homes of the workers with ease, killing five people, including eighteen-year-old Juan Fiorini, who was "inside his house drinking maté with his mother."[23] The massacre outraged the workers of the city, who overwhelmed union offices across Buenos Aires. The cry of vengeance was in the air, and by January 9, the day of the funeral procession for the victims of the massacre, the city awoke completely paralyzed, following the call for a general strike.

By 2:00 p.m., the massive funeral procession was underway, "led by a vanguard of 150 armed anarchists, which grew progressively as armories along the route were looted."[24] The procession marched to the Vasena steelworks, where an enormous confrontation took place, claiming an unknown number of victims. The next major clash of day would take place around 4:00 p.m., as demonstrators attempting to set fire to a church clashed with the armed firefighters protecting it. Eventually what was left of the procession after the succession of armed clashes, numbering not more than a few hundred, reached its destination at the Chacarita Cemetery. Accounts of the number of casualties of the day's clashes vary, ranging from thirty-nine to eighty-five.

A vehicle is overturned and set on fire at a workers' barricade during Semana Trágica clashes.

Unrest was clearly spreading, and with the sympathy and even active participation of broad sectors of the working class, anarchists and syndicalists interpreted that they were in a potentially revolutionary situation, with *La Protesta* proclaiming loudly that "the people are ready for revolution!"[25] But where there is uprising and attempted revolution, there is also reaction and counterrevolution. As workers erected barricades across the city, allowing only vehicles flying the red flag to pass, Argentina's right wing, its nationalists, and its upper class were decrying the uprising led by a "seditious minority." Just as with the civil rights movement of the 1960s or the George Floyd uprising in the US in 2020, as with almost any left-wing or progressive movement of the last century, the bourgeois press declared that the country was in the midst of an "international Russian Jewish conspiracy with the aim of establishing a Soviet in Argentina." As the *Buenos Aires Herald*, English-language newspaper of the prosperous British community of Buenos Aires, claimed that "Buenos Aires faced its first test of Bolshevism," right-wing and anti-Semitic organizations took to the streets proclaiming that "where there is a barricade of rebels there should be a barricade of Argentines."[26] The bourgeois panic quickly lent free rein to the already latent anti-Semitism of Argentina's well-to-do classes.

Patriotic youth from upper-class families on patrol in private vehicles, looking for Jews, strikers, or foreigners. Notice the police officers accompanying them.

Following a further failed attempt on January 10 by armed workers to take the Vasena steelworks, again suffering heavy casualties, the combined forces of police, military, and armed groups of right-wing civilians gradually began to retake the city. By nightfall, what would come to be known as the White Terror, which would take thousands of lives and culminate in Latin America's first and only anti-Jewish pogrom to this day, was in full swing. It was on this day that the far-right fascist Liga Patriótica Argentina was born (although it was initially called the Comisión Pro Defensores del Orden), and its mobs of upper-class patriotic youths began sweeping through the city, together with police and military.

To cries of "Death to the Jews!," "Death to the anarchists!," and "Death to the workers!" the patriotic mobs began raiding party offices, union spaces, anarchist centers, and everything they associated with being foreign and proletarian, lynching whomever was unfortunate enough to cross their paths. The objective was to exert a "punishment they would remember for fifty years" so as to preempt any further uprisings.[27] That night, the raids would increase in scope and ferocity, as paramilitary gangs "raided homes without judicial authorization, murdering and beating occupants, raping women and children, destroying goods, and burning books."[28]

It's difficult to convey how massive, murderous, and sadistic the White Terror was without entering into pages and pages of eyewitness accounts. But the account of young Jewish journalist Pedro Wald, who was jailed and tortured during the Semana Trágica under the almost comical accusation of having been selected to be the president of the impending new Argentine Soviet, is particularly illustrative, as detailed in his 1929 book about the events, *Koshmar* (Nightmare):

> The actions of the "good boys" of the Patriotic League were savage, as they marched chanting for death to maximalists, Jews, and other foreigners. Refined, sadistic, they tortured and programmed orgies. One Jewish person was captured and after the first blows blood began flowing from his mouth. Next they ordered him to sing the national anthem and, as he didn't know it because he had just arrived in the country, he was promptly liquidated. They didn't discriminate: they struck and killed anybody with a beard who seemed Jewish and they were able to get their hands on. As they captured a passerby they ordered him to "yell that you are a maximalist." "I'm not," he pleaded. A minute later he lay on the ground in a pool of his own blood.[29]

The anti-Semitic fury of the nationalist mobs eventually culminated in two separate nights of pogroms in the predominantly Jewish neighborhoods of Once and Villa Crespo, in central Buenos Aires. Led by the Liga Patriótica Argentina, mobs set fire to synagogues as well as the Poalei Sion and Avangard movement libraries.[30] Jews were indiscriminately arrested, or simply beaten, tortured, and killed on the streets of Buenos Aires. In the daily Jewish newspaper *Di Idische Tzaitung*, José Mendelson wrote:

> The pogroms of Europe are nothing next to what was done to Jewish elders by civilian gangs in the streets, inside the 7th and 9th District police stations, and in the police headquarters. Jockeys dragged naked elderly Jewish men through the streets of Buenos Aires, pulled them by their beards ... while the sables and whips of the men on horseback beat them and fell intermittently against their bodies....
>
> Fifty men, growing tired of beating, would alternate for each prisoner, as executions continued from morning until past noon,

Smoke billows from the fire at the Vasena steelworks.

from afternoon into evening, and from evening until dawn. With matches they burned the knees of the arrested, dragged needles through their open wounds ..., urinated into their mouths. The torturers yelled, "Long live the Fatherland, death to maximalists and all foreigners!"[31]

As the pogroms raged in Once and Villa Crespo and the White Terror spread across the city, anarchist-led workers counterattacked. A group of strikers shot and killed an army sergeant while nearby the commander of a firing squad and a right-wing civilian were also killed by strikers. Elsewhere a military battalion was ambushed by strikers and forced to resort to the use of a heavy machine gun in order to fend them off. Most significantly, an infantry regiment was forced to intervene in order to liberate four hundred strikebreakers who were trapped in the Vasena steelworks and had been surrounded by anarchists, who threatened to set fire to the building with the strikebreakers inside. On the morning of the 13th, strikers intent on pursuing the armed uprising attempted to loot a police station armory, only to be repelled by a marine

The bodies of fallen workers, left outside a public assistance hall.

firing squad, one of thousands of military reserves that had descended on the city.[32]

Parallel to the clashes and pogroms, the government was negotiating with both the anarchist FORA and its socialist counterpart as well as with the owners of the Vasena steelworks to attempt to bring an end to the conflict. President Hipólito Yrigoyen himself ratified the liberation of all arrested workers, with the exception of those accused of serious crimes (including Simón Radowitzky, whom anarchist unions had demanded be released along with workers detained during the current uprising), a 40 percent pay increase, and a reduction in the workday. The president then summoned Alfredo Vasena, the steelworks owner, and communicated to him that his acceptance of these conditions must be unconditional.

By the time the unions called an end to the strike and the clashes were over, the human toll of the fierce repression of the workers and anarchist movement, one possibly without precedent in Latin America, was immense, with the US embassy putting the number at 1,356 dead and the French embassy estimating over 4,000 wounded and 50,000 arrested.[33]

Anarchism in Argentina never fully recovered—although the era of Severino Di Giovanni and the anarchist expropriators was still ahead, as well as that of the agrarian uprisings of La Patagonia Rebelde—and would never again reach the same degree of implantation in society that it previously had. There were ebbs and flows, particularly around the Spanish Civil War years, but the general trajectory from the 1920s on is downward. To be fair, as in the US, it would be reductionist to attribute this solely to the effects of state repression. Societal factors, particularly concessions made by both the state and capitalists—concessions of course obtained through the sacrifice, struggle, and blood of workers' struggles that anarchists more often than not led—made the anarchist position that the state was nothing more than an instrument of the ruling class less instinctively relatable for wide swaths of society. Likewise, trade unions began to be integrated, and the (by definition) combative and antagonistic conception of anarchist unions appealed to fewer workers.

Its influence and infrastructure was progressively decimated during the course of the twentieth century by successive waves of repressions and dictatorships; its ideological sphere of influence on the working class was reduced by the Bolshevik victory in the Russian Revolution and subsequent defeat in the Spanish Civil War; and it was finally pushed to the fringes of society and the working class by the galloping advance of Peronism, which remains the dominant force among the Argentine working class to this day. Anarchism had all but disappeared from the political and social landscape of Argentina by the 1950s. The once vibrant anarchist movement lay dormant—if not dead then barely breathing. What had once been the terror of the state and bourgeoisie was now something reduced to a handful of aging militants and a few libraries, to be studied with condescending curiosity by academics.

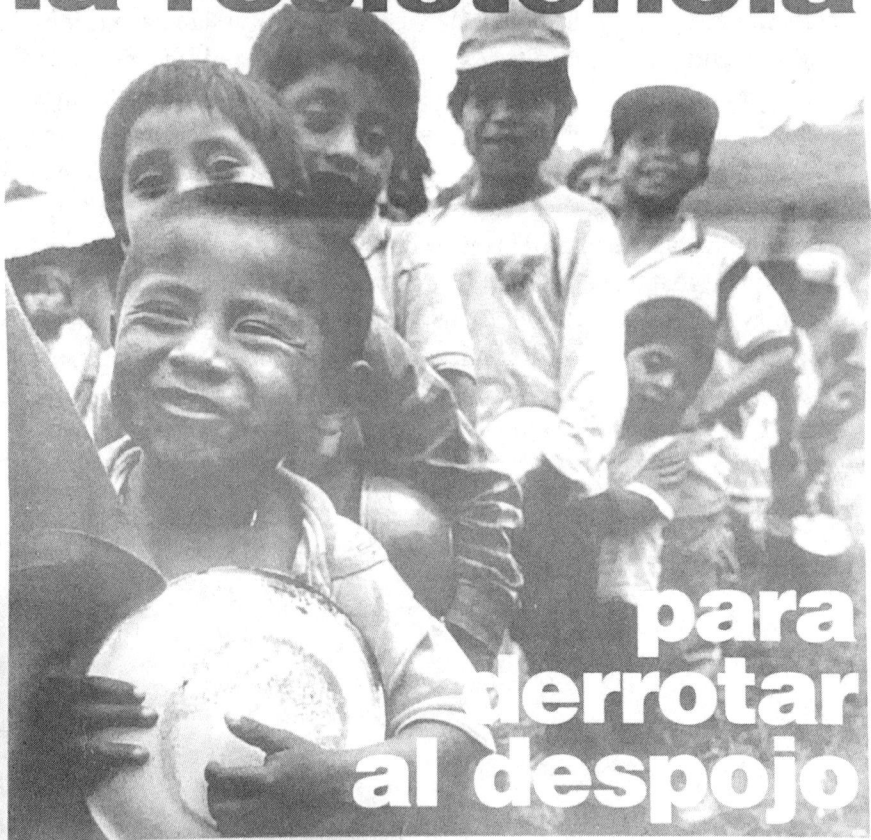

ÓRGANO DE DIFUSIÓN DEL ANARQUISMO ORGANIZADO

EN LA CALLE

AÑO 4 NÚMERO 42 • NOVIEMBRE-DICIEMBRE DE 2001 • VALOR $1.00

Organicemos la resistencia

para derrotar al despojo

Cover of the last issue of *En la Calle* before the uprising of December 2001: "Let's organize the resistance to the plundering."

2

The Biblioteca Popular José Ingenieros

Villa Crespo, Buenos Aires, Sometime Early 1997

Porque este juego es	*Because this game is*
lo que siempre fue,	*what it's always been,*
una bota pateando el tablero	*a boot kicking the chessboard*
de ajedrez	

—Los Violadores,[1] "Más allá del bien y del mal"

*It happened in a matter of seconds. A plume of white smoke shot into the calm blue skies... and red flames engulfed the entire building immediately. It was as if they had scored a heroic victory, as if they had put a man-eating monster to death. The well-to-do crowd sang and danced around the enormous bonfire that devoured the printing press of that newspaper—*La Protesta*—which had been set up at the cost of untold exertions and workers' tears. "We've torched it!" "We've avenged Falcón!" It was like they had killed a mythical beast.*

—*Ideas and Figures*, no. 34, October 1, 1910

Sometimes what seems incredibly, almost unimaginably distant is connected to you much more directly than you think. An eternity has passed since the nationalist mobs set fire to the offices of *La Protesta*, and it has been just over one hundred years since the anti-anarchist and anti-Semitic pogroms of 1919. But in the Buenos Aires neighborhood of Villa Crespo, where I happened to spend most of my days in Buenos Aires, two of the remnants of the influence of the anarchist movement and workers' self-organization of that era—beyond pastries—lay hidden in plain view. Testaments to an idea and a movement that refused to die.

Not the 1910 attack against *La Protesta* described in the epigraph on the previous page, but yet another attack on an anarchist press—this time by the police, the night of January 14, 1919.

The first of them I came to discover in the most unexpected of settings. I would call it sheer dumb luck, but once again it seems to be an example that when you are constantly thinking of and talking about something, your enthusiasm pushes the hand of fate. The scene: the weekly Sunday family lunch at my great aunt's house. An event I rarely attend, and when I do my participation is in the form of a brief guest appearance before rushing away to Avellaneda for the Racing game. The roundtable of the family lunch sports a deeply middle-class and upper-middle-class Jewish cast, of first- and second-generation immigrants from Germany. There's my grandfather and his sister, who still speak to each other in a German that sounds like it escaped untouched from a 1930s time capsule. They fled Nazi Germany as children, but only barely escaped. My great-grandfather was a Jewish German World War I veteran, the kind who couldn't wrap his head around the idea that his country, the country of which he considered himself a patriot and for which he had fought, could declare him an "other" and persecute him. He only eventually came to his senses about the acutely impending danger when one of his kids was brutally beaten on the train for being Jewish. Shortly thereafter, arriving first in Paraguay before moving to Argentina, he and my great-grandmother quickly started a business and managed to build comfortable lives for themselves and their numerous children. To be clear, this is not the working-class, labor-unionism, "my ancestors were anarchists and communists in Europe" kind of German Jewish crowd.

Yet I, young and evangelical about my anarchism, make mention of it during lunch in some context or another that I can't recall. Immediately two things—one more unexpected than the other—happen. First, Albert—my great-aunt's likewise German Jewish husband and a pretty successful capitalist—begins waxing poetic about what he experienced as a young man in the anarchist revolutionary Barcelona of 1936: "I remember people offering whatever food they had to others, chocolates and such, on the tram. And that the fancy restaurants were suddenly open for everybody." As it turns out, their escape from Germany involved an extended stay in Barcelona, and his account of the almost immediate and radical changes in society could have come straight from the pages of George Orwell's *Homage to Catalonia*, if Orwell had witnessed revolutionary Barcelona through the eyes of a child.

Still trying to process this aging Jewish businessman's idyllic recollections of his life experience with anarchist revolution and socialist collectivization, and because German Jewish Sunday lunches aren't exactly quiet affairs, I barely catch it when my second uncle's wife blurts out, "Oh yeah, my stepfather is an anarchist." Once I've processed what I think I've just heard, I turn in her direction, squinting confusedly, the gears in my head slowly grinding as they try to make sense of what I'm hearing. I mean, I'm used to hearing, "Oh yeah, so-and-so is also an anarchist" when I broach the topic. It's just that usually it's somebody's mom talking about some teenager who has heard of the Sex Pistols and has a circle-A patch because "Anarchy, dude!" or whatever. While math is no strong suit of mine, I'm fairly certain that the stepfather of this thirtysomething woman with two children who is sitting across from me is, um, unlikely to be a punk rock teenager. "Oh yeah, yeah, Patricio. He's been an anarchist activist all his life. I'll give him your number so you can get to know each other. I'm sure he'd love to meet you."

A few days later, a man gets off the number 55 bus at the stop where Patricio and I have arranged to meet. I'm not sure how I'm supposed to recognize him, but I look anarcho-subcultural enough that I'm not worried: he'll find me. Soon enough, as a bus speeds away and several people get off, I hear a gruff older voice behind me. "Tomas?" I turn to find what my adolescent eyes can only interpret as an ancient person. Which is how I would always experience him, as "ancient," although some basic math tells me that he was actually in his fifties when we met. Patricio wears dress shoes, nice pants, and a dress shirt. As we make our way the few short blocks toward our destination, I continue to fixate on the fact that this is just a standard, nondescript, regular human being, much like the ones I ran into in Paris from the CNT in exile. Lifelong worker, printer by trade, not an inkling of subcultural or anarchist youth-culture ghetto on him. Almost as quickly, it becomes clear to me that he is an incredibly well versed, well read, eloquent, and committed lifelong anarchist—who is also open and enthusiastic toward me, clearly excited at the prospect of new generations taking up anarchist ideas.

I'm not aware of it in that moment, or at least not as acutely as I am today, but his enthusiasm—aside from being a reflection of his good nature and anarchist ideals—is understandable. Patricio's generation of anarchists, who probably came of age around the 1950s, was brutally small in numbers and the first to be faced with an anarchism almost completely relegated from any sort of relevance in Argentine society at large, swept away along with the wave of Peronism's influence on the Argentine working class. Not only that, but they also had to contend with the military dictatorship of the 1970s and its brutal repression, which touched even those few remnants of active and organized anarchism that remained. Patricio's generation resisted, maybe even subsisted, as best they could. When possible, they edited journals, among other things keeping *La Protesta*, born in 1897 and today the world's oldest still-running anarchist publication, alive, although with understandably irregularly appearing issues.

They also, against all odds, kept some of the self-managed educational and social spaces of the anarchist movement's heyday open. Patricio and his generation nurtured the fragile flame of the anarchist idea, sustaining it inside the few physical spaces they were able to maintain—much like the Spanish old men of the CNT in exile in Paris—so that when a next generation were to come, they might find it still burning. They fought against the hands of time, the pain of marginalization, and the danger of repression to preserve the remnants of the anarchist movement. Thanks to their efforts, the next generation of anarchists would find a space to organize in and a previous generation to learn and draw from. Quite literally, they kept the lights on and held the door open for us.

And it's through that unassuming door, painted red and black, in the middle of a nondescript residential street in Villa Crespo, which if not for Patricio I might not have found (or at least not as quickly),

A lunch or dinner at the anarchist Biblioteca Popular José Ingenieros, in the Buenos Aires neighborhood of Villa Crespo, sometime in the 1990s.

that we enter … into the general assembly of the Biblioteca Popular José Ingenieros. There's maybe fifteen to twenty people sitting around a conference table in the middle of a brightly lit room, which is filled floor to ceiling with books everywhere. Yellowing books in a room that looks as if it hasn't changed one bit from the early '70s, when the library entered the space. The library was originally founded in 1935, with "two objectives: on the one hand to participate in the internal activity of the anarchist movement while at the same time consolidating itself in the neighborhood where it's located through loaning books, public conferences, practical workshops, movie screenings, etc."[2] Through the decades, aside from sheltering numerous anarchist groups and initiatives, it has been the operational center of the *La Protesta* editorial group as well as a meeting space for the leadership of the FORA in clandestinity, a task apparently made difficult not as one would expect because of the cops, but because "the neighborhood kids would play on the street until late and upon seeing the arrival of 'strange' people would start banging on the shutters and chanting that 'the anarchists are meeting!'"[3]

The crowd tonight is an eclectic mix of young people in their late teens and early twenties, and then the "olds," who range from their forties all the way to well into their seventies. It's not lost on me that there's next to nothing in the middle, but this is common in Argentina among the left and anarchists. Missing is the generation swallowed by death and exile during the dictatorship. But the folks at that general assembly, the main decision-making body of the library, represent a cross-section of Buenos Aires anarchism and all the people whom I would fall in with for the next year or so. There's the dreadlocked crusty kids from the downtown fanzine fair, which takes place every Friday in front of Congress and serves as a de facto weekly gathering for the young anarchos. From there we'll often head to a radio show some of the folks put on, or to whatever concert the thriving Coordinadora Straightedge Libertaria (Libertarian Straight Edge Coordinating Committee) might be holding that weekend. (Yeah, you read that correctly. It was a thing, and it was a big thing.)

Among the "olds," there are a few women, and a man who, to my great surprise and excitement, speaks Spanish with an unmistakable US accent. The BPJI apparently boasts its own in-house gringo anarchist. Why he lives in Argentina or how he ended up here I'll never find out (or most likely have forgotten, since it seems like a pretty obvious question). But he is a regular day in and day out at the library, and we will quickly become good friends, as although his Spanish is good I will find that he is very happy to have a fluent English speaker around.[4]

Another "old" sitting at that table is none other than one of the most prolific and best historians of anarchism of recent decades, Osvaldo Bayer. He is the author of *Rebellion in Patagonia*, *The Anarchist Expropriators*, and *Severino Di Giovanni: El idealista de la violencia* (The idealist of violence), to name just a few of the hits. As I stare at this living piece of anarchist history, a framed letter on the wall catches my eye. It is nothing less than a handwritten note signed by Peter Kropotkin. The room exudes the past and present of the anarchist movement.

Speaking of anarchist movements present and future, there are also a few folks from Grupo Anarquista CAIN (Anarchist Group CAIN). I don't remember how or when, but I soon begin to regularly attend their meetings. I will be a little intimidated by the older comrades, rarely speak, and not contribute much of anything ever—but I will listen, learn, and witness the beginnings of the process through which CAIN will mutate from a relatively diffuse group to what will eventually become the openly platformist Organización Socialista Libertaria (Libertarian

Public meeting of the Organización Socialista Libertaria, sometime in 2000.

Flyer from Grupo Anarquista CAIN, just as timely in the 1990s as it is today: "Slave factory seeks workers willing to: work rotating twelve-hour shifts; get paid bonuses and vacations in installments; pay their indemnity out of their own pocket; work weekends and holidays without protest; work free overtime." The text ends with a sarcastic jab at the bureaucratic unions and a call to "Organize and struggle!"

Fábrica de Esclavos

SOLICITA
OPERARIOS DISPUESTOS A:

Trabajar turnos rotativos y de 12hs.

Recibir fraccionado el aguinaldo y las vacaciones en cuotas.

Pagar de su propio bolsillo su indemnización.

Trabajar sin protestar los sábados, Domingos y Feriados

Trabajar horas extras gratis.

Si ud. es el desafortunado que reúne estos requisitos, presentarse en Avenida Flexibilización Laboral, entre CGT y Gobierno

Caso contrario
ORGANIZATE Y LUCHA

C(A)IN GRUPO ANARQUISTA

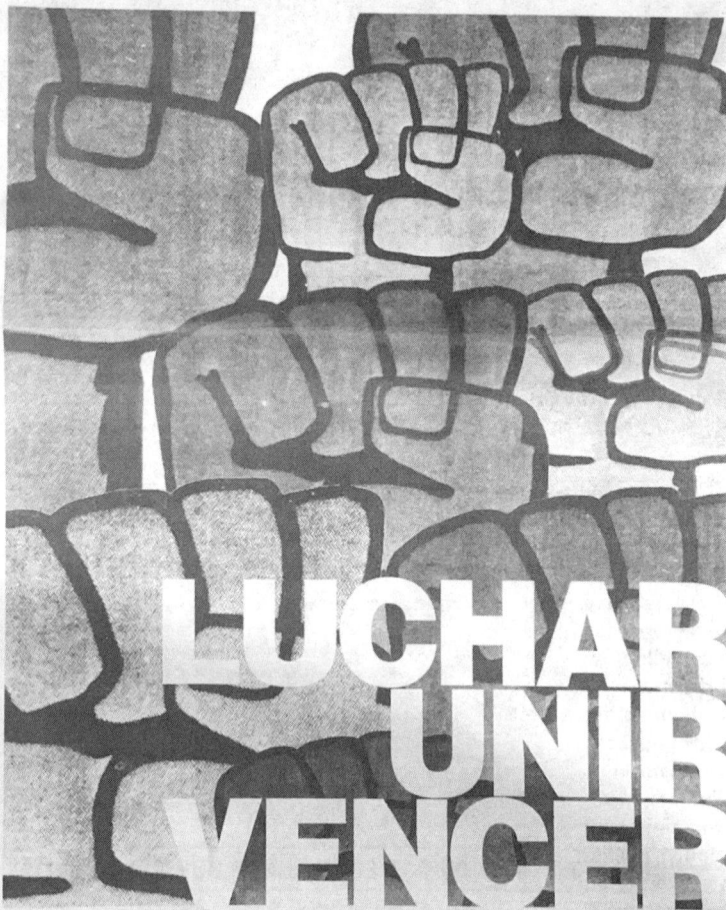

Cover of the March–April 2002 issue of *En la Calle*: "Struggle. Unite. Win."

Socialist Organization). Their debates and actions, their conviction that anarchism needs to again become a player in social struggles, to discard subculture and enter the battles in the streets and neighborhoods, will forge my positions as well, making it no coincidence that on my return to France I will find myself solidly in the CNT, and on arriving in the US in the platformist Northeastern Federation of Anarcho-Communists.

CAIN believes in an "organized anarchism" that is "part of the left," and in the necessity of implanting anarchism in the popular struggles of the time, of going "away from the libraries and into the streets."[5] Together with a few other like-minded groups, such as AUCA (meaning "rebel" in Mapuche) from La Plata and Organización Anarquista de Rosario (Anarchist Organization of Rosario), in late 1997 they begin editing an agitational periodical by the unsurprising name of *En la Calle* (In the streets): "En la Calle was a collective, and conflictive, creation.... These three collectives reached an agreement in the decision to develop anarchist political organizations that ... would have their militancy within popular organizations. Originally, the call was simple, ambitious, and also arrogant as to the state of the anarchist movement of the day: return anarchism to the streets."[6]

En la Calle rapidly blends iconography of the traditional left, positive references to clearly nonexplicitly anarchist revolutionary processes across Latin America, and the incorporation of pieces on anarchist theory and practice into its pages. We find ourselves deep in the era of Menemism (the neoliberal ideology of President Carlos Menem) and convertibility, with "the Menemist government advancing the implementation of neoliberal policies while the dominant sectors attempt to impose the postmodern ideas of the end of history and the triumph of capitalism."[7] Parallel to this, and while we are still unaware of what it will eventually dramatically spill over to, we are seeing some of the first stirrings of discontent and popular organization—particularly among the unemployed workers who will give rise to the *piquetero* movement, a spectrum of different unemployed and class-struggle-oriented groups and organizations whose umbrella name of *piqueteros* literally translates as "those who picket"—eventually leading to the explosion of December 2001. Revolutionary anarchists, while few in number, are not foreign to these developments.

At the same time, "the first steps begin to be taken in neighborhood activism, with AUCA and Grupo Anarquista CAIN taking part in

FURIA. Carros hidrantes y gases lacrimógenos para dispersar a los manifestantes.

A 21 AÑOS DEL ULTIMO GOLPE MILITAR

Nueve heridos y 20 detenidos

Fue en Plaza de Mayo • Grupos de jóvenes enfrentaron a la Policía • Los incidentes comenzaron cuando actuaba Mercedes Sosa • Todos los heridos son policías. PAG. 14

Clarín, March 25, 1997: "21 Years After the Military Coup. Nine arrested and 20 injured.... Groups of youths clashed with police.... All injured are police officers."

the first Meeting of Social Organizations, which takes place in La Plata in November 1997 with the participation of fifty organizations from different fields: labor, students, neighborhoods, human rights, etc."[8] Interestingly, none of the parties of the traditional left are present. In yet another sign of the growing organizational drive of Argentina's marginalized and impoverished, that same month over a dozen organizations take part in the Second National Meeting of Unemployed Workers, attended by over three hundred people and taking place in the heart of the working-class district of La Matanza. *En la Calle*, in an article titled "For Work, Land, and Freedom, Not One Step Backward!," describes it as follows: "We are more and more in the hands of fewer and fewer. This grotesque realization clashes directly with the advances in science and technology, with the philosophy of egalitarianism, with the concepts of civil society, and with the sacrosanct principles exuded by democratic institutions. But in this context a new protagonist is arising: the unemployed worker and his organizations. Without the hegemony of party apparatuses."[9]

Every once in a while, we feel the burning sensation of tear gas and hone our skills battling the cops, usually during clashes on the anniversary of the military coup or at mobilizations outside the homes of convicted murderers from the dictatorship, who walk free among us thanks to pardons received in the 1980s. But by and large, the explicit remnants of the once powerful and broad ecosystem of anarchism in Argentina are limited, and if anything more symbolic than practical.

A nonexhaustive list of some of these remnants, besides the BPJI, would include the once mighty FORA, which formally still exists. The (commendable) work of its adherents is more agitational than organizational, and the organization has a headquarters in none other than the traditional neighborhood of La Boca, not far from the world-famous and mythic stadium known as La Bombonera, home of Boca Juniors. The Federación Libertaria Argentina (Argentine Libertarian Federation), originally founded in 1935 as the Federación Anarco-Comunista Argentina (Argentine Anarcho-Communist Federation) before changing its name in 1955, also still exists and has a space where it conducts activities in downtown Buenos Aires. The journal *La Protesta*, which was once the organ of the FORA and reached a daily circulation of one hundred thousand, remains in existence to this day, despite some publishing interruptions throughout the course of the decades.

But despite some valiant efforts and budding initiatives, the reality is that anarchism in 1997 is still primarily relegated to concerts and fanzines, our few libraries and social spaces, and a very incipient participation by some comrades on the neighborhood, unemployed worker, and student fronts. It is far removed from the massive anarchist labor struggles at the beginning of the century, from the era of the Severino Di Giovanni and the expropriators, or even from the antifascist clashes and black blocs erupting or about to erupt in Europe and the United States.

But there's one name I keep hearing: "El Urubu." The younger anarchos speak of him in hushed, longing tones of respect and sadness, as if talking about a recently deceased folk singer in the movement. The older crowd is respectful of his memory, although in private they are understanding but critical. One night, while walking with Patricio to the bus station, I ask him who exactly Urubu was and how he died. Patricio usually gives me patient, thorough, and illustrative answers. Tonight his reply is curt and stern, something to the effect of, "They did something dramatic, romantic, and out of context, and he was killed by the cops."

As it turns out, El Urubu, whose legal name was Sergio Terenzi, was murdered by the Argentine police on June 7, 1996, in La Matanza, on the west side of the greater Buenos Aires area. On a cold winter night, he was "murdered in the process of carrying out an expropriation together with other comrades. Apparently, the cops were waiting for him. Apparently his weapon malfunctioned that night."[10]

Some upheld his memory as that of a comrade "who died fight-ing" and "an apostle of social revolution and of his libertarian ideals" while discreetly omitting the armed act that claimed his life.[11] But other comrades, quietly but surely, interpreted the decision of El Urubu and his comrades as simply another tool in the anarchist arsenal, just as aligned with the history and practice of our movement as any other. The book and the gun. The library and the armed conspiracy.

Patricio was having none of it. "Our movement has always had to carry a burden of solidarity with the most adventurist among us. We do it out of principle, and because we all can understand the urge to action that drives anarchists to feel that their conscience demands action. But sometimes it's simply bad decision-making, and in the past it's often been the perfect pretext for our enemies to defame and repress us. It was the case with the assassination attempts way back when, and back then at least there was some kind of basis of support and sympathy in society. Today there's nothing."[12] An older me might counter that a healthy and growing anarchist movement is and will always be threatening enough to the powers that be, and history has shown that if we don't provide the "justification" for repression they'll manufacture it regardless. But at the time I don't have the courage, and anyway it seems unwise to argue.

It dawns on me that this comrade, Patricio—who has been at the service of the anarchist idea for decades and who has experienced who knows what terror and proximity to death and suffering during the dictatorship—is likely speaking from experience. He could very well have been introduced to anarchism when he was my age, by an older comrade, just as he is guiding me into our movement. I can't recall if I ask him about it that night, or any other night. (And Patricio is no longer among us today to tell me his story.) But it's completely plausible, and if that was the case, then that comrade could very well have been a veteran of the Semana Trágica, the founding of the BPJI, or the era of Severino and the anarchist expropriators. There's potentially an entire century of history of the anarchist movement, of its beautiful aspirations and tragic defeats, held together by one single solitary degree of separation. The world may have changed, and it might feel like an eternity separates us, but maybe there isn't as much space as it seems between the anarchists building barricades in 1919 against cops, bosses, and nationalist mobs and those of us who would in a few short years be storming the skies at the presidential palace, hunting fascists, and hurling fire at the summits of the dictatorship of capital.

The only reminders of the once powerful influence of anarchist ideas on society are in the structures we still maintain, the names of our pastries, and in one just as unexpected area. Unbeknownst to me, yet another of those remnants lives in my neighborhood.

PRIMERA B

POR SERIOS INCIDENTES SE SUSPENDIO ATLANTA-DEFENSORES DE BELGRANO

Guerra en Villa Crespo

Hubo choques entre los hinchas y los visitantes rompieron el alambrado que bordea el **campo** de juego. Muchos criticaron la pasividad policial. El saldo: 12 detenidos y 8 heridos leves.

Otra tarde de violencia. Algo tristemente usual en el fútbol argentino. La pelota estuvo ausente en el partido de Atlanta contra Defensores de Belgrano (debía jugarse ayer, pendiente de la 29ª fecha). Todo comenzó apenas cinco minutos antes que empiece el juego, cuando en la esquina de Humboldt y Padilla, por donde ingresaban los hinchas de Defensores, se cruzaron ambas parcialidades, ante la pasividad de la policía y la extraña falta del vallado correspondiente.

Fueron cinco minutos de piedrazos, enfrentamientos cuerpo a cuerpo y palazos. La policía entró en acción, con palos y gases lacrimógenos, y separó a los violentos. Pero eso fue sólo el principio.

Cuando los hinchas de Defensores entraron al estadio, exaltados por la represión policial, comenzaron a derribar el alambrado periférico. Los bomberos reprimieron con agua, pero la gente ya había arrancado paneles del alambre.

Cuando los hinchas visitantes intentaban ingresar al campo de juego –también con cantos antisemitas–, la hinchada de Atlanta derribó una reja y corrió por un lateral para enfrentarlos. Otra vez los piedrazos y los gases lacrimógenos de la policía ganaron la escena.

El final ya se presentía: el árbitro Eduardo D'Amico suspendió el partido por falta de garantías. "El subcomisario me dijo que con el alambre roto no se podía jugar", afirmó D'Amico. Entonces, los hinchas visitantes abandonaron el estadio pero no su actitud violenta. Los golpes y los piedrazos se trasladaron desde el estadio hasta la Avenida Corrientes.

El partido era de alto riesgo (hace unos años los hinchas de Defensores tiraron jabones a los Atlanta, en un acto racista), los incidentes eran previsibles, pero nadie hizo nada para evitarlos, y si lo hizo, le salió mal. "El operativo tuvo muchos errores. La policía tiene que aceptar que se equivocó", afirmó Emilio Mehtce, presidente del fútbol profesional de Defensores de Belgrano. En presidente de Atlanta, Jorge Rubinska, dijo en cambio: "Tanto el informe del árbitro como el de la Policía indica que el partido se suspendió por disturbios en la tribuna visitante".

"El operativo no tuvo errores. No se colocaron vallas porque estas son un arma de doble filo, la pueden agarrar entre diez y tirárselas al personal policial", se excusó el encargado del operativo, Subcomisario Nicolás Belusci. Atlanta pagó por la prevención 2.500 pesos, por 85 efectivos.

La violenta tarde de Villa Crespo dejó como saldo a 12 detenidos (en la Comisaría 29ª), 5 policías con heridas leves –trasladados al Hospital Churruca–, 3 heridos por los piedrazos y destrozos en los automóviles estacionados en el lugar.

Y los que fueron a ver fútbol se volvieron a sus casas con las manos vacías. Todas las voces apuntaban a la ineficacia de la policía, pero lo cierto es que los violentos dicen presente en cualquier lado donde haya una pelota de fútbol. Y ayer fue otra de esas tardes tristes.

DESTRUCCION. Hinchas de Defensores rompen la reja para "combatir".

Hubo fútbol en tres canchas

Además de Atlanta-Defensores, se jugaron otros tres partidos pendientes de la Primera B Metropolitana.

Merlo 3-Almirante Brown 3. De la 31ª jornada. Partidazo. Con el resultado abierto hasta el desempate. Cardozo (35m PT) y Carlos Ramírez (12m ST, de penal) abrieron la cuenta para el local. Brown reaccionó y llegó al empate a través de Ojeda (33m ST) y Bazán Vera (35m ST, de penal). Merlo desequilibró otra vez gracias a Tourn (43m ST). Y en el último minuto, volvió a igualar Bazán Vera.

Español 3-Morón 2. El duelo de los Deportivos fue para el local. Barreto (24m PT) marcó la apertura para los visitantes. Empató Aspitía (37m PT). Español dio vuelta la historia con Franco Romero (13m ST) y Pablo López (21m ST). Descontó Sergio Zapata (37m ST).

Italiano 1-Talleres 2. En cancha de Colegiales, pendiente de la 26ª fecha. El local tenía controlado el partido. Hasta se había puesto en ventaja rápidamente, con un gol de Marcelo Bruno (12m PT). Sin embargo, la expulsión de Luis Sosa (31m PT) complicó todo. Y Zárate Aguirre (35m PT) y Villamayor (40m PT) revirtieron el resultado. En el complemento, el Sportivo no tuvo contundencia para igualar. Solchaga (44m ST), de Talleres, y Barros (45m ST), de Italiano, vieron la tarjeta roja.

Clarín, April 8, 2001: "War in Villa Crespo." Newspaper account of a match between Atlanta and Defensores de Belgrano, called off due to clashes both inside and outside the stadium.

3

"We're Going to Kill Jews to Make Soap"
Villa Crespo, Buenos Aires, Saturday, April 26, 1997

*En Villa Crespo, el que manda
soy yo ...
azul y amarillo es mi corazón,
y soy de Atlanta hasta el cajón*

*In Villa Crespo, I'm the boss ...
blue and gold is my heart,
and I'll be an Atlanta supporter
until the grave*
　　　　　—Guardia Negra,[1] "Bohemios"

"**G**o, go, go!" The huge metal gates slide open, the cop line in front of us finally parts, and we're off to the races. Maybe one hundred of us, if I'm generous, are participating in this weekend's edition of the famed Urban Athletics 400 Meter Sprint Challenge. Four hundred meters. The estimated distance between us and the Villa Crespo train station. The objective: sprint to the station and reach it before the next train does, thus thwarting the escape from the neighborhood of the other hundred or so folks who had a few months ago been waving a swastika flag at us and today spent several hours behind police protection chanting, "Ahí viene Hitler por el callejón, vamos a matar judíos para hacer jabon" (There comes Hitler down the alleyway, we're going to kill Jews to make soap).

As we near the station at full sprint, rocks begin to fly in all directions, while tires screech as panicked motorists stuck in the crossfire speed away. In the middle of the street, a little winded and completely focused on my target, I fail to notice that somebody has come up on me from behind, until I feel a hand grab my wrist tightly. As I spin around and manage to break his grip, I'm confronted with a burly, bearded man, well into his thirties. I can't make out if this is a cop or, um, "non-state actor opponent." But I do make out the rodlike metal object in his other hand, just in time to feel it come crashing into my back as I speed away.

TRES HERIDOS GRAVES

Feroz pelea en un recital de rock

Fue en parque Rivadavia ◆ Un grupo se apartó del público y atacó a "cabezas rapadas" que allí venden revistas y libros neonazis ◆ Después apedrearon las ambulancias ◆ Y el recital no se suspendió ◆ Cuando se desconcentraron, rompieron la vidriera de una vinería y la vaciaron ◆ La Policía no intervino ◆ La ironía es que el espectáculo fue para pedir justicia por Walter Bulacio, un joven muerto hace cinco años, luego de estar detenido en una comisaría. PAGS. 32 Y 33

Salvajismo. Un joven patea a un "cabeza rapada", que estaba caído.

Clarín, April 29, 1996: "Savage clash at a rock concert: . . . Skinheads selling neo-Nazi books and magazines were attacked." It's likely the man on the ground is Marcelo Scalera, poised to become a Nazi martyr.

★

You're assuming, not unreasonably, that I'm describing some clash between antifascists and Nazis in Buenos Aires. It's a fair assumption, and for the record there were some pretty significant ones during the 1990s. In fact, just a year earlier, after a series of escalating confrontations and ambushes by a group of neo-Nazis who had a book stall in Parque Rivadavia, a group of antifascists, leftists, and punks attacked the thirty or so Nazis who were guarding the stall as a leftist open-air concert took place nearby, killing neo-Nazi Marcelo Scalera.

You're assuming wrong, though. While the people desperately trying to escape my neighborhood did gleefully engage in anti-Semitic taunting, enraging me and lending my actions a veneer of antifascism, they were in fact visiting fans of Estudiantes de Buenos Aires, from a neighborhood on the west side of the greater Buenos Aires region. And my fellow sprinters were the *barrabravas*, essentially the Argentine version of hooligans or ultras, of my neighborhood club, Atlanta. Our nickname was "the Bohemians," but to rival fans we were simply "the Jews." And this scene was nothing more than just another weekend's adventure for me in and around the terraces of the lawless Wild West that is Argentine second-division football in 1997.

All Boys fans, from the Floresta neighborhood, hold a banner with an anti-Semitic play on words. "Yo nací en Floresta" means "I was born in Floresta," but with the z instead of the c it becomes "Me, a Nazi from Floresta."

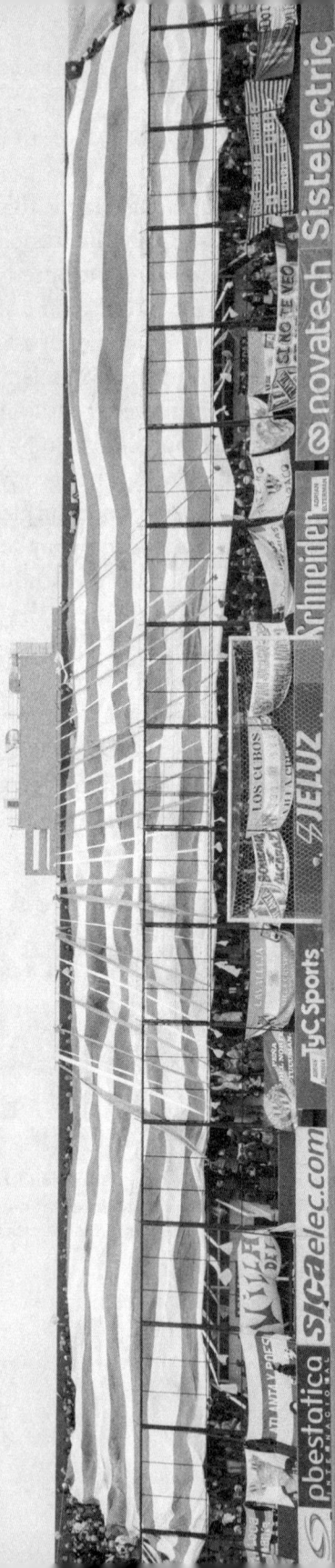

The terrace at an Atlanta match.

4

El Barrio No Se Quiebra
(The Neighborhood Doesn't Go Bankrupt)
Club Atlético Atlanta, Villa Crespo, Buenos Aires, Saturday, February 15, 1997

> Estas calles son mías,
> todas caminadas con el
> corazón
>
> These streets are mine,
> I've walked them all with my
> heart
> —La 25, "Chico común"

The streets of our cities and neighborhoods are always trying to tell us their stories. You just have to look hard enough. Stare between the lines as you look at a seemingly inexplicably shuttered and abandoned building in front of you. Speak the language of the graffiti furtively scrawled on its walls late at night. Decipher the codes. These, sprayed across my neighborhood in tones of blue and yellow, scream of a time past. Of resistance to a seemingly inescapable fate.

The decline of anarchism in Argentina, and the scene I find in 1997, is by no means an outlier, largely following patterns similar to the decline of the anarchist movement during the course of the late nineteenth to mid-twentieth century in the United States as well as other countries where it once held significant sway over the working class. But its resurgence in Argentina, be it in the 1970s and '80s or during the course of the rise of the antiglobalization movement of the late '90s and early 2000s, has been significantly milder than in a lot of those same countries. I'm fond of the dedicated, caring, and tight-knit community I have hopefully succeeded in lovingly sketching in the preceding chapters. A community that is inarguably devoted, but just as inarguably painfully small, particularly for a city of ten million inhabitants. While I quickly become a regular at the library and at anarchist events, I'm still a teenager with too much time to kill, and my activist drive is also somewhat tempered by the knowledge that my presence in the country is probably temporary.

So I walk these streets every day, or at least I do in the year or two in my teenage years during which I again find myself living in Argentina. Which is how I ended up at the scenes described above—walking the streets of the working- and middle-class neighborhood of Villa Crespo, which holds not only the BPJI, but also my grandmother's apartment as well as my dad's place of work. There are the commercial streets of Corrientes and Scalabrini Ortiz, where I spend an embarrassing amount of hours at the arcade playing football games and an almost equal though less embarrassing amount of hours ducking in and out of its bookstores seeing what, if anything, they have on anarchism or revolutionary history. I make my way to my grandmother's apartment, located where Scalabrini Ortiz gradually becomes more residential, almost never failing to pause and stare at the headquarters of the Communist Party of Argentina and the huge hammer-and-sickle billboard atop its several-story-tall building.

Let's just say the prime Buenos Aires real estate it owns has very little to do with a representation of its popularity or influence in society—and much more to do with the generous financial support once upon a time extended by the USSR to this profoundly Stalinist and pro-Moscow party. Every time I see the building I remember that as Trotskyists and other revolutionary communists were fighting, dying, and disappearing at the onset of the military dictatorship in 1976, these geniuses were marching those of their activists who were still free and alive into police stations to try to explain to the cops that it was all just a big misunderstanding. I always imagine the dialogue in my head, comical if not for how tragic it was: "You've made a terrible mistake arresting our comrades, officer. We're not like the ultras from the armed groups. We're a legal party and in favor of the civic-military convergence to put an end to the adventurists and preserve democratic stability in the country." I imagine the officer looking incredulously at the poor soul in front of him, exchanging a quick nonverbal "this can't be for real" glance with whoever is sitting at the desk with him, before answering, "Sure, whatever you say, buddy. But since you're here, why don't you just sit here in this cell too while we go figure this out."

I sigh, shake my head disapprovingly, and continue on my merry little way to Grandma's house with whatever haul of candy, newspapers, and magazines I've invested in for the day. After visiting Grandma,

I'll continue my stroll through gradually more residential parts of the neighborhood. It's Saturday today, which means I'll be passing a lot of observant Jews on their way to and from temple. We are, after all, in Villa Crespo, which is together with Once one of the two epicenters of Jewish life in Buenos Aires—and this says a lot, Buenos Aires being home to the largest Jewish population in Latin America, and one of the largest in the world.

The neighborhood's Jewishness is all around me. There's a Jewish restaurant, clearly Jewish names on several storefronts, and the occasional orthodox Jew walking completely at ease down the street. It's not lost on me that these are the same streets where some of the horrors of the Semana Trágica and its pogroms took place, when the nationalist and anti-Semitic mobs, after receiving some basic military training at a naval center, stormed the neighborhood to the cry of "If the Jews ... don't dare to come downtown, we'll attack them in their own neighborhoods."[1] While the pogrom may seem distant, incredibly even unknown and lost in history to many in this very community, the danger of anti-Semitic terror most certainly is not, as less than three years ago, in 1994, the Jewish social and cultural center AMIA, located only a few short kilometers from here, was bombed—taking the lives of eighty-five innocent people.

As the neighborhood again becomes more commercial, I reach the end of Avenida Warnes and its seemingly endless amount of car repair and spare parts stores, arriving at where my father works. He's also in the car business, and he works most Saturdays. It's barely 2:00 p.m. and I've already played at the arcade, wandered through bookstores, visited Grandma, eaten junk food, read magazines and newspapers, and pondered the ills of Stalinism. We have now reached the "I am bored and bemoaning that if I were in Athens or Paris right now I'd be at a demonstration and this would not be happening" phase of my day. But this Saturday, as I sit bored on the sidewalk trying to protect myself from the late summer heat under a tree, I notice a constant stream of people in blue-and-yellow jerseys walking past me, all headed in the same direction. I remember that we're maybe five blocks from the stadium of Club Atlético Atlanta, who currently find themselves in the second division of Argentine football.

Fast-forward maybe fifteen minutes. Never one to require much convincing to go on a potential new adventure, I find myself in the

The entrance to the shuttered and abandoned social center of Atlanta, once a focal point of community life in the Villa Crespo neighborhood.

terrace section of Atlanta's stadium, which has a total capacity of around thirty thousand spectators. Sound impressive? Sound nice? No, trust me, it isn't. If I'm generous, there's maybe one thousand of us in the stadium, three-quarters of which is composed of wooden stands that bend perilously as the ultras behind the goal jump and sing. The club, deeply linked to the Jewish community of its home neighborhood, has most definitely seen better days.

Almost next door to the stadium, maybe a block or so away, is a huge abandoned and decrepit property—itself probably the size of an entire city block. I walked by it a few weeks earlier, noticing the huge blue-and-yellow graffiti on its walls: VAMOS A VOLVER and EL BARRIO NO SE QUIEBRA, translating to "WE'LL BE BACK" and "THE NEIGHBOR-HOOD DOESN'T GO BANKRUPT." I made mention of it later that day while having dinner at a neighborhood friend's house and was caught off guard by the emotional reaction from his mother. "It makes me so sad to walk past there. And angry. It was auctioned off to real estate speculators after Atlanta was declared bankrupt in '91, and it just sits there abandoned since then. It's Atlanta's social and sporting center." She paused. "Er, it was, I guess."

María grew up in Villa Crespo, and while Jewish, she is most definitely not religious. Which apparently is unsurprising in this case. Villa Crespo is the part of Buenos Aires where "Jewish people are most 'integrated,' less tied to the religious aspect, which is also probably why their connection to Atlanta began to grow," according to Federico Kotlar, a journalist, Atlanta fan, and author of a book on the club's history titled *Atlanta: Una historia de valientes*.[2] María continued, "I grew up in that place. For decades it was the heart of the neighborhood. We'd play sports there, hang out at the pool, spend time after school." I thought she might be about to start crying, which teenage me found deeply and unacceptably awkward, so I quickly changed the subject.

As it turns out, the slow-moving drama of a neighborhood losing its local club, which lay at the heart of the community and which carried with it decades and decades of memories, not to mention it being a collective nonprofit social and sporting experience, has been playing out across Buenos Aires during the course of the decade: "For many, the neighborhood club is a temple filled with memories and affections. These institutions fulfilled, and to this day fulfill, the parental role of connecting and educating each generation that passes through them."[3] As Federico Chiapetta, subsecretary of sports for the Province of Mendoza, puts it, they are "a social instrument by definition" and provide functions that "not even the state can replicate," particularly in more impoverished neighborhoods.[4] These potential institutions of community dual power, where neighborhoods self-organize to advance their needs and interests outside of the sphere of both the state and capitalist logic, are experiencing rapid decline. Indeed, from their peak of over six hundred in the Buenos Aires region at the beginning of the twentieth century, the number has dwindled to just over half that by the beginning of the twenty-first.[5]

It's an apt metaphor of the general decay of community infrastructure during the 1990s. Club after club, unable to sustain rising operational costs, bleeding members as customs and lifestyles change and become more and more individualized. Bankrupt. Shuttered. Auctioned off. Closed.

Back at the stadium, which I would soon learn was the only asset of the club allowed by the bankruptcy judge to remain operational and not be auctioned off—along with its professional football squad—Atlanta loses 2–1 to Deportivo Italiano, another troubled but historic club,

ATLANTA La Unica Solución es Vender la Sede

Deudas

La Comisión Directiva de Atlanta comenzó 1992 con un verdadero desafío. El más duro desde que inició su gestión, allá por setiembre del '90. Es así que la institución de Villa Crespo, actualmente presidida por Ezequiel Salomón Kristal, ve peligrar la continuidad de la sede social, enclavada en pleno corazón de ese porteñísimo barrio, en la calle Humboldt 374, muy cerquita de la bohemia avenida Corrientes. Porque para mediados de este año (mes de junio), se deberá poner al día con los acreedores (la deuda, con "todo incluido", alcanza los 2 millones y medio de dólares), caso contrario, el predio social será rematado. Atlanta se encuentra en estado de quiebra, y sus dirigentes están agotando todos los esfuerzos para mantener el patrimonio del club. Pese a la ausencia del presidente Kristal (recién llegará mañana de Mar del Plata), quisimos saber cómo está la situación hoy, a poco menos de seis meses para conseguir el cancelamiento de la deuda. Y para eso conversamos con Emilio Varela, gerente de Atlanta, quién amablemente nos explicó cómo están encarando este grave problema económico-financiero que atraviesa la institución.

"Para que Atlanta se ponga al día con los acreedores y logre un momentáneo desahogo económico, no hay más remedio que poner en venta la sede social. Y si no, hagamos números. El club debe unos dos millones y medio de dólares, y el predio está valuado en casi cuatro millones de dólares. La cosa está bastante clara. Nos sacaríamos de encima las deudas y, encima, quedaría a nuestro favor cerca de un millón y medio de dólares, los que luego serían utilizados para construir una nueva sede, en el estadio. Ofrecimientos para concretar la operación tenemos varios, casi todos provienen de inmobiliarias, y los estamos estudiando minuciosamente. Tampoco queremos "regalar" la sede. De todas maneras, la venta es la única salida viable para mejorar la economía del club."

— Los dirigentes quieren vender la sede, pero, ¿cuál es la opinión de los asociados? ¿Están de acuerdo con la negociación? ¿Se resignarán a perder un predio que tiene pileta, canchas de tenis, gimnasio y otros salones que se utilizan para la práctica del deporte?

— Mire, el tema de la venta de la sede tiene, como todas las cosas, su lado negativo y su lado positivo. Negativo, porque nos desprendemos de un predio que fue construido con mucho esfuerzo, para que los socios pudieran disfrutar sus comodidades y sentirse allí como en su propia casa. Para que se practicaran la mayoría de los deportes y también para unir cada vez más a la familia. A los chicos, a los grandes, a todos. Pero tenemos también lo positivo. Porque con la operación, Atlanta podrá salir a flote en materia económica. No más deudas. No más dolores de cabeza. Sería como empezar a crecer nuevamente. El socio de Atlanta es inteligente. Sabe que si no se vende la sede, el club podría desaparecer. Y eso nadie lo quiere. Entre todos, levantaremos a la institución y la pondremos nuevamente en el lugar que alguna vez ocupó. Pero ya que nombramos a los socios del club, lamentablemente tengo que decir esto: no hace mucho, en 1983, teníamos 12 mil asociados. Ahora sólo hay apenas mil, de los cuales unos 800 son los únicos que pagan la correspondiente cuota. El socio de Atlanta se fue alejando de la institución. Cada vez más. Muchos se fueron a

otros clubes. Hoy por hoy tenemos poca gente que se acerca a nuestras instalaciones. Eso no nos ayuda para nada, pero seguiremos trabajando para recuperar el caudal societario, la columna vertebral para que una institución funcione bien.

— ¿No quedó ninguna posibilidad de arreglo con la convocatoria de acreedores?

— No, ya no. Las negociaciones fueron intensas. Buscamos todos los caminos para llegar a un acuerdo y lograr una forma de pago más accesible y así evitar el tener que llegar a esta situación límite. El acuerdo no llegó, y ahora no tenemos otra alternativa: vender la sede antes de que sea rematada. Entre los principales acreedores figura Futbolistas Argentinos Agremiados, UTEDYC y Obras Sanitarias. Muchos se refieren a juicios entablados por ex jugadores y ex empleados del club.

— Pasemos ahora a la parte futbolística. ¿Cómo están preparando el plantel para la reanudación del campeonato?

— Está quedando un "chiche". Tenemos que dejarlo en excelentes condiciones para que no tengamos más

que jugar en otra cancha que no sea la nuestra. Sólo nos falta colocar algunos alambrados y enrejados, más otras tareas menores, para que nos den el visto bueno. Calculo que en una semana más estarán terminados los trabajos.

— ¿Y al plantel cómo lo están manteniendo económicamente?

— Siempre hay algunos socios y allegados que se acercan y nos dan una mano. Así estamos afrontando los gastos que demanda la mantención del equipo. Los muchachos están poniendo una voluntad digna de elogio. Además, hacen un gran esfuerzo. Porque eso de jugar tres partidos por semana para ponerse al día con los partidos pendientes no es cosa fácil de soportar. El 15 de enero volverán al trabajo, en el estadio, siempre con la conducción técnica de Fernando Zappia. Para encarar la parte física tenemos contactos para traer a Adolfo Mogilewski, quien trabajaría junto al hermano de Patricio Hernández.

— Volviendo al tema sede, usted nos dijo que si se produce su venta se podría construir otra nueva en el estadio. Explíquenos eso es...

— Claro, las oficinas ya las tenemos instaladas en el estadio. Quedarían por rehacer todo lo que se utiliza para la práctica de los distintos deportes. Por ejemplo, canchas de tenis y paddle, gimnasios para básquetbol, fútbol, vóleibol y demás disciplinas. Y otros sectores, que serán destinados para confiterías, juegos de salón y para realizar espectáculos. Eso, lógicamente, llevará su tiempo y mucho dinero. Pero, como le dije antes, con la diferencia que nos quedaría con la posible venta de la sede, tendríamos dólares como para afrontar las obras, para beneficio de toda la familia de Atlanta.

Atlanta y su desafío. Los dirigentes y su ilusión de sortear este duro escollo económico, que pone al viejo club de Villa Crespo (fue fundado el 12 de octubre de 1904), en un delicado momento institucional. Su sede social corre peligro. La venta sería la única solución, según sus directivos. Mientras tanto, todo el barrio de Villa Crespo está pendiente de lo que pueda suceder con su querido club. Ese club que hoy, como nunca, necesita de su gente. Para que no agonice. Para que no se vaya muriendo día a día sin que le tiendan una mano...

Imagen de la sede de Atlanta. Su venta sería la solución...

Newspaper clipping illustrating the plight of many neighborhood clubs in the 1990s: "The only solution is selling the social center."

representing Argentina's Italian immigrant community. The game on the pitch and its result are anecdotal. What's striking, and not in a good way, is how this once vibrant center of the community and the neighborhood has been reduced to nothing more than a decrepit football stadium (which the city would indeed go on to shut down only six years later, deeming it unsafe). A place once full of people of all ages, kids, families, activities, and vibrant community life is now pretty much only visited once every couple of weeks by a couple hundred aging neighborhood men who rant and rave about past glory while vociferously lamenting the current spectacle taking place both on and off the pitch, and another one or two hundred neighborhood youths who make up its barrabrava.

Unsurprisingly, I'm in. What else are you going to do on a Saturday afternoon? Racing Club, my first-division club, plays on Sundays—so it's either this or watching old men haggle over the price of used car parts. By the next weekend, some of the neighborhood kids "convince me" to travel by train with them and the hooligans to an away game on the west side of Buenos Aires province, in Caseros—and by "convince" I of course mean "mention to me once that it was taking place." Stones rain down on the closed metal shutters of our train compartment both as we arrive and depart Caseros, but what I see inside the stadium cements my relationship with Atlanta from there forward. In the opposing terrace, the home fans proudly display a swastika flag while chanting about how they were going to be walking down the alleyway with Hitler, killing Jews to make soap. A few years later, opposing fans will even go as far as to throw bars of soap onto the pitch as Atlanta players make their entrance. The anarchist and antifascist in me is enraged and has found justification for the many confrontations to come. It's a chicken-and-egg situation, I'm aware. But although everybody around me would probably fight each other anyway over absurd neighborhood affiliations fueled by the social cannibalism of capitalist alienation and testosterone-driven macho culture, the undeniably explicitly anti-Semitic overtones of many of those wearing the differently colored jerseys week in and week out coat all the adventures to come with a veneer of antifascism that turn me into a willing and enthusiastic participant.

★

A postcard of the club's desperate measures to make ends meet: Atlanta players train while workers dismantle the stage after a concert by popular Argentine rock band La Renga.

In the span of at most a year, I took what I can only describe as an advanced course in practical antifascism, mass street combat, urban confrontation tactics, you name it. Most of all, I developed a proximity to violence that cured me definitively of the sense of entering unexplored—and often frightening—new territory most anarchists might feel when first confronted with physical combat against the state or fascists. The lower divisions of Argentine football in the '90s were a veritable no-man's-land, and in that incredibly short span of time I was caught and forced to kneel on train tracks as I was called a "fucking Jew" before being miraculously saved from who knows what fate by other Atlanta fans who happened to witness the situation, was ambushed by fans of Deportivo Morón who—I kid you not—flew dramatically out of the back of a refrigerator truck while throwing stones in the middle of a Villa Crespo avenue, found myself in the middle of a mass battle as fans of some team none of us had ever really even heard of saw our bus passing their neighborhood, and had to jump into a moving car to escape rival Nueva Chicago fans. Not to mention the situations where, in all honesty, we were the aggressors—such as the ambush of opposing fans at the Villa Crespo train station I already mentioned, or when we knocked down the gates separating us from the Arsenal de Sarandí fans on the other side, eventually chasing them clear out of the stadium, but not before I caught sight of not one but several knives brandished by the opposing hooligans.

The adventures were "great and all"—or at least I hold them no resentment, most likely because I was lucky enough, or skilled enough, or most likely a bit of both enough, to somehow escape all of them pretty much unscathed, and the antifascist in me felt vindicated every time I saw some lumpen who had just been yelling anti-Semitic slurs get put on the run. If anything, when I mentioned to the young comrades that I couldn't make this or that event on a weekend because I was alternately attending an Atlanta or Racing match, I was often met with playful derision at best. Even in Argentina, soccer was frowned upon by most anarchists. Aside from the admittedly shallow veneer of antifascism, the world of anarchism and antifascism and the world of my soccer clubs were worlds that to my knowledge didn't much intersect.

And while this was essentially true at that moment, little did I know that all this too could be traced back to the influence of the anarchist movement of yesteryear—extending beyond the names of some pastries and into the collective fabric of organizations that were replicated hundreds of times over across the neighborhoods of the country. That while their explicit connection to anarchism and workers' self-organization may have been severed as the decades passed—if not the influences implicit in their modes of organization—once upon a time things had been radically different. That the vestiges not only of workers' self-organization but also of anarchist influence still reverberated across the landscape of Argentine sporting and social clubs.

A collage inside Defensores de Belgrano's clubhouse shows the red-and-black-draped ultras section as well as its players and their red-and-black uniforms.

5

An Unlikely Heritage: The Immigrant, Radical, and Anarchist Origins of Argentine Football Clubs

El vil clero a la cara te escupe	*The vile clerics spit in your face*
y el que manda te aplique su ley	*the rulers apply on you their laws*
y el burgués tu sudor te arrebata	*and the bourgeoisie robs you of your sweat*
y te matan la patria y el rey	*and the fatherland and king murder you*
Viva viva la anarquía	*Long live, long live anarchy*
viva el pueblo productor	*long live the working people*
libertad, igualdad, y armonía	*freedom, equality, and harmony*
arte, paz, justicia, y amor	*art, peace, justice, and love*

—Anarchist folk adaptation of the national anthem of Argentina

The world of Argentine football is significantly different from what most people know as the world of professional sports. For starters, the team you are a fan of is actually not a team at all, but rather a *club social y deportivo* (which translates broadly to "social and sporting club") that happens to have a football team—just as it also has a basketball team, a volleyball team, a chess team, one or more social centers, a swimming pool to lounge about at in the summer, a gym you can use, a bar and restaurant to hang out in, and in a few cases even a school you or your children might attend. They are often, in every sense of the word, neighborhood clubs and social centers, intricately embedded in their communities.

Indeed, many of them can trace their origins back to the turn-of-the-nineteenth-century movement to create workingmen's social and sporting clubs.[1] Argentina was at that time in history something that seems difficult to imagine today: a land of mass immigration from Europe, a destination chosen by those seeking a new life in the Americas second in numbers only to the United States. As many of these newly emerging immigrant communities began to assert themselves and participate actively in the social activities of their new city, they organized in part along the lines of the social and sporting clubs. To this day Deportivo Armenio, Deportivo Español, and Club Sportivo Italiano reflect the legacy of immigrant communities organizing their sporting and leisure activity based on their nationality of origin, with the latter two even using exact replicas of their national teams' jerseys until well into the 1990s.

A further example, of course, is that of my neighborhood's Club Atlético Atlanta, a historic first-division club who have found themselves languishing in second or third division for going on forty years now. The anti-Semitic chants and displays of Nazi symbols from opposing fans I've already referenced even often resulted in match play being temporarily stopped by officials until the chants from the stands ceased. In one particularly heinous act of anti-Semitism during a match on February 26, 2000, opposing fans threw bars of soap onto the field as Atlanta players entered the pitch—alluding to one of Nazi Germany's most horrific crimes against humanity—as they chanted, "There comes Hitler down the alleyway, we're going to kill Jews to make soap."[2]

Other clubs formed during that era were organized very explicitly not only along lines of class or ethnic background but also of political affiliation. Given the size and strength of the anarchist movement in Argentina at the turn of the nineteenth century, it's unsurprising, then, that several of the social and sporting clubs formed during the first decade of the twentieth century were visibly and vocally anarchist, and some of those are still in existence to this day. Anarchism was deeply embedded in Argentine society, and this was reflected beyond the spheres of labor struggle and conflict with the state. In what they saw as their quest to uplift the human spirit and plant the seeds of a new society, anarchists articulated their movement into a rich tapestry of cultural, educational, and social manifestations.

As Juan Suriano outlines in his excellent portrayal of Buenos Aires anarchism of the period, *Paradoxes of Utopia: Anarchist Culture and Politics in Buenos Aires, 1890–1910*, the anarchist message "went beyond mere economic demands"—and conflict with the state—"to point toward the quantitative transformation of society. Workplace battles were merely a first step; their real goal was to rouse workers' sleeping consciences and build a different society. It was to that prospect that they devoted their best efforts."[3]

Coming of age "between the turn of the century and the Centenary Celebrations" (that is, the centennial of Argentina's independence), the anarchist movement "created a substantial number of centers and cultural circles where its militants delivered lectures, performed theatrical works, and held parties; published periodicals, pamphlets, books, flyers, magazines, and even a daily newspaper; spurred the creation of rational, free schools; and were crucial to the organization of tenement dwellers."[4]

The thriving anarchist press and the presence of its once numerous educational and social centers, numbering anywhere between thirty-five and fifty in the city of Buenos Aires alone during the first decade of the twentieth century, had the purpose of providing a constant educational, informational, and agitational presence.[5] These objectives are well summarized by the stated goals of one of the first such centers, the International Social Studies Circle, who outlined their objectives in *La Protesta Humana* (which would soon be renamed *La Protesta*) in 1901:

> To prepare the proletariat for emancipation, cultivate its moral and intellectual cohesion, and ready it for social struggle.
> To spread the principles of modern economic science among the proletariat.
> To support the foundation of a library, lecture hall, and a libertarian school for children, facilitating the education of workers and their offspring.
> To offer itself to workers' societies for all types of sociological and social propaganda.
> To hold propaganda meetings and debates in order to study the roots of underlying social problems.[6]

But anarchist participation in the world of workingmen's social and sporting clubs was initially by no means a given, as the original position of many anarchist activists of the time toward this new game was similar to that of the anarchists of today. The rise of the new sport alarmed anarchists, as "instead of attending the workers assemblies or ideological picnics, workers would spend their Sundays at the stadiums."[7] It was seen not only as a distraction, but also as running counter to the embodiment of the human spirit that anarchists sought to foster, in the same vein as other activities of the time of which they disapproved, such as the circus, drinking, dancing, gambling, and most of all the yearly carnival season.

The anarchist critique of carnival is interesting, because it largely mirrored the modern anarchist critique of soccer. The "cathartic, unbridled revelry of the Carnival made it easier for people to go back to work in the factories and workshops, where they were exploited with impunity." Anarchists held that it was an activity that embodied "myriad social blights (lechery, prostitution, triviality, alcoholism, and ignorance, among others), prevented the rationalization of behavior, and squandered revolutionary energies."[8] A 1904 issue of La Protesta stated, "We should not lower anarchy to men's vices, but make them shed their vices and rise to anarchy. Workers' events should provide instruction and recreation."[9]

Central to this conception were the anarchist veladas, multifaceted and often all-day events that blended elements of both elite and popular culture with a specifically anarchist model, often beginning with a collective singing of a revolutionary anthem like "El Hijo del Pueblo" or "The Internationale." Veladas were the anarchist attempt "to respond to workers' social needs and engage their non-working hours with a cultural project that was fun and also instructed them in the libertarian ideal. To do this, they deployed refined artistic and educational practices—such as theater, musical performances, and lectures—as well as more traditional recreational pastimes like games and festivities."[10] Veladas and parties quickly became "foremost among anarchists' strategies for engaging free time" in the hopes of not only advancing the libertarian ideal but also discouraging workers from "patronizing bars, brothels, cabarets, Carnival celebrations, and other sites that supposedly promoted debauchery and alcoholism."[11] It's also important to note that even though the anarchist movement of the time was deeply patriarchal (as were all political movements and society in general), it was "constantly stressed that anarchist parties were family affairs and encouraged the participation of women and children."[12]

But just as was the case with dancing, which, certainly to the relief of Emma Goldman, was originally resisted but eventually incorporated into the anarchist veladas, with even some famous tangos carrying the anarchist message despite the initial rejection of the "lascivious dance," many anarchists eventually reached the conclusion that the leisure space of the social and sporting clubs was no longer one they could or should cede to rival political factions or, worse, the growing influence of nationalist associations who sought to assimilate workers and inculcate them with patriotism through the clubs. The anarchists of the time "had to organize against this, and thus they decided to jump onto the pitch and became key players in the formation of some of the first neighborhood clubs of our country. Thinking tactically not only about how to win the match, but also, what will the club be named? What color will the jersey be?"[13] And so, the anarchist sporting and social clubs began to proliferate.

The first anarchist club in Argentina, by the name of Club Atlético Libertad (Liberty Athletic Club), was born in 1901 in an unlikely place: the city of Salta in the far north of the country, significantly far from the urban centers where anarchism was most influential. The humble club, which exists to this day, was founded by "anarchist workers and artisans." It quickly became much more than a mere sporting club, as "the founders of the club managed to practically convert it into a unionization space" in which workers of all trades and fields gathered to "debate about politics, revolution, communism, and anarchism; to set prices for labor, discuss and plan social activities, exchange infor-mation about different trades or about working conditions."[14] Closely aligned with the anarchist FORA, the club was "almost permanently subject to attacks from Salta's oligarchy," who also promptly founded the rival club Gimnasia y Tiro de Salta, currently in the second division of Argentine football, as a hurried response to the growing influence of the anarchists.[15]

Just as Club Atlético Libertad still proudly sports the red-and-black crest of its anarchist founders, two neighborhood clubs today partici-pating in Argentina's second division still sport red-and-black jerseys harking back to their anarchist origins. The first is Chacarita Juniors, born on May 1, 1906, in an anarchist library.[16] The second, founded less than a month later, is Defensores de Belgrano, whose red-and-black colors were chosen to represent "the socialist and anarchist ideals of its founders."[17] Ironically, the club is today located directly across the street from the former ESMA (Escuela de Mecanica de la Armada, or "Navy

The anarchist red and black of Defensores de Belgrano's club crest.

Graffiti reading "Defe and Nothing More" ("Defe" being short for Defensores de Belgrano) on the gates of the infamous ESMA center, used by the Argentine military to torture and exterminate thousands of "subversives" from 1976 to 1983.

The entrance to the terrace section of Defensores stadium, named after disappeared Montoneros militant Markitos Zuker.

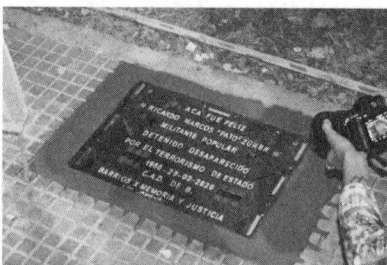

"On this spot, Ricardo Marcos 'Pato' Zuker, popular militant detained and disappeared by state terrorism, knew happiness. Club Atlético Defensores de Belgrano. Neighborhoods for Memory and Justice." Plaque located at one of the entrances to Defensores de Belgrano's stadium.

School of Higher Mechanics"), one of the largest and most infamous torture and murder centers of the Argentine military during the last dictatorship—now a museum to remember and expose the crimes and horrors committed there.

Since May 25, 2001, the terrace section of Defensores stadium, which its ultras drape in red and black every match day, carries the name "Markitos Zuker" in honor of a club member and fan who was disappeared by the military junta. A member of the Montoneros, the largest guerrilla organization in Argentina at the time, Zuker was held for forty-six days in 1977. Incredibly, he was released and managed to flee the country—first to Brazil and then to Spain. In 1979, he made the decision—as part of a larger Montoneros operation—to return to Argentina, and on February 29, 1980, "he was captured by a task force of the First Army Corps and the Intelligence Battalion 601."[18] He was never seen again, joining the ranks of Argentina's thousands of dead and disappeared during the military dictatorship. Although his body was never found, it is believed that he was executed together with three others at the nearby torture and extermination center of Campo de Mayo.[19]

Less than two years after the 1906 founding of Defensores de Belgrano, in April 1908, came the founding of yet another Buenos Aires club, with the explicit name of Libertarios Unidos (United Libertarians). Legend says that on learning of the name of the newly founded club, none other than the infamous Colonel Ramón Falcón—later assassinated by Simón Radowitzky's bomb to avenge the eight fallen anarchists killed by Falcón's repression—"suggested" the club change its name.[20] The club apparently resisted that pressure, until it was renamed in 1919 "by government decision ordering the name change, anarchism being a prohibited idea."[21] Club Atlético Colegiales is currently in the second division of Argentine football, and while it no longer sports the red and black colors on its jersey, having traded them in during the late 1920s for a red, yellow, and blue inspired by the Spanish republican flag, its stadium still proudly carries the name of Libertarios Unidos.

The list goes on, with the 1915 founding of El Porvenir (The Future) in Gerli, to the south of the greater Buenos Aires area, by anarchist workers, "as anarchists realized that football was being embraced by the popular classes they aspired to represent" and clubs began to appear as "trenches of resistance during times of fierce repression against those considered dangerous to the established order."[22] El Porvenir's activities

The inside of the stadium still bears the original red-and-black club crest of Libertarios Unidos (United Libertarians), the club's original name.

Some of the club crests of Colegiales through the years: Libertarios Unidos, followed by Sportivo del Norte after anti-anarchist repression forced the name change, and finally the present-day Colegiales.

The seated section of what is still officially Estadio Libertarios Unidos (United Libertarians Stadium). The tricolor scheme of the current club crest and seats is said to be an homage to the Spanish republicans.

included wrestling, weight lifting, boxing, figure skating, athletics, volleyball, chess, and many more, including, of course, soccer (they are currently in the fourth division). Its founding members would also go on to open a workers' library in the area as well as the local offices of the anarcho-syndicalist FORA.[23]

While the name might not sound like an explicit reference to anarchist ideals, it was very much in keeping with a prominent theme among anarchists of the time, which was the firm belief in science and progress—an enlightened future—as emancipatory forces in society, the advance of which would inexorably help guide humanity toward anarchism. Many social centers had names similar to El Porvenir's, "pointing towards science's centrality in the construction of the new society: Labor and Science, Light and Progress, Initiative, Forward, New Directions, Creation, Aspirants to the Ideal, New Era, and Evolution."[24]

The current name of one of the last clubs founded by anarchists in Argentina, Club Atlético Florentino Ameghino from the Patagonian city of Comodoro Rivadavia, is also a reference to the "scientific, ethical, and spiritual convictions that informed the materialistic, positivistic, and secular foundations of the socialist discourse."[25] *Socialist* and *anarchist* are used here interchangeably, and the name was a veiled reference to the scientific convictions of Florentino Ameghino. The club was originally founded on February 12, 1919, by workers from the local oil fields under the name of Club Atlético Germinal, in reference to the epic novel by Émile Zola about a coal miners' strike in 1860s France. The bosses and the nationalist organization Liga Patriótica Argentina also had a club, and "incidents between the players and spectators were recurrent" when the two faced off against each other, necessitating that "police perform patrols around the field of play" in order to keep both sides at bay.[26] In 1923, General Alonso Baldrich, on being designated as administrator of the state-run oil field, called the club and stated to them that "either you change the name or you disappear"—leading them to adopt the less explicitly anarchist name of the scientist Florentino Ameghino.[27]

Just as one Germinal was changing its name, the last of the anarchist clubs of Argentina was being founded by almost the exact same name, this time in the nearby city of Rawson, the capital of the province of Chubut. That Germinal, Club Atlético Germinal, bears the same name to this day, which was chosen to represent the "anarchist and syndicalist sympathies" of a founder.[28]

Argentinos Juniors players pose with a banner reading "In Homage to the Martyrs of Chicago" for May Day, 2021.

I've left the most famed of the anarchist clubs for last: Argentinos Juniors of La Paternal.[29] Argentinos Juniors, Diego Maradona's first club, three-time Argentine national champions, and 1985 Intercontinental Cup finalist, was founded in 1904 in the Buenos Aires neighborhood of La Paternal and traces its origins back to a fusion of two clubs, one of socialists by the name of Sol de la Victoria and the other of anarchists by the name of Mártires de Chicago (Martyrs of Chicago, after the Haymarket martyrs). While Argentinos Juniors might seem like an odd name choice for a club of anarchists and socialists, it is logical in the context of the very real anti-anarchist and "foreign-born radical" hysteria and brutal repression of the time and was chosen to prevent drawing undue and unwanted attention from the state or reactionary patriotic mobs. Its actual members, though, joked that the club's initials, AAAJ (standing for the full name, Asociación Atlética Argentinos Juniors), actually stood for "Adelante Anarquistas Avancemos Juntos," meaning "Forward, Anarchists, Let's Advance Together."[30] Their choice of "association" rather than "sporting club" is also no coincidence, referencing their desire for the club to go beyond the sporting realm and also serve as a space to discuss labor, life, and political issues.

One of the many murals in homage to Diego Maradona around AAAJ's stadium, which bears his name: "From La Paternal to the World—Land of God.

Another mural around AAAJ's stadium, in memory of the disappeared during the dictatorship: "Memory. Truth. Justice."

A mural marking the intersection of soccer and anti-imperialism: Maradona's "hand of God" against the British during the 1986 World Cup, four years after the war between the two countries.

While little to nothing is left today of the explicitly political character of these clubs, and even less of their original anarchist character, their foundational status as such—or, to be precise, as "civil associations," as is their legal status in Argentina—does still carry over to their actual ownership and operating structures. To be clear: There is no owner. The clubs are owned collectively by their members, who pay their monthly dues and in exchange can participate in the activities the club organizes, play on its teams, use the facilities, and, in most cases, attend football matches in the terrace section free of charge. Finally, much like any other kind of club, management from president on down is democratically elected by the dues-paying members.

This creates a sense of both belonging and participation, which is to a large degree difficult to replicate elsewhere. While there are, of course, other professional football teams in other countries that are also part of larger clubs with similar structures (although this is sadly less and less the case as more and more clubs become privatized), rarely do these have the degree of activities that Argentine clubs do, much less their own schools.

While I could never muster the enthusiasm to care too much about which billionaire's hobby project wins a particular game or event, or

The neighborhood club spirit summarized: "In the name of nobody, for the benefit of everybody."

The five-a-side soccer and basketball court at Racing Club's Villa del Parque social center, where we hung out endlessly. The banner reads, "It's a prolonged kiss that my heart gives you."

The enormity of a Racing Club match in the 1990s. This banner was, back then, the largest football banner in the world.

wrap my head around the very American phenomenon of entire teams just packing up and leaving for another city on the whims of a business-man, I identified strongly not just with my particular clubs but with the world of clubs in general. I am specifically a fan of my neighborhood club, Atlanta, with its Jewish community ties and the practical lessons in antifascism it forced on me during my teen years, and the giant Racing Club de Avellaneda. But while my fandom for those particular two has to do greatly with the luck of the draw (my Jewishness, the neighborhood I lived in, and a first-division club I pretty randomly chose at a young age), what drew me to them and kept me there applies to the world of Argentine social and sporting clubs generally.

It was a world of endless days spent playing soccer with your friends until you couldn't stand or they finally turned off the lights, of hanging around at the pool or eating yourself silly at barbecues. And, of course, of weekends spent going crazy singing and yelling at the stadium, or of unspeakable adventures traveling around Buenos Aires on away days. In my specific case, it was a world that represented something close to the only stability in my life. I lived most of my childhood outside of Argentina, and the club, its centers, and its stadium was a world that I knew I could always return to and find just as I left it, no matter how far or how long I wandered. A home that would always and forever be there for me.

Or so I thought.

Olé

diario deportivo

Los suples de Independiente y San Lorenzo

El paraíso terrenal que los hinchas del Rojo y del Ciclón esperaban, llega con Olé todos los viernes.

¿Lo vamos a dejar morir?

La Justicia ordenó liquidar todos los bienes de Racing y el domingo ya no juega. Debe 60 millones pero lo cerrarán por no pagar una deuda de 300 mil. Le queda una sola carta: apelar a la Corte Suprema. La AFA esperará y reprogramará todas las fechas. Los hinchas, reunidos en el club, agredieron a Lalín.

Olé, March 5, 1999: "Are we going to let it die?"

6

Solo Entiende Mi Locura Quien Comparte Mi Pasión

(My Insanity Can Only Be Understood by Those Who Share My Passion)

De pendejo te sigo	*By your side since I was a kid*
junto a Racing siempre a todos lados	*together with Racing always everywhere*
nos bancamos la quiebra	*we stood up to bankruptcy,*
el descenso, y fuimos alquilados	*relegation, and [the club] being rented out*
no me olvido ese día	*I'll never forget the day*
que una vieja chiflada decía	*that a crazy old lady was saying*
que Racing no existía que tenía	
que ser liquidado	*that Racing no longer existed, that it had to be liquidated*
si llenamos nuestra cancha y no jugamos	*we filled our stadium with no match being played*
defendimos del remate nuestra sede	*we defended our social center from being auctioned off*
si la nuestra es una hinchada diferente	*our fans are different*

—Los Rodríguez, "Para no olvidar"
(Racing Club terrace version lyrics)[1]

On March 4, 1999, my fanaticism increased exponentially, as that world I had imagined to be eternal threatened to fall apart with the words "Racing Club civil association has ceased to exist." We all remember exactly where we were when it happened, the same way people in the US remember where they were and what they were doing at the moment of the Kennedy assassination or the September 11 attacks. A faceless weekday afternoon like any other when Liliana Ripoll, until that moment some bureaucrat working in relative anonymity managing Racing Club's bankruptcy proceedings, declared on live television that since the club's continuing operations had no reasonable prospects of turning a profit and advancing toward paying its creditors, the only logical next step was to cease operations, dissolve the club, and proceed to the auctioning off of its physical assets.

Within minutes hundreds, and later thousands, would converge on the streets of Avellaneda outside our social center—one of two social centers operated by the club, the other being in the more central and middle-class Buenos Aires neighborhood of Villa del Parque, and along with our stadium one of the three principal physical assets to be auctioned off. Grown men cried inconsolably as if grieving the death of a loved one, others walked around as if in a dazed stupor, seemingly unable to comprehend that this could actually be reality, while still others hugged and consoled each other as best they could. But even then, in the immediate aftermath of the announcement and in an atmosphere of acute confusion and grief, the first signs of resistance began to appear. One man, his voice repeatedly cracking as he held back tears, spoke passionately into a journalist's camera and to anybody close enough to hear: "We've been brought to this by decades of corrupt politicians and club managers, they've made millions getting rich off of our passion. No politician will save us, no businessman will rescue us. We, the people of this club, have to get organized and defend it."

Eventually, Daniel Lalín, the club's president and the person who actually filed for Racing's bankruptcy, depending on whom one chooses to believe either as some desperate measure to try to reduce the burden of its $60 million debt or as part of a cynical ploy to have the club privatized and then try to become its owner, emerged from the building to speak to the crowd. He didn't make it ten seconds before a huge drum flew through the air and into his face, leaving him bleeding and forcing him shortly afterward to abandon his attempts at a speech. The message was unmistakable: We're done with politicians and business interests. This is about passion, about defending our club and by doing so a pillar of our community. A space that defies reason and the logic of profit. Racing's greatness is in its people, and you'll have to get past us to close it.

Over thirty thousand people attended our stadium on the first Sunday following the announcement. It was the largest attendance at

Clarín, March 1, 1999, three days before bankruptcy is declared: "Racing fans can only watch and wait in the face of the club's economic crisis.... They suffer a lot, and as is their tradition, they don't lose hope."

QUIEBRA Y LIQUIDACION

¿Será verdad que Racing ya no existe?

Es un club símbolo, y fue el primer campeón mundial argentino • No gana un título desde 1966, pero su hinchada sigue siendo enorme • Como no puede pagar, iría a remate • La esperanza: un acuerdo con los acreedores. **PAGS. 51 A 55**

RADIOGRAFIA DEL DERRUMBE

1 En 1996 bajan la deuda de 28 millones a solamente 12.

2 En 1998 salta a 52 millones y el presidente Lalín pide la quiebra.

3 El juez sólo reconoce 34 millones de deuda. Parece que hay salida.

4 Pero no. Y anoche, le tiraron un redoblante en la cara a Lalín.

NESTOR SIERRA / Clarín

CORAZON HERIDO. Mariano Merlo, 26 años, ayer, frente a la sede. La gente lloraba.

Clarín, March 5, 1999: "Is it true that Racing has ceased to exist?"

any football stadium in Argentina on that weekend, with one particularity to the stat: There was no match. It was just tens of thousands of people, of all ages and from all walks of life, coming together in the first steps of what would become a largely self-managed and autonomous movement of club members and fans proclaiming that "passion cannot go bankrupt, or be legislated out of existence." I wasn't there that day, or on the day of the announcement, as I was still living in Paris. It made the feeling of impotence, helplessness, and rage all the more powerful. For hours I sat in my room in an almost catatonic state, and for days if someone asked how I was (my nonexistent poker face already hinting strongly at "not well") I was placed in the somewhat awkward position of trying to explain to a European, probably an anarchist to boot, that I was constantly on the verge of tears because, um, "a football club might be closing." Unlike those in Buenos Aires, there was no social center or stadium at which I could grieve, mourn, or organize collectively.

My decision to drop everything and temporarily move back to Argentina a few short months later was motivated in no small part by my desire to be an active participant, rather than a helpless spectator, in

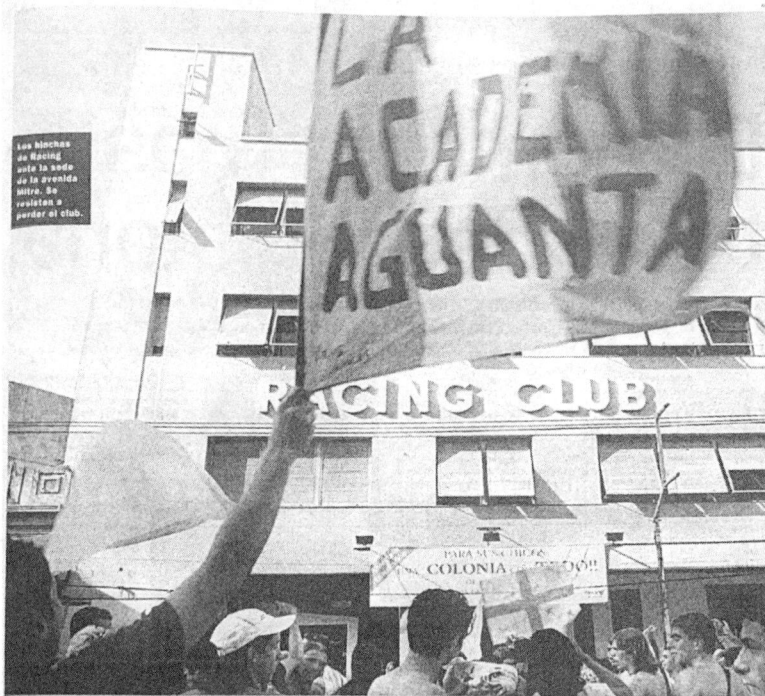

Los hinchas de Racing ante la sede de la avenida Mitre. Se resisten a perder el club.

RACING Y EL MOMENTO MAS TRISTE DE SU HISTORIA

¿SER O NO SER?

La Justicia decretó la liquidación de Racing. El acuerdo de los acreedores es la única salida. Los hinchas se concentraron ante la sede. Lalín quiso hablar y fue agredido.

Clarín, March 5, 1999: "To be or not to be? Racing and the saddest moment in its history." Fans congregate outside the Avellaneda social center following the announcement.

Daniel Lalín, Racing president who declared the club's bankruptcy, is hit by a drum as he tries to address the crowd in Avellaneda.

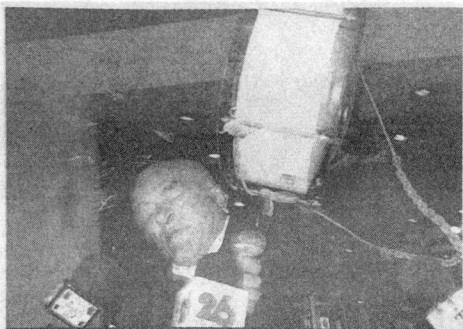

LA AGRESION. El redoblante pega de lleno en la cara de Lalín. Sus anteojos vuelan en mil pedazos.

Olé, March 7, 1999: "A Sunday without Racing: It could never happen, but it happened. Football has started and Racing watches from the sideline."

Olé, March 8, 1999: Despite the team not playing that Sunday, "almost 25,000 people attended Racing's stadium. The resistance remains unbreakable." Many estimates put the number at more than thirty thousand.

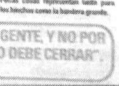

the fight to save our club. It turned out to be an eighteen-month-long struggle, similar in many ways to many of the explicitly social and political struggles I had experienced previously in Paris. And while it might sound surprising on the surface, it actually makes sense: In many regards, just as was the case with the *sans-papiers* ("illegal" immigrants) or unemployed movements, this was nothing other than a community organizing to take the initiative over matters that concerned them, to protect an essential aspect of their social and recreational life (not to mention several hundred jobs) and make use of their collective strength to defend their interests. All of it in a self-managed capacity, free from the influence of politicians or businessmen.

Much the same as in an autonomous or anarchist struggle, we made use of a variety of tools and strategies. We leafleted outside the courthouse. Demonstrations of thousands snaked through downtown on their way to Congress, proclaiming loudly that the corrupt politicians responsible, those who had intentionally mismanaged the club and lined their pockets at its expense, should be the ones held accountable for the club's situation. Still others began, in a stunning display of mutual aid and optimism in the face of a most uncertain future, converting a barren wasteland that was property of the club into yet another sporting and social center, funded exclusively by the force of their own time and labor.[2]

When the day came, in August 1999, that the state-sanctioned auctioning off of the club's physical assets was to begin, including the auctioning of our social center in the Buenos Aires neighborhood of Villa del Parque, there was direct action and militant confrontation. Thirty people had barricaded themselves inside the building the previous night, and another five hundred gathered outside in the morning to block the entrances—only to find police behind metal barricades already there as they arrived. When word spread that the police and auctioneer were about to try to enter the building, a confrontation quickly ensued, by the end of which six police officers were injured, five people were arrested, the auctioneer was chased away and saved himself by hiding inside a parking garage, and I was laid flat on the ground with a policeman's boot literally on my head.

Not only did I gloriously manage to somehow evade arrest immediately following that less-than-promising scene (and eventually be voted my school's "Most Likely to End Up in Prison" as that image made

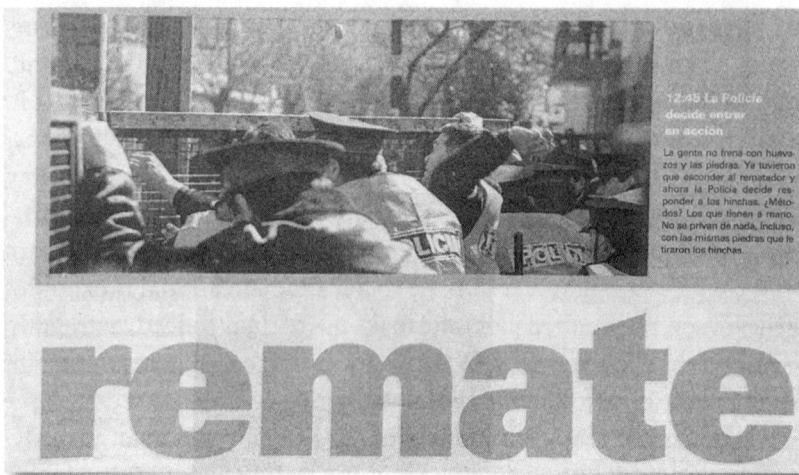

Olé, August 13, 1999: "Auction." Police officers throw stones at Racing fans who are trying to storm the entrance of the social center in order to stop it from being auctioned off.

the front page of the next day's newspaper, next to a headline reading "Despite the pressure, Racing resists"), but also, most importantly, there was no auction that day, nor any other day. Thanks to the popular pressure, a law was eventually passed in Congress that protected our club, and many other smaller ones in similar situations, from bankruptcy and disappearance. Part of the cost of this was that a period of privatized management followed, one in which we indeed temporarily ceased to be a club and became a business, a fact fans from our neighborhood rival club from across the street love to remind us of. And there was a yearslong, and eventually successful, struggle against that reality as well, but that story is deserving of another book unto itself.

As is, of course, a comprehensive and honest discussion of some of the world-famously extremely negative aspects of the world of Argentine football and clubs, which I have either completely glossed over or only mentioned in passing. The clubs' importance as social anchors in their neighborhoods means that the conflicts between club fans often take on an almost gang-like character, generating a phenomenon of football violence that is much more widespread and entrenched than in most other countries. Not only is this violence often of poor versus poor, a kind of completely needless mass social cannibalism, but in the last decades the barrabravas, which again is the Argentine term for football hooligans or ultras, have often been weaponized as shock forces

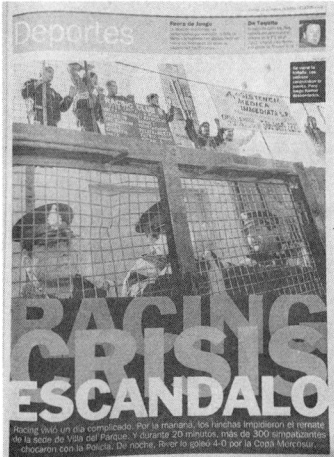

Clarín, August 13, 1999: "Racing. Crisis. Scandal." Fans who have barricaded themselves inside the social center can be seen behind the police line.

Olé, August 13, 1999: "Despite the pressure, Racing resists." Under the policeman's boot, the author of this book in one of his less glorious moments.

VILLA DEL PARQUE

Aunque le pesa, Racing aguanta

Cuatrocientos hinchas impidieron el remate de la sede. Hubo escándalo, 8 heridos y 5 detenidos.

Summer camp at the Villa del Parque social center, 2024.

Plaque in honor of those "who with their courage and fortitude prevented the auctioning off of this social center."

The entrance to the Villa del Parque social center. The floor decal reads, "Together Forever."

answering to one politician or another, intimidating and beating political opposition in both the political and the trade union spheres. And, of course, the club nature of Argentine football absolutely does not make it exempt from the multibillion-dollar industry that is football globally, an industry that is well known for its corrupt nature—and Argentina is not only no exception, it is probably one of the most flagrant cases.

None of this changes the fact that to this day, when I walk past Racing Club's Villa del Parque social center, instead of the inevitable parking garage or shopping center that would have replaced it had the auction we prevented on that August morning in 1999 been successful, I am greeted by the shrieks of happy kids playing around at the swimming pool.[3] Inside, there is a constant stream of families coming and going with their children, either to take them to one of the many activities the club offers or to enjoy a meal or a barbecue together. And somewhere inside that building and its maze of children, families, and activities is something that will forever tear at the strings of my little anarchist heart. As anarchists, our struggle is often selfless, and even when successful, rarely are we thanked or recognized for our efforts and sacrifices. We organize and fight in anonymity, both as a matter of principle and as a matter of security. So the plaque that reads, in part, "to the fans and supporters of Racing Club who with their courage and fortitude prevented the auctioning off of this center ... our most sincere gratitude" not only serves as a permanent reminder of the risks taken and the sometimes very tangible rewards obtained in exchange, but also allows me to feel both recognized and thanked for my efforts. It's never been the motivating factor, but I would be lying if I didn't say it feels nice.

With all that said, when I go to the stadium, my main concern is still not whether the eleven mercenaries who currently happen to have contracts to wear our jersey will do a better job of kicking a ball into the goal than the eleven mercenaries with a different jersey who are protecting it. But it would be dishonest to claim that I don't care. I still seem to care deeply, and aside from the obvious "it makes the party and the atmosphere better when we win," I can't really explain why. In the end, the players don't represent me. Who does represent me are the people in the terraces and in the stands. Our banners, our flags, and our chants that speak of decades of road traveled together. I'm fanatical not about what happens on the field of play but the community that exists outside of it and around it.

It's also possible that everything I have just told you, while factually true, might still be a complete farce—nothing more than an elaborate lie that I have told myself, and others, for decades. It is completely plausible that it is just the attempt of a politically overactive mind (and a lifelong attempt at that!) to retrofit a piece of its personality with a political or social justification in order to desperately try to make it fit into a puzzle where it seems to by no means belong. Maybe the reality is that despite all my years abroad, or perhaps ironically due to them, I am simply a culturally deeply Argentine creature. Happiest at daylong barbecues where the so-called world's worst drink, Fernet and Coke, flows endlessly, and at home in a culture where the Rolling Stones tongue is still a symbol of youthful cultural rebellion and their

What exists outside of and around the actual pitch in Argentina.

concerts are marked by giant mosh pits and flares on the inside while riots against the cops rage on the outside. Most of all, the child of a place where football stadiums are cauldrons of passion to which for decades we flocked not so much to watch what happened on the pitch but to be protagonists of the collective mass ritual that took place in the stands. And protagonists we were, on our best days unfurling record-breakingly huge banners that blanketed the entire stadium or covering the pitch in insanely unimaginable amounts of shredded paper, paper

El festejo final de Racing por un punto que puede resultar decisivo: la felicidad de Maciel, Milito, Pezzutti y Ubeda

Racing se acerca al título

Igualó 1 a 1 con River y mantiene los 5 puntos de ventaja, a 9 del final

En el partido del campeonato, el líder consiguió uno de los dos resultados que le servían: Racing empató 1 a 1 con River, su rival directo, y logró mantener los cinco puntos de ventaja, cuando restan 9 por jugarse, lo que desató otra fiesta de su gen-

te en Avellaneda.

Al equipo de Ramón Díaz, que abrió el marcador a los 44 minutos del primer tiempo con un gol de Cambiasso, no le alcanzó con el peso de sus mejores individualidades para sostener la diferencia. Retrocedió

en el campo y Racing, con su habitual voluntad, llegó al empate a través de Bedoya, a los 41 minutos de la segunda parte.

En su regreso, tras la caída en Japón, Boca perdió con Banfield por 1 a 0 y quedó a 10 puntos del líder. **Deportes**

Early December and it looked like less than two years after "ceasing to exist," the first championship since 1966 was imminent. *La Nación*, **December 3, 2001: "Racing is close to the title."**

rolls, and flares, and on our worst needlessly stealing banners and flags from others and attacking other workers and youths for no reason other than that they were from a different neighborhood or wore a jersey with different colors—and generating scenes of mass violence the rest of the world had long ago mostly banished from its stadiums.

Maybe I, and probably most people, should simply find peace with the idea that not everything in life needs to have a logical and reasonable explanation.

Either way, in mid-December 2001 there were only a couple of matches left in the season, and with Racing in first place, one of the twin utopias seemed within reach. If I had traveled down so much of this road together with this club and its people, if I had been there through all the dark times, through bankruptcy, "disappearance," demonstrations, relegation, actions, and putting our bodies on the line to secure its existence and future, having only left Argentina again once the club's continuity had been secured, how could I not be there when finally, after thirty-five years, it seemed the tide was finally turning? It wasn't *le grand soir* of social revolution and liberation, but for the community around this club it might as well have been, and I dropped everything and jumped on a plane to be there.

Clarín, December 20, 2001: "Everything for Racing: Clashes, anger, and chaos during the ticket sales at Racing."

7

The Golden Ticket

Avellaneda, December 19, 2001, 10:00 a.m.

No me hablen de la suerte,	*Don't talk to me about luck,*
no creo en eso, señor	*I don't believe in that, sir*

—La Furia de Petruza, "Santos de mi devoción"

The looting had been multiplying for a week, but on December 19, the same morning in which the Racing fans were trying to obtain their match tickets, the bomb exploded. They were thousands upon thousands, driven by misery, trying desperately to get their daily bread from mini-markets, super markets, and wholesale markets. It was happening across the country, but the epicenter was the greater Buenos Aires region. The Argentina that for years had been kept hidden under a veneer of supposed prosperity suddenly came to light. The news channels captured the events with their cameras in breathless tones as if they were covering the apocalypse. Shutters pried open, barely lifted just enough so as to enter and exit with bags and boxes; men and women crashing into each other, making the most of every second to take what they could: anything, from food to drink; bathroom items; dairy and fruits; televisions, refrigerators, and appliances. The press reported in horrified tones because they weren't taking from the shops only basic food items and the basics of subsistence, but rather also boxes of beer and expensive wines. As if poverty somehow eliminated human desire. People were taking what was available. What they could. What capitalism made them desire.

—Alejandro Wall, *¡Academia, Carajo!*

Cinco víctimas fatales y gran cantidad de heridos

La muerte no faltó a la cita

Cinco muertos -en el Gran Buenos Aires, Rosario y Santa Fe- y un sinnúmero de heridos fue ayer el lamentable saldo del caos generado por los saqueos que se registran en todo el país, desde comerciantes y policías salieron a resistir a balazos el vaciamiento indiscriminado de supermercados y otros comercios.

El primer episodio lamentable ocurrió a las 17 en la localidad de Villa Fiorito, partido de Lomas de Zamora, donde el dueño de un supermercado chino, identificado como Lui Yian Kuing, de 26 años, atacó a balazos desde una terraza a un grupo de personas que pretendía saquear su comercio.

De acuerdo a las fuentes, el hecho ocurrió en la calle Recondo 450 y a raíz de los balazos resultó gravemente herido Diego Avila, de 24 años, quien recibió un impacto en la cabeza y otro en la pierna. El joven fue trasladado de urgencia al Hospital Allende, donde murió antes de que pudiera ser intervenido quirúrgicamente.

Efectivos de la comisaría quinta de Avellaneda apresuraron al comerciante, quien debió ser alojado en la seccional de Ingeniero Budge debido a que los vecinos de su barrio intentaron lincharlo.

En la localidad bonaerense de Libertad, partido de Merlo, un comerciante mató a balazos a un hombre e hirió a otro al resistirse anoche a que saquearan su local.

El hecho ocurrió cerca de las 20 cuando un grupo de personas intentó ingresar por la fuerza al supermercado Stelli, ubicado en Gamboa y Helvecia. El suegro del dueño que estaba armado con una pistola atacó a balazos a la muchedumbre hiriendo a dos jóvenes. Uno de ellos, Eduardo Lejembre, murió cuando era trasladado al hospital de la zona.

Caos y sangre

Otra de las víctimas de los saqueos de ayer fue un menor de 15 años, quien fue abatido en Santa Fe por un balazo de un comerciante minorista cuando se dirigía hacia un supermercado.

El hecho se registró en la capital santafesina, donde un grupo de 400 personas marchaban hacia un supermercado de la cadena Bienestar, ubicado en la calle Blas Parera al 5800, según indicaron voceros de la policía provincial.

Según se indicó, el disparo habría sido efectuado por un comerciante particular que tenía su local en las proximidades del supermercado, aunque esto aún no fue confirmado en forma oficial.

De acuerdo con la versión policial, el comerciante -quien sería propietario de una farmacia- se defendió a los tiros un intento de los manifestantes por entrar a su local.

En ese marco, el comerciante hirió con un balazo al menor de 15 años, quien murió mientras era trasladado al Hospital Cullen, de esta ciudad.

Un policía aparece en actitud de custodia en un comercio saqueado por habitantes de Ciudadela

Diario Popular, December 20, 2001: "Five fatal victims and many wounded" during looting on December 19.

"**C**an't. Breathe. Not dying for this." José struggles to say the words audibly, clearly gasping for air under the pressure of thousands of bodies. He and Carlos are both tough kids, lifelong friends of mine whose footballing adventures over the years have included being shot at, being chased through the streets by rival gangs, a few fights, and more than enough confrontations with police. He isn't easily frightened, and it is impossible to overemphasize the significance to us of the golden tickets we are currently apparently quite literally dying to get our hands on. So I'm not sure which is worrying me more, his fear or that he is consciously saying that this can't be worth it.

We're only meters away from the ticket booth, maybe ten or twenty or so. But nothing has ever been closer and yet still so far. José starts to panic, his face flushed bright red, and his flailing can't be described as wild only because the crush of people has his arms pinned to his body, making flailing impossible. He looks like a dying fish writhing in somebody's hand, and it's not a pretty sight. We're being crushed by the weight of thousands of bodies pushing us against the little cement building that is the stadium's ticket booth. A literal human avalanche, and those who know about footballing history know that these can and will kill you. I mean, it also happens to be how we celebrate goals in

JUEVES 20 DE DICIEMBRE DE 2001 | **DEPORTIVO** | CLARIN | 3

RACING

MUCHOS DE LOS QUE HICIERON COLA EN EL ESTADIO DESDE EL DIA ANTERIOR FUERON DESBORDADOS POR LOS QUE SE COLARON

Las populares volaron en medio de incidentes, broncas y descontrol

DESBANDE. CAE EL ALAMBRADO Y SE DESATA EL CAOS. SUSTOS Y PROTESTAS DOMINARON LA MAÑANA FRENTE AL ESTADIO DE RACING, DONDE LA ORGANIZACION FUE DEFICITARIA.

Clarín, December 20, 2001: The fence is toppled and chaos erupts.

LA PENULTIMA

▶Foto insólita ▶Todo vale

El señor se propuso llegar a la boletería para conseguir su entrada para ver Racing-Vélez y decidió hacerlo como fuera. Se preparó con los cortos y las zapatillas de aerobismo y la emprendió contra los cientos apiñados desde el martes en el estadio de los de Avellaneda. Pisó cabezas y hombros pero, cuando estaba por llegar, algo o alguien lo hizo caer. Lo verá por tevé.

Clarín, December 20, 2001: "Anything goes." Crowdsurfing in front of the ticket booths.

the *popular*, Argentine for "terrace," launching ourselves wildly down the steps into a frenzied human heap of joy and celebration, but even those sometimes result in sprained ankles or broken bones. But when the press of human bodies has nowhere to go at its end point, things can end tragically, and we know this very well.[1]

José begins trying to push his way toward the sides, out of the stampede. It crosses my mind that we might very well die here. Of all the confrontations, riots, and general wealth of life-threatening situations I've successfully navigated, apparently I'm going to die attempting to get a ticket to a football match. It's not the death I was expecting. Not a fascist's knife or a policeman's bullet. Not only is it a horrible way to die, being crushed to death, but for an anarchist militant it's also not particularly glorious. I'm actually more than a little afraid, and yet in another worrying display of my self-preservation instincts possibly not being what they ideally should be, the next sentence out of my mouth is, "José, José, give me your money," which he is luckily somehow able to do. We already lost Carlos at the beginning of the chaos, and I need José's cash to have any chance of buying three tickets. As I lose sight of José, another crushing wave of pressure from people farther back trying to reach the ticket booth hits me.

Whatever mental image you might have of some sanitized and modern structure on the outside of a First World sports stadium— imagine the exact opposite of that. As much as I love our club's stadium, this is South America, where football fans are treated worse than cattle and the infrastructure is usually anywhere from simply unpleasant to flat-out deadly. This is a small cement structure, not three meters high, with a few small "windows" through which to do business. And by "windows" I of course mean small openings with no glass, just vertical steel bars. On both sides of the structure there is a chain-link fence attached to metal poles, probably at least six meters high, a fence whose purpose on game days is precisely to act as one of many lines of defense to keep the ticketless hordes at bay.

I don't know what miracle happened, but as I gasp increasingly frantically for air, the wave carries me to within arm's reach of the ticket booth's metal bars. I manage to grab on to them for dear life, while still holding the money in one hand. Don't ask me how, but I somehow use the leverage from the bars to pull myself upward, and I weirdly end up parallel to the ground, above the crowd. Like a crowd surfer, but holding

Scenes from the chaos on the day of the ticket sales.

on to the bars so as to avoid being swept away by the ebbs and flows of the human tide. I yell at the ticket seller, "Three tickets, please!"

"Sorry, kid, maximum two per person."

On the verge of tears, I respond, "Please, we're dying here, I need three, please." My last words to him were "Just keep everything," as I let go of one bar to slip the money to him. This being Argentina, the tip did the trick, and without another word I had the three tickets in my hand.

I'm pulled up out of the crowd by the arms, lifted upward by those standing on the roof of the ticket booth who are frantically rescuing people, some with tickets but most without, in a scene reminiscent of saving people from a sinking ship. As I'm taking a moment to catch my breath and compose myself, I take in the enormity of the scene around me from my elevated position. It's the culmination of thousands of people standing in line, or more precisely camping in line, for days for tickets to a match that, for the record, is neither today nor even at this stadium.

We find ourselves in Avellaneda, officially its own city on the south side of the greater Buenos Aires area, but Buenos Aires's urban sprawl being what it is, it's essentially a suburb with a population of several hundred thousand people, connected to downtown Buenos Aires by a highway and a bridge. Most importantly, it is the home of Racing Club de Avellaneda—the club of which I am a fanatical supporter and which, in a twist of fate unimaginable little more than a year earlier, with just a tie in the last match of the season, in an away game at Vélez Sarsfield four days from now, can obtain its first national championship in thirty-five years.

Behind me, separated from the crowd by the ticket booth, the fence, and a distance of maybe forty meters, is our stadium, the Estadio Presidente Juan Domingo Perón, a picture postcard of stoic enormity, a sixty-five-thousand-spectator-capacity behemoth, and the second-largest stadium in the country. Directly behind it, less than one city block away and only possible because Argentina is an insane country, lies the forty-thousand-spectator-capacity stadium of Club Atlético Independiente, our neighbor and archnemesis.[2] We play home games on staggered weekends to avoid fans from both clubs running into each other, and even with that precaution, trying to ambush groups of opposing fans as they head to or from matches is a sadly popular neighborhood pastime.[3]

Just last night, as the three of us sat on the sidewalk, in our case about five blocks away from the ticket booth, which was how long the line already stretched when we arrived more than forty-eight hours prior to the start of ticket sales, word spread that we would be paying "the Ashtray"—as we derogatorily refer to Independiente's stadium due to its architecture, which lacks stands on the corners of the structure—a visit. As excitement about this prospect grew among the young and criminally minded among us (not going to lie, my childish mind was excited at the idea of taking home a piece of their stadium as a souvenir), Carlos raised a not-irrelevant concern. "Are you crazy? What if the cops show up? Imagine if we get arrested and don't get tickets because of something stupid like that!"

A woman sitting in line a few meters down from us, who had a little portable radio she kept putting to her ear to pass the time, overheard us and chimed in. "I don't think any cops are coming. I keep hearing on the radio about more and more looting in the area. They seem busy with that. Pretty sure it's also why there's no cops here either." I took note of the news approvingly, as an anarchist should, but didn't think much of it at the time. Sporadic holiday-season looting is a bit of a tradition in Argentina, and it didn't seem surprising that it would be somewhat more widespread this year. Not only was the country experiencing record rates of unemployment and poverty, but in an attempt to prevent further panic

RACING

A pura bronca por los precios

Los precios en las plateas tuvieron un efecto negativo en el público. Muchos hinchas manifestaron ayer su malestar por los excesivos valores asignados a esas localidades ante la poca cantidad de populares visitantes y la disposición de la cancha de Avellaneda como único punto de venta, cuando en principio se creyó que también se podrían adquirir entradas en el Luna Park.

Populares y plateas comenzarán a venderse hoy de 11 a 18.30. Los socios deberán adquirir sus populares en las boleterías de la calle Colón. Los no socios podrán hacerlo en las ventanillas de la calle Alsina. Las plateas deberán comprarse todas en los trailers ubicados en la calle Italia.

Los precios son los siguientes: populares, 12 pesos; plateas sur alta, 50 pesos; platea norte alta, 60 pesos; y plateas sur baja, 80 pesos.

Los hinchas también hicieron oír su voz durante el día: "Se aprovechan porque saben que la cancha se va a llenar igual", dijeron.

PIEL MORENA. LA PAREJA ESPERA SU TURNO Y APROVECHA PARA PASARSE BRONCEADOR. LOS SIMPATIZANTES COPARON LOS ALREDEDORES DE RACING.

DE LA COLA A LA OFICINA. EL NI SE CONMUEVE PESE AL SACO Y LA CORBATA. TODO POR RACING.   LOS PRIMEROS. LEONARDO, SEBASTIAN Y LAS CARTAS QUE IDENTIFICAN SUS LUGARES EN LA HILERA.

LOS HINCHAS ESTAN HACIENDO COLA DESDE EL LUNES A LAS 7 DE LA TARDE PARA CONSEGUIR UNA UBICACION

Porque el amor es más fuerte

Clarín, December 19, 2001: "Because love is stronger." The day before ticket sales, with tens of thousands in line. When it was all still peace and love.

runs at the bank as rumors spread of an imminent devaluation of the peso—which had been tied to the US dollar at a rate of one to one since 1991—the center-left government of Fernando de la Rúa had a few weeks earlier established something called the *corralito*, a series of economic measures severely limiting the amount of cash individuals were able to withdraw from their bank accounts. As *Barricada*, the Boston-based anarchist monthly magazine I at the time coedited, reports:

> These entailed that for a period of 90 days, people would be allowed to withdraw no more than $250 per week from the banks, that one could leave the country with no more than $1,000 (and that leaving the country was not an excuse to be allowed more

Front pages of Argentina's two largest newspapers, *La Nación* and *Clarín*, announcing the limits on cash withdrawals from the bank of $250 per week.

money from the bank …). A cap was also placed on money transfers outside the country, and people were limited to two bank accounts (in order to prevent people from opening multiple bank accounts and thus sidestepping the $250 limit).[4]

These moves had triggered a bit of an uprising from middle-class and upper-middle-class *ahorristas* (a term that can be translated roughly as "those with savings"), who could be seen protesting with their pots and pans outside banks, fearful of losing their savings in a potential upcoming currency devaluation. But the move triggered, or at least accentuated, another crisis. Large sectors of Argentines exist outside the formal economy and depend on the flow of cash from those slightly better off for their day-to-bay bare minimum of existence. If you make your money to survive by selling snacks or small items at traffic lights to middle-class folks in their vehicles, but the middle-class people in those vehicles no longer spend any cash because they are concerned about their access to it, your situation goes from dire to untenable very quickly.

And so it is that hunger, anger, and looting have become even more than usual the themes around Buenos Aires this holiday season. So when we did eventually pay a visit to the Ashtray later in the night (because, you know … adventure over intellect, I guess), the cops who are usually so eager to chase us on horseback or randomly shoot at us were nowhere to be seen. If we had succeeded at opening one of the gates,

The golden ticket to the championship match!

I'm pretty sure we could have busted out a football, picked teams, and played a pickup game on the field and no cops would have appeared. It was the first clue that something was definitely very, very off.

As I turn again toward the chaos from which I have just emerged, the second indication that something very out of the ordinary is afoot, not just here but around the city, is strikingly obvious. The throng of people, swaying back and forth in waves against the ticket booth and the fence, numbers comfortably in the several thousands. It is what remains of what was for days a relatively orderly line, until the moment tickets went on sale. At that point, many of those toward the back began to panic, and eventually all hell broke loose as we arrived at the human stampede scenes I am lucky enough to have just escaped. Not that the presence of police would necessarily be very helpful, as Argentine cops usually tend to add to the chaos by riding their horses through crowds and indiscriminately beating, gassing, and shooting people, but whether we think of it as a positive thing or not, from my perch above the crowd I can make out maybe five police officers, not the several hundred that something like this would normally draw.

I eventually succeed in reuniting with Carlos and José, smile an exhausted smile, and flash them our three golden tickets before hiding

A mural on the Avellaneda side of the Pueyrredón Bridge, which connects Avellaneda to Buenos Aires, remembering Darío Santillán and Maximiliano Kosteki—murdered during the police repression of a bridge blockade in 2002.

them safely away. As we walk away, still wondering to each other where all the cops might be, my last memory of the scene is of the gigantic fence finally being toppled by the crush of the crowd.

The club will later put out a statement, making clearer what we are still unaware of but are starting to suspect:

> The Pueyrredón Bridge [one of two bridges leading from downtown Buenos Aires to Avellaneda] was blocked by piqueteros and there was looting taking place only a few blocks from there. We requested police presence, and they sent us what they could. The country is in a critical situation, and we did the best we could in that context.[5]

8

Sleeping Through the Uprising
Somewhere in Buenos Aires, December 20, 2001, 3:00 a.m.

Considero muy loable cortar	*I consider it very*
calles por el hambre	*commendable to blockade*
y el que no lo considera tiene	*streets due to hunger*
llena su heladera	*and who doesn't consider it so,*
	has a fridge full of food

—Salta la Banca,[1] "Considero"

"**G**et off the streets, moron," a random passerby in a car yells at me out his window. Seems like an odd thing to yell at me, especially since it's one of the rare occasions where I'm in the streets, you know, not making any trouble. I'm quietly walking down the sidewalk, not even wearing any identifiable club or political attire, which would be the other usual catalyst for randoms screaming at you out of their cars in Buenos Aires. Whatever, I shrug it off. This is, after all, the big city, and it has more than its fair share of random crazies.

It's the middle of the night and I've just woken up about fifteen minutes ago. Maybe it's because I fell asleep in the middle of the afternoon, collapsing the moment I got home from the cocktail of emotion, physical exertion, and days spent "sleeping" on the sidewalk. Or it might have been because the measly fan by my bedside was no match for the summer heat. Either way, I had woken up, with no hope of falling asleep again. So I've decided to enjoy one of my routines from when I used to live here: walk the two blocks from my apartment in the middle of the night to the newspaper stand and purchase the fresh-off-the-presses edition of the coming day's newspaper, together with some midnight snacks. Probably not the healthiest routine in the world, and probably

The front page of *Clarín*, December 20, 2001: "Looting and 7 deaths.... A never-before-seen protest.... State of emergency for one month."

also explains why I would so often fall asleep on the train to school in the mornings and wake up at the other end of the city.

In any case, it's a more or less residential part of the city, and the streets are quiet except for the rude interruption a few moments ago from the passing car. I'm savoring the tranquility of my nighttime tradition, especially since I'm only here for two weeks this time, having dropped everything and spent all of my savings to be here for the final match of the season.[2]

★

The short stay was also why despite my normally very high expectations of myself in regard to organizing and political engagement, I was pretty disengaged from the tumultuous days we'd been experiencing. My sympathies with the ahorristas were limited—of course, having banks essentially confiscate and eventually steal a significant chunk of the savings you've worked hard your whole life for is condemnable, but on the other hand the socioeconomic demographic these people represented (namely middle to upper middle class) had a strong tradition of being very much enabling to the most repressive and reactionary elements in Argentina.

But there were also the piqueteros, whose presence, actions, and numbers had been growing over the last several years. The pickets usually took the form of militant blockades of highways, bridges, central avenues, and other strategic aspects of economic activity as an instrument of resistance. It would be unfair to assign one political framework to all piquetero groups, as within them there was (and still is) a wide spectrum of ideas as well as practice. But the one aspect they all had in common was that they were a mechanism for the excluded and marginalized by the neoliberal order in Argentina, those who either due to unemployment or because their labor was in the informal economy did not have the recourse of a union or a traditional political structure to assert and defend their interests.

As an anarchist, the Movimiento de Trabajadores Desocupados (Movement of Unemployed Workers) seemed particularly likable and was indeed a structure in which many local anarchist organizers were active. While by no means a specifically anarchist organization, with members coming from diverse traditions including, for example, liberation theology, anarchist principles ran visibly through the organization: popular self-organization and direct democracy in the form of an assembly system of decision-making, organizational autonomy in direct opposition to the often vertical nature of many workers' organizations in Argentina, and, finally, direct action as a form of concrete intervention in struggle, free of intermediaries. In the words of one MTD activist, "We organize by way of neighborhood assemblies, with general assemblies as the highest instance of discussion and decision-making, with representative memberships, with revocability for leadership whenever the assembly determines it ... direct action and a politics independent of the state and the political parties."[3] Ines, an MTD militant from a Buenos Aires shantytown without prior explicit political organizing experience, sums it up perfectly when she says, "We don't have a boss, we work how we want, we all decide everything.... This is what's good [in the MTD], that we don't have a master."[4]

Anarchist forms of organization and action in these organizations are unlikely to be mere coincidences and probably have a lot to do with the strategic efforts of class-struggle anarchists since 1997 to agitate and organize from within popular organizations, in a concerted manner and with explicitly anarchist politics. Writing in March of that year, *En la Calle* succinctly sums up the objectives:

> The intervention of libertarians in the class struggle has as its objective the elimination of all exploitation, and the constitution of a free and socialist society as its strategic project, for this we build and participate in the different social organizations and moments of struggle. All year, in every roadblock put up by unemployed workers or state workers, we've seen the most dynamic sectors of our class taking part in this stage of resistance.
>
> These roadblocks of hunger frame the immediate task at hand, the demands of the moment. But we need to advance toward an organized resistance, capable of overthrowing empires and constructing a real future with justice, freedom, and dignity for all, in a project that begins in neighborhoods and workshops but that has a continental dimension and a global projection. Comrades, brothers, sisters ... let's go![5]

★

A general assembly of Movimiento de Trabajadores Desocupados women on the Pueyrredón Bridge during a blockade, 2003.

But I am only here for fourteen days, and I have promised myself that I will devote them strictly to football, friends, and eating obscene, unhealthy, and kind of worrisome amounts of pizza, ice cream, and *asado* (barbecue, sorry). 2001 has been, to put it mildly, a pretty busy year politically for the anarchist militant, as we find ourselves at the peak of the antiglobalization movement. In my case, my collective and I have been instrumental in several of the large mobilizations—and ensuing militant confrontations—of the past year. After the Bush inauguration, chasing Nazis around Connecticut, and the fierce clashes during the FTAA summit in Quebec City, as well as those in Gothenburg and Genoa, at the EU and G8 summits respectively—not to mention the stresses of editing what was then the only monthly anarchist periodical in North America—I felt that I had more than earned myself a break, and unlike many other comrades am also privileged enough to be able to afford one. And a well-timed break can go a long way in keeping one motivated and avoiding burnout. But beyond my personal need for a short break, and much more importantly, Argentine social movements aren't exactly crying out for polit-tourists who live abroad to drop by to say hi and check things out.

So while I am definitely a strong sympathizer of the piqueteros and can't help but smile every time I learn of a road being blocked or a supermarket looted, I have to admit I'm probably not thinking much about them as I stare at the odd and unexpected sight of the closed magazine kiosk in front of me. It's supposed to be a twenty-four-hour place, but whatever, it's almost Christmas and I guess they are, after all, entitled to a few days' vacation, even if it scandalously inconveniences me and my need for midnight newspapers and candy.

I head back home. Bored. Hungry. Having still spoken to no one since waking up and having seen no one on the street aside from the jackass who yelled at me. I turn on the TV, expecting Brazilian evangelical pastors yelling and crying in Portuguese about salvation, or maybe '80s sitcom reruns. I understand nothing of the breathless, live, dramatic commentary coming from the anchor on the twenty-four-hour news channel. All I see is that there are thousands of people at the Plaza de Mayo, the square on which Argentina's presidential palace is located, as well as in front of Congress, fighting pitched battles with the police.

Did I sleep for years? Have I woken up in a parallel dimension? As the fog of confusion slowly lifts from my brain and I begin piecing together the information from the news channel, it becomes apparent. An insurrection has erupted—and I slept placidly through its first hours.

9

While You Were Sleeping

Late Night of December 19 and Early Hours of December 20, 2001

*Volvió la mala, fue corta la
primavera
cerdos miserables comiendo lo
que nos queda
se llevaron la noche, nuestra
última alegría
gente "poniendo huevo" para
salir de esta ruina*

*The hard times are back, the
spring was short
miserable pigs eating what
little we have left
they've taken even the night,
our last joy
people struggling to get out of
these ruins*

*Se viene el estallido
se viene el estallido
de mi garganta
de tu infierno, también,
¡vamos!*

*The uprising is coming
the uprising is coming
of my voice
of your hell, as well
let's go!*

—Bersuit Vergarabat, "Se viene el estallido"

Vladimir Lenin is said to have noted, "There are decades where nothing happens; and there are weeks where decades happen."[1] Judging from all that has apparently happened in the ten or so hours during which I was asleep, I would go him one further and posit that there are also hours in which weeks happen.

The first thing I eventually learn is that, faced with the increasingly uncontrollable social anger in the streets, President de la Rúa went live on all the broadcast channels at around 10:00 p.m. What was expected to be a plea for calm and an attempt to display empathy was instead a four-minute speech in which the first sentences out of his mouth were:

Foto Gustavo Fidanza

Miles de personas salieron a la calle, haciendo un gigantesco cacerolazo.

Foto Hernán España

Tras la represión a los manifestantes se produjo un incendio en dependencias del Ministerio de Economía.

Quemaron el subsuelo del Ministerio de Economía

Un grupo de manifestantes que participaba de la movilización en Plaza de Mayo prendió fuego el subsuelo del Ministerio de Economía.

Los manifestantes también arrojaron piedras a los efectivos policiales que participaron de la represión en la plaza, a pocas horas de que comenzó la protesta.

Por otra parte, los manifestantes que se retiraban de la Plaza de Mayo apedrearon esta madrugada los vidrios de la Jefatura de Gabinete, ubicada en la esquina de las avenidas Belgrano y Diagonal Sur. Los cientos de personas que habían participado de la manifestación espontánea que se produjo en horas de la noche expresaron de ese modo su malestar ante la violenta represión policial que se había producido minutos antes.

Diario Popular, December 20, 2001: Demonstrators in front of Congress, and the basement of the Ministry of Economy on fire on the night of December 19, 2001.

"Countrymen, a difficult day comes to its end. Acts of violence have taken place across the country that endanger persons and property.... I want to inform you that, for this reason, I have declared a countrywide state of emergency."[2] It is only the third time since the fall of the military dictatorship in 1983 that a state of emergency, which among other things forbids all public gatherings of three or more people, has been declared (and the two previous were both during the 1980s).

★

The "Argentina Erupts" report from the January 2002 issue of *Barricada* describes what came immediately following the announcement:

> This was the final mockery. The breaking point. Minutes later, in every neighborhood, on every street, from every balcony, and from every street corner, the pots and pans began to sound. People took to the streets. Several thousand converged on the presidential residence in Olivos, over four thousand converged outside of the home of Economy Minister Domingo Cavallo in the upscale neighborhood of Palermo, tens of thousands converged in from of the Presidential palace (the Pink House) at the Plaza de Mayo, tens of thousands more converged in front of the congress, and innumerable thousands more on every street corner of every neighborhood in the nation.
>
> Soon after 11pm, the news came that Economy Minister Domingo Cavallo had resigned, and a resounding cheer rose from all the thousands that had spilled onto the streets. But the people were not content, and wanted more. The looting continued, and the thousands upon thousands remained in the streets. It became clear that this was not a protest simply against one or another particular politician, it was a protest against the Argentine political class as a whole, be it of the Partido Justicialista, or the UCR. It was a protest against a ruling class that, for too long, has dedicated itself to looting the future and livelihood of Argentines. A ruling class that put the nation at the mercy of a neoliberal economic policy that could serve only the interests of a select few, at the expense of the many.
>
> The chants said it, crudely and clearly. "Idiots, the State of Emergency, Shove it Up Your Asses," "Menem and De la Rua are the Same Shit," "Out with All of Them," etc.[3]

BARRICADA

JANUARY 2002   REVOLUTIONARY ANARCHIST MONTHLY   ISSUE #13 $2

From Brussels...

The Struggle Advances!

...To Buenos Aires

Inside: A Barricada Exclusive on Argentina
from our on-the-ground correspondent

Cover of the January 2002 issue of *Barricada*: "From Brussels to Buenos Aires:
The Struggle Advances!" Anarchists also mobilized against an EU Summit in
Brussels, Belgium, in December 2001.

The events during the course of the day that had led to this announcement had been far more agitated even than what the absence of cops in Avellaneda had led us to suspect, and are described in the same article as follows:

> The first news was of sporadic looting in some provinces and in the outskirts of the city of Buenos Aires. Next, came word of heavy fighting in the city of La Plata, pitting leftist groups and municipal workers against the police after attempts to take over a municipal building. The rubber bullets and tear gas were flying, the barricades burning, and the bank windows crumbling.
>
> Minutes later, news came of even more looting, and masses of people, sometimes dozens, sometimes hundreds, sometimes thousands, gathering around supermarkets, begging for food, and if they were not given it, taking it. On the heels of this, news of fighting between municipal workers and police in the city of Cordoba after state workers partially set fire to the state house. News of police ... shooting tear gas into a building belonging to the Luz y Fuerza union where young children were practicing ballet. Children coughing and in tears, being rushed away in ambulances, amidst screams and the distant sound of rubber bullets.
>
> In the meantime, the looting crept closer and closer to the capital. Sometimes, police watched helplessly, or chose not to intervene, others, it ended with bullets and gas. Sometimes those of us watching on television could cheer as the downtrodden and forgotten of Argentina took what they needed from the multinationals and large corporations in order to make their lives better, if only for a few days. Other times, we were left almost in tears as we watched what threatened to become a war of poor versus poorer.[4]

Apparently, the sea of people converging from all directions at Congress and in front of the presidential palace following the speech and the declaration of the state of emergency was an incredible sight to behold. A spontaneous expression of such a broad spectrum of society that even twenty-six-year-old Martín Vitali—a professional soccer player on the Racing Club squad—found himself "feeling the adrenaline of rebellion shooting through his body" as he raced in his car toward downtown from the western suburb of Morón, where he lived.[5] By his

Un día de furia, saqueos y lágrimas al borde de la Autopista del Oeste

Clarín, December 20, 2001: "A day of fury, looting, and tears on the edge of the western highway." A local shopkeeper whose neighborhood market has been looted cries.

Una noche de saqueos y violencia

Clarín, December 19, 2001: "A night of looting and violence." Looting on December 18 and 19, not just in Buenos Aires but throughout the country.

own admittance, when you are a professional footballer "you live in a bubble," and he had never in his life attended a demonstration.[6] But that night, like thousands of others and despite being on the cusp of winning a historic championship for his club, he felt the compelling need to be there:

> Martín Vitali, the defender who was about to be a champion, saw the Plaza de Mayo overflowing and was overcome with emotion. . . . He had only gone there to see what it was all about. Maybe the thousands marching alongside him had thought the same thing. They came from everywhere, with nobody summoning them, and their destination needed no explanation, because it's the place where people go to make their voices heard. The Plaza de las Madres ["Plaza of the Mothers," in reference to the mothers of the dead and disappeared during the last military dictatorship]. Vitali couldn't know that. It was nighttime but it was still too early. So he walked and walked, sang and yelled, and saw people joining. He saw how they appeared from one side and the other, women, men, families, couples, grandmothers and grandfathers.
>
> "I understood then that something big was happening, but I didn't image everything that was still to come," says Martín. "I didn't imagine the deaths."[7]

★

I will eventually hear of endless personal stories like that of Vitali's. I'll also be told the cacophony of pots, pans, and car horns that rang out across all the neighborhoods of the city as soon as de la Rúa's speech ended was pretty impressive. I wouldn't know, though, seeing as how I have slept gloriously through all of it.

And at some point in the night, this mass protest transitioned into the ferocious pitched battles I am now witnessing on TV. But I know neither when nor how this happened and have no idea what is happening in the surrounding areas. (This is a source of controversy even to this day.) Some will say it was an unprovoked police attack on the crowds, while others will say they were responding to provocations from "leftist groups" who began attacking Congress.

Either way, my first instinct, obviously, is to put my clothes on and head downtown as well. But in an uncharacteristic display of good judgment, or at least caution, I force myself to decide against it. These are South American cops, after all, and who knows if maybe even the military is out there as well, and both of those can, do, and will kill *zurditos de mierda*, the catch-all derogative term for "piece-of-shit leftists," as they like to call us. The idea of running into a horde of cops or soldiers on a dark street in the dead of night because I am unaware of what areas are being controlled by whom seems too dangerous. My only possible defense if running into them would be, "No, no, please don't hurt me, I swear I haven't done anything … yet. I was sleeping and got here late," which seems like it probably won't be very effective.

So instead, I'm on the phone. "Um, yes, buenas noches, how are you?" is my characteristically poetic opening line. Some of the larger organizations in the alphabet soup of Argentine authoritarian communist groups and parties have a fair amount of offices and centers, and the Communist Party even owns a pretty impressive property near downtown, not unlikely a consequence of solid party coffers thanks to their decades-long stellar relationship with Soviet Moscow. I had assumed, correctly it seems, that the left-wing parties might be gathering their militants in order to plan their next moves, so it wouldn't be unreasonable to think there might be somebody there during the dead of night. While I am definitely not that stripe of communist, at the same time I would really much rather find myself among them, where it is also likely that piqueteros and maybe some anarchists will not be far off, than to just merrily make my way downtown on my own, considering all the possible dangers. So I've just tried calling one of the Communist Party offices and, lo and behold, got somebody on the line! It is a bit of an awkward conversation to say the least. "Yes, um, I'm seeing what's happening on TV and was wondering if the party was calling for any demonstrations or gatherings or anything?"

There is what I can only assume is a distrustful silence (as they're not terribly popular, so I doubt they get too many random late-night callers phoning and asking for the party's guidance). But, finally, I get what I am looking for: "We are meeting at the demonstration at 1 p.m. in front of Congress."

10

La Plaza es de las Madres
(The Plaza Belongs to the Mothers)
Plaza de Mayo, December 20, 2001, 10:00 a.m.

Van	*They go*
en ronda mareada	*in dizzying rounds*
remando en silencio	*rowing in silence*
a orillas de un tiempo	*on the shores of an era*
de grises y ausencias	*of gray skies and absences*
de niebla en la voz	*of fogged voices*
van de pie con las heridas altas	*they stand tall, wounds held*
convidando memoria	*high*
y andarán contra mugre y	*offering memory*
perdón	*and they'll continue against*
aunque duren los cuervos	*dirt and forgiveness*
llueva este asco	*though the crows persist*
y pesen los pies	*though it rains incessantly*
	and their feet are heavy
Van	
pañuelos curtidos	*They go*
de llantos inmensos	*faded headscarves*
de soles de inviernos	*of immense cries*
diciendo los gritos que nadie	*of winter suns*
gritó	*voicing the outrage that*
	nobody screamed

—Los Caballeros de la Quema, "Madres"

Fate smiles on the bold. How else can we explain that the morning after the fierce repression falls on a Thursday? Thursday. The one day of the week on which, since the darkest times of the dictatorship in

Repression begins in and around the Plaza de Mayo on the morning of December 20.

The Mothers of Plaza de Mayo and sympathizers begin their traditional circular march at Plaza de Mayo, around 10:00 a.m. on Thursday, December 20, 2001.

1977, the mothers and grandmothers of those abducted and disappeared by the military junta gather to hold vigils and demand justice for their children. Every. Single. Thursday. To my knowledge, without exception, rain or shine, they are there with their iconic white headscarves, marching in dignified and defiant silence in front of the presidential palace, at the Plaza de Mayo.

And so on the Thursday morning of December 20, sometime after 10:00 a.m., the Mothers of Plaza de Mayo, as this association of women is called, arrived at the plaza. This was some five hours or so after a tense calm had finally returned to downtown Buenos Aires, as the police action eventually succeeded in dispersing the tens of thousands of people on the streets—although not before the crowd apparently managed several attempts at storming Congress. That night could have been the beginning and end of the "Battle of Buenos Aires."

But as the morning wore on, scattered attempts had already been made to start retaking the plaza, or at least to regather in the face of the prohibition of public gatherings. A young man could be seen on TV, imploring people to come down, to not go to work, to take a day, an hour, a moment to help change the course of history. But as the Mothers

Shortly after the Mothers and their supporters arrive at the Plaza de Mayo, the police repression begins.

Repression begins in and around the Plaza de Mayo on the morning of December 20.

arrived, there were probably no more than one or two hundred people there.

Shortly after they arrived, the police were given the order to disperse the one or two dozen Mothers and the hundred or so supporters present. Old ladies, many of them in their seventies and eighties, stood bravely against mounted police charges and whippings. Little old ladies, frail looking on the outside but carrying with them decades of unbreakable courage and conviction, facing off against the unhinged violence of a dying government. Armed with nothing but their dignity. And the country watched it all unfold on live television.

I don't know if the Argentine uprising needed another spark, or if the prairie fire was by then already spreading out of control. We will never know. But I do know that the impact of those scenes was immeasurable. If a final spark had been missing, then these scenes were it. They were also—and I'm sure exactly this experience was replicated thousands of times over—the last images I saw before heading downtown myself.

Compañerxs de Línea Anarco Comunista y de Resistencia Libertaria

¡PRESENTES!

EN NUESTRA LUCHA Y NUESTROS CORAZONES

Son 30 mil
Fue genocidio

24 DE
MARZO
1976

ASL
Acción Socialista
Libertaria

"Comrades of the Línea Anarco-Comunista and Resistencia Libertaria ... Present! In Our Struggle and in Our Hearts." Graphic by Acción Socialista Libertaria.

11

The Long Shadow of the Past

Congress, December 20, 2001, 12:30 p.m.

Al pueblo nadie lo asfixia,	*Nobody asphyxiates the people,*
que acabe la caridad	*the time for charity is over*
y que empiece la justicia	*let justice begin*

—Los Olimareños,[1] "Cielo del 69"

A left-wing demonstration with an energy and enthusiasm not seen for quite a while among the Argentine left. Well over two thousand people were in attendance, and the spirit of battle was in the air.

—*Barricada*, "Argentina Erupts"

I stand there looking at the sea of red flags and hooded faces. Combativeness and rebellion are palpable all around me. They are felt in the passion and rage of the chants and are visible in the improvised batons and slingshots everywhere in the crowd. It would be a tempting lie to say that we knew what was in store for us that day. How momentous, inspiring, and, as is often the case, at the same time tragic the hours to come would be. But the state of emergency coupled with the images we had just seen on TV of the repression against the *madres* made it abundantly clear that combat was what lay ahead for us, and that in one way or another it would be in the context of a historic day. And I couldn't help but think about the long and painful road that brought us, the broad collective "we" of leftist social and popular resistance in Argentina, to this point.

Movements are organisms, and just like people they carry the scars of their past battles, which is what makes this moment as surprising as it is inspiring and encouraging. The whole broad spectrum of the

Argentine left—from Marxists to anarchists to left-wing Peronists—had been left badly scarred by the armed struggle of the 1970s and the fierce, no-quarter Dirty War waged against it by the military dictatorship. The resulting thirty thousand dead or disappeared, the tens of thousands who passed through the network of clandestine concentration camps of the dictatorship, and the unknown number, probably in the six digits, of those forced to flee to safety in exile.

The political landscape of radical movements, resistance, and left-wing politics in the Argentina of the 1990s was very much a reflection of the toll of the last few decades, of audacious, possibly ill-advised struggle followed by savage, murderous repression, of a generation literally gone missing, followed almost immediately by the collapse of the Eastern bloc and the seemingly unstoppable march of victorious capitalism. It was not a promising landscape. The genocide and Dirty War carried out by the country's military dictatorship in the late 1970s and early '80s were so thorough and destructive that almost twenty years after the fall of the military junta, you could still clearly notice the lasting consequences among the general "left" of the country.

Internationally, there is significantly less awareness as to the nature of the Argentine dictatorship and Dirty War than, for example, the Pinochet dictatorship in Chile. And there are specific reasons for this that are well worth looking into. First of all, Argentina's dictatorship lasted "only" seven years, from 1976 to 1983, while Pinochet's rule in Chile began in 1973 and held until almost the 1990s. Second, the coup in Chile targeted the not only democratically elected but also explicitly socialist government of Salvador Allende, which had risen to power with the support of a broad front of popular organizations. The political affinity with the left-wing character of the Allende government made campaigns of international solidarity among the left-wing movements of Europe and North America arise more organically and powerfully than with Argentina, where the overthrown government was the relatively weak and unpopular one of Juan Domingo Perón's widow, Isabelita Perón.

Which also brings up the issue of Peronism and the rifts within it in the previous years, which are fundamental to understanding not only the buildup to the military coup but most of Argentine politics of the last seventy or so years. The ideology of Peronism is named after the populist general who in 1955 had once been removed from power a few months after Argentina's military bombed Peronist civilians from the sky in downtown Buenos Aires, killing hundreds, with the tacit approval of the country's traditional oligarchy, who felt threatened by Perón's pro-worker message and policies.

Peronism itself is an exceedingly complex particularity of Argentine politics. Perón was seen as a champion of the interests of Argentina's oppressed and working class and devised a doctrine of social justice (*justicialismo*, the term Peronists use to this day) stipulating in essence that capital should be reined in by a strong state, as well as enshrining vertical and bureaucratic trade unions into the machinery of capital in order to ensure that the benefits of a strong national industry and economy would also benefit the masses of society. Either out of sincere political conviction and analysis or out of strategic opportunism, movements on both the far left and far right of the political spectrum, as well as everywhere in between, claimed (and still claim today) to be the rightful ideological heirs of Peronism and its legacy. This despite the fact that, once forced to flee into exile, Perón's choice of refuge was none other than Francisco Franco's fascist Spain. If Perón's choice of country of exile wasn't strong enough of a hint as to where his sympathies lay, on his return to Argentina in 1973 following eighteen years of exile, several million people turned out to greet him outside Buenos Aires's Ezeiza International Airport, in what has come to be known as the Massacre of Ezeiza. Right-wing Peronists and nationalist snipers opened fire on masses of left-wing Peronists, killing at least thirteen and wounding several hundred. The architect of this massacre was none other than Perón's personal secretary and right-hand man, José López Rega, who would later go on to found the feared Triple A (short for Alianza Anti-Comunista Argentina, or "Argentine Anti-Communist Alliance") death squads.

This divorce from Perón and the realization that the general was in fact not an ally in the struggle for a "socialist and anti-imperialist Argentina" meant that the Montoneros, the left-wing Peronist guerrilla organization, the country's largest, continued and even intensified its activities after the return of Perón and democracy in 1973, originally two of its principal stated objectives.

So while the coup in Chile was aimed at an unquestionably democratically elected government and justified solely and exclusively with the argument of Cold War–era anticommunism, in Argentina, while the overthrown government was in theory democratically elected, the

"Neither Victims nor Forgotten! Combatants!" Demo on the anniversary of the military coup d'état, March 24, 2023.

pretext for military rule was to neutralize the threat of Argentina's two largest guerrilla organizations of the time, the Montoneros and the Trotskyist ERP (Ejército Revolucionario del Pueblo, or "People's Revolutionary Army").

It's important to state clearly that these two organizations did indeed mount a concerted, principled, and significant campaign of armed struggle against the Argentine government and military. At their peak in the mid-1970s, the two organizations together probably had several thousand armed combatants, organized in both urban and rural fronts, plus a wide network of supporters and sympathizers. Structured into a strict military hierarchy, as was typical of the Marxist-Leninist guerrillas of the time in South America, they carried out "smaller" actions such as kidnappings of prominent business figures or politicians, bank expropriations, and actions to obtain weapons from armories or isolated squads of police or soldiers, much like the European urban guerrillas of the time. However, in displays of their collective strength, they also carried out large-scale military operations, ranging from the hijacking of cargo trucks with food, in order to subsequently redistribute the goods to inner-city slums, to spectacular attacks on military barracks involving hundreds of armed combatants.

The character of the heroic and eventually desperate struggle waged by Argentina's armed left, despite whatever ideological or tactical differences with them we may have as anarchists, is an important point to make. Over the last fifteen years or so, particularly with the center-left Kirchnerists (a left-wing Peronist tendency; see chapter 15) in power, there has been a state-sanctioned attempt to revise the history of the militants of these organizations, in order to present them as mere victims of the military dictatorship and its Dirty War.

This is dishonest and a disservice to the sacrifices made and risks taken by these brave and committed revolutionaries, especially because both assertions are in fact true: It is just as true that they were absolutely not innocent and helpless victims, having consciously chosen the path of armed struggle, as it is that they were also eventually victims of a depraved and sadistic Dirty War. It is generally accepted that within the conflict, the insurgents were largely respectful of the laws of war, and while innocents did perish in bombing attacks, the guerrillas neither explicitly targeted noncombatants nor did they engage in torture of captured enemy combatants. The ERP even made it a point to not liquidate or needlessly harm conscripted soldiers carrying out their military service.

Their military opponents, however, employed a wide array of vicious and brutal techniques of torture (many of which they had learned in training at the School of the Americas, in Georgia), including barbarities involving electric shocks, the introduction of rats into women's vaginas, and the gutting alive of prisoners. Prisoners in any one of the wide network of clandestine detention centers were kept alive and tortured until their captors believed there was no longer any information to be obtained from them, at which point they were drugged and thrown alive from helicopters into the Río de la Plata. Those pregnant at the time of their capture were often forced to give birth before being subsequently murdered and their newborn baby given to a military

Demonstrators wheat-paste images of Norma Arrostito and Mario Roberto Santucho with the text "Heroes of the Working Class" during a demonstration, March 24, 2024.

Norma Arrostito

Norma Arrostito was one of the first women in the Montonero leadership. Captured in January 1977, she was kept prisoner at the infamous ESMA concentration camp for over a year, during which she was savagely tortured and, because of her importance to the organization, often paraded around to lower morale among other prisoners. Prisoners who escaped the ESMA recall that "she carried herself in a dignified and heroic manner throughout her captivity," often exclaiming that she would "neither collaborate nor surrender." She was eventually murdered on January 15, 1978, and her body was never found.

Mario Roberto Santucho

Mario Roberto Santucho was the secretary-general of the Trotskyist Partido Revolucionario de los Trabajadores (PRT, or "Revolutionary Workers' Party") and commander of its armed wing, the ERP (Ejército Revolucionario del Pueblo, or "People's Revolutionary Army"). He was killed in battle on July 19, 1976, together with other members of the PRT's political leadership. In a 2012 interview, the dictator Rafael Videla admitted to disappearing Santucho's body. "He was a person who inspired hope. If his body appeared, it would lead to tributes and commemorations. He was a figure who had to be eclipsed."

family. This treatment, of systematic and prolonged torture followed by murder, was extended not only to armed fighters but to sympathizers and anybody whom the military viewed as part of what they termed the "tree of subversion," whose "branches" were varied enough to include everything from "university student" to "psychologist." This wide view of "subversion" explains the disparity in numbers: only a few thousand armed combatants but thirty thousand dead or disappeared, and countless more in exile. It also discredits the "theory of the two demons," which attempts to create a moral equivalency between the two sides, asserting them both to be equally dangerous and violent elements that converged to force the country into conflict and eventually dictatorship.

In fact, the commonly accepted argument that the military coup and subsequent dictatorship and Dirty War were somehow necessary to defeat the guerrillas and spare Argentina from socialist revolution is also completely false, as by late 1975 both of these organizations were significantly weakened, having suffered a series of devastating military setbacks. The final major blow was the failed attempt by the ERP to take the military barracks at Monte Chingolo, in the south of the greater Buenos Aires area, in December of that year. It was an audacious action, involving approximately three hundred armed combatants and the simultaneous occupation of nine bridges to cut off access to the area from other parts of the city in an effort to expropriate several tons of military weapons and ammunition. Unfortunately, the ERP was unaware of an informant embedded in a strategic organizing position of the operation, and they decided to proceed with their plans despite intelligence from the Montoneros warning them of the risk that the military was aware of the impending attack. With no element of surprise, the ERP walked into a trap, and the result was the death of over ninety militants, sixty-two of them falling in combat and another approximately thirty being murdered by military forces after being detained and disarmed.

While the bulk of the armed struggle in Argentina was carried out by the different tendencies of the Marxist left, the small anarchist movement, largely erased from the history of this era, played its part as well. Indeed, the fate of those involved was a smaller-scale version of the end met by the participants in the broader popular movement of armed struggle in the country from 1976 onward. If anything, in line with the sadly very anarchist tradition of heroic struggle in the face of impossible odds, their story is particularly poignant.

Cover of the book *Resistencia Libertaria*, one of the first attempts to rescue the memory, struggle, and history of Resistencia Libertaria.

The participation of organized anarchism in the struggle of the 1970s in Argentina was primarily by way of an organization called Resistencia Libertaria (Libertarian Resistance), which viewed itself as "an anarchist political organization with a class character, promoting the constitution of workers' power.... In pursuit of that objective, they developed a strategy of a 'protracted people's war' to be waged on all fronts, including military."[2] The organization grew out of a group of younger anarchists mainly centered on the city of La Plata and originally organized in the collective of significantly older anarchists who published *La Protesta*, one of the world's longest-running anarchist periodicals and the once official organ of the massive anarcho-syndicalist FORA, until their expulsion. The younger comrades took an increasingly positive opinion of the wave of armed struggle in Latin America, in stark contrast to the views of the older generation, who interpreted them as an adoption of some elements of Marxism. The younger anarchists eventually stated in a March 1971 article in the paper that

> the urban guerrilla is an insurrectional response to the murderous and eliminationist project of the modern world. As such, we

view it as difficult but positive. From within or outside of the armed struggle, our two enemies will always be the two poles, both the system that must be destroyed as well as the forms of action that perpetuate human practices that are an obstacle to the achievement of a true revolutionary transformation. If we enter the struggle with this clear objective, with an antitotalitarian definition of the processes underway, we should not hesitate to insert ourselves within them just as we do in any other front.[3]

Some two years later, Resistencia Libertaria was officially formed in the course of a countrywide anarchist conference, eventually incorporating militants from another anarchist organization of relevant size, the Línea Anarco-Comunista (Anarcho-Communist Line). The RL viewed itself explicitly as a cadre organization, and its members worked on several fronts broadly defined as labor, neighborhood, student, and military, agitating and organizing to the end of "developing workers' power," which we would probably refer to today as "building dual power."

In a 2002 interview, Fernando López, one of the organization's few surviving members, describes its activities on the various fronts. On the labor front, "Our participation was focused on rank and file workers, on the formation of classist groups. We participated in the national labor movement, organizing unions, internal commissions of classists and revolutionaries in distinct factories in the whole country, and the Coordinators of Unions in Struggle. We did a lot of work in this between 1974 and 1976. And in 1976, under full military repression, we even went so far as to occupy the Alpargatas factory in Florencio Varela for two weeks, during which we were surrounded by the army." On the other fronts, "The neighborhood front attended, above all, to the poorest neighborhoods. The activities of the neighborhood groups had to do with demands for water, sewage, the construction of housing, parks, etc. (the various distinct demands of poor neighborhoods). In the student front we worked on the traditional student demands around study programs, classroom materials, and grades: the usual issues of the time."[4]

Its military actions were obviously on a smaller scale than those of the larger Marxist guerrilla organizations. Not only due to the logical limitations imposed by its smaller size and less developed military front, but also because, unlike the authoritarian organizations, Resistencia Libertaria's armed actions were intended to achieve purely tactical

"Detained-Disappeared Comrades from Resistencia Libertaria ... Present! We'll Return on All Roads." Graphic by Acción Socialista Libertaria on the anniversary of the kidnapping and disappearance of approximately twenty Resistencia Libertaria militants between May 31 and June 8, 1978.

or propagandistic purposes, and its members did not see themselves as attempting to build a "mass people's army." Their actions usually consisted of either activities necessary to finance the cost of operations as a clandestine organization by way of kidnappings of businessmen for ransom, or actions termed "armed propaganda," such as shooting at police stations, arson attacks against police and military infrastructure, and the erecting of flaming barricades.

Resistencia Libertaria's militants paid dearly for their efforts, and it is estimated that a significant majority of its members did not survive the military dictatorship. In a particularly tragic turn, María Esther Biscayart de Tello, a militant of RL whose three children, Marcelo Rodolfo, Pablo Daniel, and Rafael Arnaldo, were also all in the organization, was able to escape to exile in France, but all three of her children were murdered and disappeared by the dictatorship.[5] Marcelo Rodolfo was disappeared and never seen again only a few weeks before the military coup, in March 1976, while Pablo Daniel and Rafael Arnaldo were both disappeared the day before the start of the 1978 FIFA World Cup in Argentina, as the junta, having largely finalized its dismantling of the larger guerrilla organizations, turned its attention to the smaller Resistencia Libertaria.

Acción Socialista Libertaria tells the story of the capture and torture of Rafael and Pablo and fellow RL members:

> May 31, 1978, was not just another day in Argentina. It was the day before the start of the World Cup, and most people were busy making plans to get together to watch the opening ceremony, which, according to the military authorities, promised to be breathtaking. After the ceremony . . . the national teams of West Germany (the reigning champion) and the powerful Poland played to a 0–0 draw in the cup's first match. It was four in the afternoon in San Fernando [a suburb of the greater Buenos Aires area] and the workers of the afternoon shift at the Quarton shipyard were finishing their workday. That Wednesday was for the shipyard workers the much anticipated biweekly payday.
>
> But neither the World Cup nor the meager pay that they would have in the bags they kept in their lockers could mask the particularly asphyxiating atmosphere in the air: The entire union steward committee had been kidnapped at the start of the dictatorship.

Two brothers with ample experience in the trade worked as carpenters at Quarton: Pablo and Rafael Tello. Both were clandestine militants of Resistencia Libertaria (RL) and had significant union experience in the shipyards of Berisso and Ensenada, especially at the legendary and combative Río Santiago shipyard.

When the soldiers stormed the plant that afternoon, the brothers knew it was them they were after. Were they reminded of their brother Marcelo, kidnapped and disappeared in Córdoba on March 9, 1976, as he was leaving a union meeting at Fiat together with his comrades in struggle Soledad García (teachers' union delegate) and Rafael Flores (secretary-general of the rubber union)? Maybe they thought of their mother and comrade in the organization—María Esther Biscayart—who was already exiled in France and to whom, in those days of clandestinity and oppression, they would write lengthy letters alternating between love, complicity, and descriptions of the political situation?

The soldier who was clearly the one in charge asked, his voice raspy and authoritarian, "Where's Tello?" When he heard "Which Tello?" he realized it was his lucky day: He had both of them. It all would go quickly. They blindfolded the workers and loaded them onto a military bus, and after a few minutes the convoy, joined by civilian vehicles with no license plates or identification of any kind, stopped. Pablo and Rafael were taken off and subjected to a mock execution.

When they were released a few hours later, the shipyard workers believed that the Tello brothers had been executed and were unaware that they had in fact been transported to be tortured at a place that would later become known as "El Banco," a clandestine torture center located ... in the heart of La Matanza.

Toward nightfall, the army kidnapped María del Carmen, Pablo's wife, known by her comrades as Bigote, at the house they rented together in La Lucila. Rafael's partner, Mariana—also a libertarian militant nicknamed Maritxu—was picked up by soldiers at their home in Ituzaingo, close to midnight. In that home, lent to them in solidarity by family members, they lived together with their three children. Rafael had told Mariana that after work he would stop by the plot of land where they were beginning to build their home, so she wasn't worried until around 11:00 p.m., when the mob kicked down her door. Both women would recover their freedom after sixteen days of torture. The five children between the two of them, in one of life's strokes of fortune, were not taken by the military mob.

At the same time, at her home in La Plata, the journalist and teacher Elsa Martínez was kidnapped, together with engineer Hernán Ramírez Achinelli. They were both anarchists, forty years old, members of Resistencia Libertaria, and not only shared ideals and militancy but had been married for years. During their kidnapping, their dog confronted the squad of soldiers and barked at them. When one of the soldiers struck the dog, Elsa pounced on him and hit him.

Hers was an anarchist life in which, even in the direst moment, no injustice could be left unanswered—and she was never seen again. The neighbors say the soldiers set up a trap at the home, to which nobody showed up [a sign that she did not break under torture]. Bored, they spent their time ransacking and looting the house for days. During their kidnapping, the couple was forced to sign over checks and their property as part of the spoils of war. The same spoils of war to which Rafael and Pablo were forced to sign over their meager paychecks.

The following days were filled with horror and terror for the members of the small but still active anarchist political organization. There was a method and a plan from the dictatorship, and in those days, while a hypnotized mass cheered goals during a perverse World Cup, they dedicated themselves to destroying it.

The next to fall were the Uruguayans "Melena" Edison Oscar Cantero Freire and "Pata" Fernando Díaz Cárdenas. Melena ... was picked up as he was leaving a union meeting in the capital, while Pata was taken at the print shop where he worked. Neither was ever seen again. The same was the case with another Uruguayan, "Flaco" Raúl Olivera Cancela, a worker at the Alvert bottling plant and father to Mauricio (six years old) and Matías (three months old), who was kidnapped on June 5 at the Liniers train station as he made his way to his home in Moreno. The three remain disappeared to this day.

The textile worker (as well as activist and delegate in the historic strike and occupation at the Alpargatas plant in 1977) Rufino Almeyda and his partner, Claudia Estévez, were kidnapped in La Plata on June 4, at Claudia's parents' house. They were held in captivity until mid-July, the same as the ATE organizer Hebe Cáceres and the textile organizer Fernando López.

Years later, Hebe testified in Madrid against the repressor Scilingo, the same genocidal murderer who—despite being condemned to 1,084 years in prison for crimes against humanity—until recently was able to walk happily and with impunity on temporary release around the capital of the Spanish State. Hebe spoke on that occasion as to the suffering that she and her comrades lived through at "El Banco." She tells of how during one night in captivity she thought she would freeze to death; at that moment Rafael approached her, gave her his blanket, and expressed that "there are two of us here, and we keep each other warm." She goes on to share that Rafael and his brother Pablo surrounded Tito Ramírez (another victim of torture, who had been his professor at the architecture school of the University of La Plata) and comforted him with their presence. There were things that, even in the worst conditions, were nonnegotiable: solidarity between comrades and the strength of their convictions.

It was the end of a vital experience: an antiauthoritarian political organization, with insertion into the workers' movement and an anarchist character. In total, around eighteen members of Resistencia Libertaria were kidnapped between May 31 and June 8, 1978; this marked the dismantling of a vital experience for organized anarchism in our country.[6]

Resistencia Libertaria, with the obviously hugely important exception of its military aspect and the extreme clandestinity and danger in which it was forced to operate, was politically and conceptually surprisingly close to the politics and organizational forms of more recent anarcho-communist or platformist organizations that arose in Argentina, North America, and Europe, such as, respectively, the Organización Socialista Libertaria (Libertarian Socialist Organization), NEFAC (Northeastern Federation of Anarcho-Communists), and the Union Communiste Libertaire (Libertarian Communist Union), to

Under images of disappeared Resistencia Libertaria militants, signs read "We Forget No Names. We Forget No Faces." Demo on the anniversary of the military coup d'état, March 24, 2023.

Posters show the faces of disappeared Resistencia Libertaria militants. Demo on the anniversary of the military coup d'état, March 24, 2023.

name but a few. A specifically anarchist cadre organization, agitating and organizing for and from within the working class to construct poles of autonomous workers' organization and power. That is to say, a Bakuninist conception of revolutionary organization and the role of its militants, which Fernando López describes as "militants that act and coordinate in order to organize the popular masses, but they do not have a directive plan for the popular masses. To say it another way, our work is the construction of power, not seizing power."[7] The Barricada Collective's identification with some version or another of this concept went to such an extent that in the December 2001 issue of the magazine we ran a not-uncontroversial article titled "The Invisible Dictatorship: Organization or Irrelevance, Revolutionary Organization and Objectives," quoting Bakuninist concepts on this matter at length.[8]

Placing its anarchism squarely in the arena of class struggle and identifying the liberation of the working class by the working class as the necessary vehicle for the emancipation of all of humanity also placed Resistencia Libertaria in the camp of the broad front of the revolutionary left—which slowly but surely begins to bring us back around to why I, revolutionary anarchist, am standing in front of Congress this Thursday afternoon, surrounded by a sea of red flags and yet feeling like I belong.

The organization considered itself broadly nonsectarian, its political orientation and work often bringing it close to other formations on the Marxist left. As López describes it, Resistencia Libertaria "got along particularly well with groups of classist character. There was the Organización Comunista Poder Obrero (Communist Workers' Power Organization), which was a New Left organization and a classist group. Although they were Leninists, even classical Leninists, we had an important enough level of agreement with them.... The agreements were functional: the coordination of efforts in the labor movement, the organization of Coordinators (fundamentally in the workers' front). At times relations were also established on the level of military defense, in operations we conducted with them. They had a military apparatus called the Brigadas Rojas (Red Brigades), which was much more developed than ours."[9]

These kinds of alliances and cooperations are of course not without controversy in modern anarchist movements, for obvious and painful historical reasons. I am acutely aware of the detrimental and counter-revolutionary role played by authoritarian left tendencies in multiple historical turning points of the last century, from the role of Trotsky and the Bolsheviks in suppressing the Makhnovist rebellion as well as the general Russian anarchist movement, to the central role of Stalinism in the defeat of the Spanish Revolution, to the brake put on revolutionary upheaval and autonomous action during the strikes and unrest of the French uprising of May '68, to name just a few of the more well-known instances.

My understanding of the danger authoritarian Marxists often pose not only to movements for liberation as a whole but also to the physical integrity of us as anarchists is not just theoretical, it's very much one of personal experience as well. If you were an anarchist in France in the late '90s, chances were good that you gained at least some practical experience dealing with the Communist Party–controlled CGT union's security service goons at demonstrations. In Genoa during the momentous battles against the G8 summit that claimed the life of Carlo Giuliani, comrades from Greece and the Barricada crew found ourselves literally facing off with iron bars against Stalinists, with the sea to our left, the hills to our right, cops to our rear, and helmeted and armed Stalinists trying to expel us from the mass demonstration at our front (and in subsequent years I would have even more dramatic encounters with the Stalinist Communist Party Youth in Greece). Even in Boston, while the balance of power was such that there were no dangers posed to the physical integrity of anarchists, the Barricada Collective and NEFAC on more than one occasion had to expel the cultists of the Spartacist League from our events, eventually even earning the dubious honor of being featured in *Workers Vanguard* in a 2001 article dramatically titled "Barricada: Which Side of the Barricades Are You On?"[10]

Yet the fact remains that in most contexts of the last several decades, at least as far as recent history as well as the on-the-ground realities of most of the times and places in which I found myself, those of us "at the heart of social movements" more often than not found one inescapable reality: Whether it be in the *sans-papiers* or unemployed workers' struggles of France of the late '90s, on the front lines of the antiglobalization movement across North America and Europe, facing off against the Secret Service in Washington, DC, or against fascists anywhere, those who shared front lines and barricades with us anarchists were almost without fail the modern-day representatives of some variety or another of the revolutionary Marxist left.

"Young Spartacus" article in *Workers Vanguard*, November 23, 2001: "Barricada: Which Side of the Barricades Are You On?"

Not only that, but even though that experience would come still later in life for me, the bulk of the groups and collectives of the "autonome antifa" movement in Germany through the '90s to this day, so famous and infamous among anarchists the world over for their tradition of militancy and (pardon the redundancy) autonomous forms of organization and struggle, are actually, contrary to what many seem to assume, not only not composed primarily of militants who would self-describe as anarchists but are in fact deeply politically heterogenous—and based on my experience in the 2000s I would even go as far as to say that the movement is composed primarily of people who identify more with Marxism than anarchism, despite having adopted directly democratic forms of organization as well as anti-state and extraparliamentary forms of struggle, which while certainly not incompatible with Marxism are usually characteristics of anarchist movements and spaces.

By and large, where anarchist movements have chosen to separate themselves, not just ideologically but also frequently physically from the greater spectrum of the left, we find small, marginalized, and often subculturally dominated anarchist spaces. In contrast, where the anarchist movement has generally placed itself within broader leftist revolutionary social movements, we find an anarchism that is more vibrant, less subcultural, and more diverse—as well as, crucially, an active and meaningful participant in the struggles of the day. This is, of course, not an argument against vehemently advocating for anarchist ideas and practice against the veritable whirlwind of reformist, statist, and authoritarian ideas and practices that abound on the left. We must vigorously defend both them and ourselves in the battle of ideas as well as physically when the need arises. Even in places where the majority of the anarchist movement relatively openly speaks of "leftists" as an "other" that has nothing to do with anarchism (Chile and Greece come to mind), anarchist blocs more often than not appear within larger left-wing mobilizations. Of course, coupling our own messaging and tactics with the fact that we find ourselves often taking to the streets with these people really does make the argument that we have nothing to do with them sound less than credible. For better or for worse, as movements we've shared struggles and barricades for over a century, and although we've fought and will continue to do so over the very real differences in our visions of the path to a free and liberated humanity, not only do we agree that in the end we shall live "from each according to their abilities, to each according to their needs," but we have forged a common collective history and identity through the jointly shared experience of desperate, dramatic, heroic, and often tragic struggle.

This is no different in Argentina, where as we've just discussed, both anarchists and Marxists share a painful recent past marked by armed struggle, dictatorship, kidnappings, torture, and death, followed by decades of almost total failure at putting any kind of effective brake on the ravages of neoliberal capitalism gone wild.

And so as I stand here, with no anarchist bloc in sight, not even a black flag to turn to, it turns out this wasn't bad luck but rather a relatively faithful illustration of the state of anarchism in Argentina. *En la Calle* describes anarchists on December 20 finding themselves "absolutely dispersed. In the street clashes one could see individuals throwing rocks and our militants sharing the organization of barricades with other forces, but these are minimal expressions of a movement that in Argentina has a debt with its people."[11]

So it's just the sea of red flags and banners, and I nonetheless feel at home as we begin to move from Congress toward the Plaza de Mayo. "Argentina Erupts" completes the scene:

We marched little more than two blocks when already the gas was clearly visible from the front. Instantly, the t-shirts became hoods, the benches and trash cans became barricades, the slingshots emerged, the pavement became ammunition, and on occasion, the banks the target when cops were not to be found. However, after not long, it became clear that a long term resistance at this location was unwise and tactically unsound, given the relatively small number of people present and the fact that the true battle was around the Plaza de Mayo, which was still quite a distance away....

We started out again along a different route. Surprisingly, the police were nowhere to be found and, aside from the occasional bank window, the march transpired in relative calm until arriving at the 9 de Julio avenue, location of the Obelisk, and only a four or five block distance away from the Plaza de Mayo.[12]

12

The Day of Revolution, Part 1
Rage: We Are the Children of Those You Killed

**Avenida Presidente Roque Sáenz Peña,
December 20, 2001, 2:00 p.m.**

> *Clase obrera nunca te olvides*   *Working class, never forget*
> *del valor que hay en luchar*   *the value of struggle*
> —Que Risa!!, "Nunca te olvides"

There is not a single conflict with the cops, soldiers, or the state—not a single stone thrown in Argentina—in which we are not thinking about the torturers and murderers who to this day live among us, and all the vengeance we are owed. Anarchists or Marxists, we carry one important reminder with us: We are the children of those they killed, the political heirs of those who gave their lives in this struggle. Suddenly, when even we least expected it, we are here to complete the work of those who came before us. Not later. Not tomorrow. Not when the conditions are declared ripe nor when The Party dictates it, but right here and right now.

This is the day of revolution.

I can't tell you the exact moment. But at some point I, and thousands around me, have a realization. This isn't any day. This isn't just a particularly intense confrontation. This is the day we have always been waiting for. Or working for. Or both. It's the day that despite our waiting and working for it, none of us could really believe we would actually see. And much less today. This specific day. Right here. Right now. This moment. The fury, the anger, the exploitation, the repression, the Dirty War, the thousands in exile, the *poverty*—it's all finally boiled over into a fury and an anger that is strong enough to topple this whole world to the cry of "¡Que se vayan todos!"

This is the day of revolution.

CARLOS BARRIA

Un helicóptero se lleva al ex presidente de la Casa Rosada. Eran las 19.52

La Nación, December 21, 2001: "A helicopter evacuates the ex-president from the presidential palace. The time is 7:52 p.m."

Masses of people put the mounted police on the run.

From the "Argentina Erupts" report in *Barricada*:

The scene at the front of Diagonal Norte and Plaza de Mayo was truly incredible, inspiring, and unforgettable. Thousands upon thousands of people, men and women, of all social and economic backgrounds, young and old, thrusting themselves straight into the gas and the bullets, not knowing if the one they shot at you would be rubber or lead.[1]

There is battle, desperate street-by-street battle. A momentous hail of rocks against tear gas and bullets. There are attempts by cops on horseback to charge into the crowd and push us back. They succeed for a fleeting moment, only for a roar to emerge from the crowd as it surges again toward the police lines. I talk to numerous other kids my age that I, "seeing them hooded and fighting in the front lines, assumed were young revolutionaries like myself, who in fact are just youths who decided that the situation had reached an intolerable point and felt compelled to spring into action. Without parties and without leaders, only with conviction and courage."[2]

The horizon beyond us is obscured by thick clouds of tear gas, and we've gotten this far by fighting our way meter by meter. We loot

Las manifestaciones en Plaza de Mayo y el Obelisco desbordaron el ánimo de la gente que -fuera de control- quemó autos y saqueó comercios.

Leftist demonstrators mix with the larger mass of people and begin erecting barricades.

As they try to reach the presidential palace, thousands face off with the police.

banks and offices as we advance, using the furniture to erect enormous barricades, along with smaller ones on intersecting streets, lest we be flanked. But as I look down a side street, that concern starts seeming increasingly unlikely. Our front, on the main avenue leading to the plaza, is thousands of people in an explosive and combative mix of leftist, piquetero, and revolutionary groups that made their way over from Congress, fused with thousands more enraged students, workers, and people young and old from all walks of life. But there are similar, if smaller, confrontations taking place on every street around us. Most importantly, we know perfectly well where we are.

> We advanced in any way we could, carrying forward desks, chairs, fences, and anything that could serve as a barricade and shield.... Step by step, meter by meter, block by block, retreating only to regroup, take respite from the gas, and advance again, growing stronger with the sight of the Presidential palace in the distance.[3]

We are now less than a block away from the Plaza de Mayo, at the end of which lies the presidential palace. The Casa Rosada. And we have them under siege. The closer we get, the more I, and I'm pretty sure those around me as well, become convinced of something unthinkable: They can't stop us. There's too many of us and our determination is too fierce. They've been charging us with horses for hours, drowning us in tear gas, and we duck and take cover constantly, as the distinctive *pop pop* of rifle fire almost never stops. We never know if it is live ammunition or rubber bullets, but we've already seen the lifeless bodies lying behind us, so we know every blast of rifle fire is potentially deadly. Indeed, the furious repression of the embattled state has already claimed two lives, one via rubber bullet to the throat, the other by way of live fire to the chest. But it hasn't stopped the uprising. If anything, it has strengthened our resolve. Short of calling the military and rolling out the tanks, what more do they have with which to stop us?

Suddenly, at the moment when the cops are shooting suspiciously small amounts of tear gas and the rumor gains strength that they might be beginning to run out of canisters, the chants around us no longer seem like over-the-top rhetoric. "Ya van a ver, ya van a ver, cuando tomemos el poder" is the chant that thunders at the barricades, accompanied by a sea of hooded faces and red flags. It translates roughly to "You'll see what's in store for you when we take power." It's obviously

Police on horseback retreat from demonstrators, back toward the presidential palace.

The bloc of the Trotskyist Partido Obrero (Workers' Party) during the clashes. The Partido Obrero is today one of the largest parties in the Trotskyist electoral front, which garnered 2.7 percent of the vote in the 2023 presidential elections.

catchier in Spanish, but I can't help thinking that I'm standing in a modern, colorized version of the storming of the Winter Palace during the Russian Revolution—and that the moment we are singing about is only as far from us as the time it will take us to fight our way onto and through the plaza. The revolution is not just within reach, it is literally in our immediate line of sight. It's not the most antiauthoritarian of sentiments, but as I imagine what might come next, I think of the tens of thousands we've lost to the Dirty War and repression, the lives wasted away in poverty, and the bodies I've seen on the streets on this very day—and I can't help being reminded of Karl Marx declaring that "when our turn comes, we shall make no excuses for the terror."

And in those instants, or those hours to be honest, with the presidential palace within reach and the prospect of power so close (or at least, in hindsight, under the delusion of its closeness), I have to admit that my anarchism (which I like to consider strong) "wavered when I thought of the prospect of entering the Presidential Palace. We would take over I thought, and even without guns we would defend it with our lives. And nobody would be able to take us out. From then on, the people would rule, and we would do things right. We would build a better future, starting right there, and with the red flag flying high."[4] The red flag, once an emblem of the anarchist movement in Argentina and banned by those who walked those same halls of power we were now close to taking, would replace that of Argentina and fly high atop the Casa Rosada.[5]

Mounted police pursue demonstrators down a side street in the vicinity of the Plaza de Mayo.

A standoff takes place during a lull in clashes around the Plaza de Mayo and the presidential palace.

Bomberos se preparan para apagar el incendio desatado anoche en Corrientes y Maipú

HERNAN ZENTENO

Fuego y ruinas en el centro de una Buenos Aires irreconocible

Bancos, tiendas y restaurantes fueron destruidos por hordas de activistas

• La City mostraba anoche una imagen nunca vista • En la Plaza de Mayo se veían cartuchos de balas de goma, piedras y basura • En el Obelisco, autos y edificios en llamas

to los vidrios de los bancos, desbaratado las obras en construcción para convertir sus piedras en municiones y sembrado de obstáculos las calles.

Al otro lado, en medio de Cerrito, como un desafío al Obelisco, un Fiat Palio terminaba de consumirse en el fuego, bajo la mirada tor-

La Nación, December 22, 2001: "Fire and ruins in the downtown of an unrecognizable Buenos Aires."

It was with this thought, that now may seem laughable and delusional, that many of us fought, and we did so like it was the last battle. We advanced regardless of the difficulty.... We threw further than we ever imagined we could throw, and we ran faster and longer than we ever imagined possible. Furthermore, we were not alone. We later learned that essentially every street leading to the Plaza de Mayo witnessed similar, and simultaneous, battles.[6]

Not to give away the plot and ruin the suspense here, but we do not succeed in overrunning the cops and taking over the presidential palace on this day, despite how convinced we might have temporarily been that such a thing was imminent. Eventually, numerous water cannon tanks roll up, and before we know it, the enormous barricades that we so feverishly built and that seemed impenetrable disappear before our eyes,

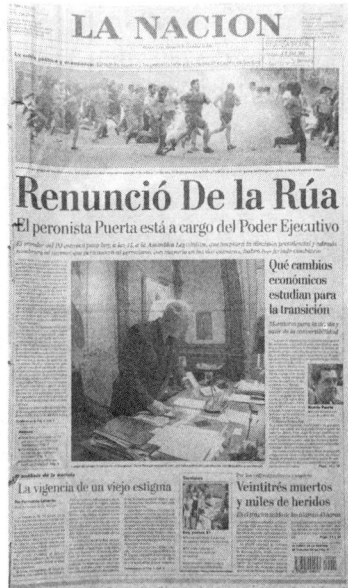

The front pages of Argentina's two main newspapers, *Clarín* and *La Nación*, on December 21, 2001. Both lead with the headline "De la Rúa resigns," while *La Nación* mentions "Twenty-three dead and thousands wounded is the tragic balance of the last 48 hours."

and with them our delusions of an immediate ushering in of a new order. (This also resolves for me the other pressing question in my mind: *If I am indeed in some kind of occupation of the presidential palace in the coming days, probably eventually under siege from the military while clashes rage in the surrounding area, how will I manage to leave to attend Sunday's game?!*)

As we retreat, destroying banks in our path and erecting flaming barricades to slow down the advance of the cops, we hear wild cheering sounds, people banging on pots, and ecstatic shouts of "¡Vamos!" in celebration from balconies above us. It's the kind of collective urban euphoria usually associated with the national team scoring a goal during the World Cup, as jubilant people spill out of their windows and onto balconies to celebrate. The time is 7:45 p.m., and we don't know it then, but apparently, although we have failed at *taking* power, we have indeed succeeded at *toppling* power. Or at least the current iteration of it. The cheering we are hearing is at the images of now-former President de la Rúa, having resigned, hastily escaping from the presidential palace in a rooftop helicopter. As it turns out, we weren't quite as delusional as it might have seemed today, as the security services determined that it was too dangerous for him to remain in the building and a land evacuation was out of the question due to the "unrest in the surrounding areas."

From "Struggle, Unite, Win," in the January–February 2002 issue of *En la Calle*:

> The insurrection of December 20 was a turning point in the history of popular struggles in Argentina. The people, fed up with humiliations, carried out a spontaneous, irreverent, and brave show of strength....
>
> The Plaza de Mayo was defended meter by meter. As the hours passed and repression radicalized the methods of struggle, the middle sectors and more moderate people gradually withdrew from the field of battle. Those who remained were those most committed, primarily youths, workers. It can be said that it was this heroic resistance that toppled de la Rúa.[7]

Diario Popular,
December 21, 2001:
"He's gone." The sign on
the ground reads, "Out
with de la Rúa."

La caída del Presidente: enfrentamientos generalizados durante todo el día

Cinco muertos en una verdadera guerra

La policía reprimió en forma brutal; la Justicia acusó a De la Rúa por homicidio e indagó al jefe de la Federal y a Mathot

• Los choques causaron, en conjunto, decenas de heridos entre los civiles. • También hubo cuarenta policías informados.

• Produjeron al presidente en inminente abandonar el país

Por Fernando Rodríguez
De la Redacción de La Nación

Imágenes del descontrol

Gases lacrimógenos en Diagonal Norte y Florida

El microcentro fue centro de la batalla

Los disturbios se produjeron desde la madrugada de ayer hasta anoche. Temprano, la mayoría de los manifestantes eran vecinos, comerciantes y empleados. Por la tarde las calles fueron copadas por estudiantes, militantes de izquierda y jóvenes sin banderías.

Una camioneta de OCA, incendiada, a metros del Obelisco

Claudia Pérez, con su hija Jorgelina en brazos, se resiste a ser desalojada

La policía montada carga contra los manifestantes en la zona del microcentro

El homicidio de un joven a manos de la policía

Recibió un balazo en la cabeza

Los gases, las piedras y las balas surcaron el cielo de la ciudad

Policías y manifestantes se trenzaron en una batalla campal

• Los sindicatos y los partidos políticos no lideraron la protesta • Grupos sin líderes aparentes tiraban con cascotes a los uniformados • Estos reprimieron y se vieron desbordados

A caballo y a pie

Rompen el cordón

En llamas

Hernán Cappiello

Rafael Saralegui (h.)

La Nación, December 21, 2001: "Five killed in a veritable war."

13

The Day of Revolution, Part 2
At the Intersection of Life and Death
Avenida Corrientes, December 20, 2001, Nightfall

¿Qué es lo que van a hacer?	*What will they do?*
¿A qué van a llegar?	*How far will they go?*
La paciencia no es eterna,	*Our patience isn't eternal,*
con el pueblo no se juega	*don't mess with the people*

—Attaque 77, "America"

The day of revolution is not just battle. It's incredible joy, selfless-ness, and courage. They exist side by side with injury and death, sometimes standing right next to each other. The greatest moments of liberation and the most tragic moments of death at the hands of murderous, desperate servants of the state are not two distant points on a spectrum. On this day, the dividing line between a life full of hope that a different world is possible and one snuffed out in its youth is charted by the invisible trajectory of a policeman's bullet. They are two sides separated by the finest of lines in the sand.

On the day of revolution, as we sit there on Avenida Corrientes, not a block away from the world's widest avenue, the Avenida 9 de Julio, heart of the city, and in view of the iconic Obelisco, it suddenly rains sweets from the sky as masked people throw fistfuls of looted candy into the air and down onto the crowd while yelling, "Merry Christmas!" On the day of revolution, I see the most marginalized and impoverished of our society, the ones white Argentina sneers at as *negros*, entering the shops of downtown and helping themselves not just to what they need, but to what they want.[1] A shirtless man, cartoonishly bad tattoos over his torso and prominent belly, probably in his thirties, approaches me with a cake in his hand as I sit on a doorstep to take a break. He offers to cut me a slice with his keychain while proclaiming loudly, "Today there's enough for everyone." On the day of revolution, scarcity has disappeared and with it the destructive instincts for survival at all costs that eat away at the human spirit under capitalism.

As I sit there on a building's doorstep enjoying my cake and taking a moment to absorb the scene around me, a woman sits down beside me. She's probably in her forties, smallish, slight build, and relatively formally dressed. I offer her some of the sweets that have just rained miraculously from the sky. We start speaking and she tells me that she is a university teacher, "and I can still barely feed my kids, and now these thieves want to steal the little money I've been able to save in my life." I can hear her voice crack with anger and can tell that she's close to tears. She quickly regains her composure and with her next sentence casually announces, "But at least today we gave them a good fight, and I was able to take back some of what they stole from me," as she shows me her shopping bag full of chocolates, groceries, and clothing items with antitheft devices still attached.

On the day of revolution, solidarity is no longer just a word, but hundreds and thousands of tangible gestures big and small all around us. Behind the front lines, the workers of a bar have opened its doors to all who need it. We sit to rest, have a drink of water, recover from the gas, and prepare for a return to the front lines.

What follows comes from "Adios se dice 'hasta siempre,' compañero" (Goodbye is pronounced "until forever," comrade), in the January–February 2002 issue of *En la Calle*:

> Each and every one of us who fought at the Plaza de Mayo, with stones, improvised slingshots, or simply with our presence standing firm, retreating, only to again occupy positions, was physically conscious of the violence of the situation that surrounded us. The violence of an insolent and despotic government and its disinterest for the population it subjugated. The cowardly violence of a criminal and cynical armed police force. And of the strength it took to protect our bodies, preserve life— the power to be free and dignified men and women writing a new page in history. We didn't think about ourselves, but about the person next to us, to care for them and pick them up should they fall next to us.[2]

On the day of revolution, the reality of the fragility of the fine line walked between poignant moments and inspiring images to take with you for a lifetime and immediate death at the hands of the guardians of the state is constantly thrust into our faces. The day of revolution is also the day of the massacre of the Plaza de Mayo, the largest killing of civilians by the state since the military bombardment of the plaza in 1955. Today the jackals are out, and they murder not at the front lines, but from behind. They do not kill in combat, they kill because they have been ordered to do so and do not value human life. Some of the acts of inspiring solidarity we see are born of tragedy. Groups of demonstrators carry away the wounded or try frantically to render first aid or summon an ambulance. Groups of *motoqueros*, essentially couriers on motorbikes accustomed to frantically crisscrossing the city, ride around the area at great risk to themselves, giving us breathless warnings of individuals emerging from unmarked cars and shooting indiscriminately at crowds. One such *motoquero* is Gastón Riva, age thirty-one and father to three children. *Clarín*, Argentina's most widely read daily newspaper, reports:

> Gastón Riva never knew what was killing him: he only felt a terrible impact in his thorax, a fire that burned him at the speed of a lightning bolt, and that was all he would know. He fell from the Honda bike he was straddling as he took stock of the spiral of violence that was shaking the streets of downtown Buenos Aires. Those who came to his aid recount that he moved a hand and his tongue. But he was unconscious. An ambulance driver picked him up at the corner of Avenida de Mayo and 9 de Julio. One of those helping to carry the weight of Riva's already dead body states the obvious in desperation: "Take him, he's dying."[3]

The time is 4:30 p.m., and as Gastón Riva lies dying, Diego Lamagna is arriving downtown. Age twenty-seven, one of the country's top five freestyle cyclists and a promising athlete, he too saw the images of the repression against the *madres*, and that final injustice pushed him to take to the streets. "Look what they're doing!" he exclaimed, alternating between shock and rage, to his seventy-three-year-old mother, María, before he left his mother's home in Avellaneda, that same Avellaneda where just yesterday we thought we might die for a chance at a ticket to a football match, and headed to the streets of downtown. María will later recall that "he told me he would be back at night, and never came home."[4]

Soon after he arrives downtown, a bullet pierces his chest, and Diego Lamagna lies dying on one of the little plazas on the Avenida 9 de Julio.

I no longer remember the chronology, nor the time it was when I saw a lifeless body in the street, with frantic, panicked people around it. I think it might have been him I saw, though the location doesn't quite make sense, as I was more often than not at the front lines and this was several blocks back. Maybe we were already retreating, but it seems too early for that. Or maybe it was during one of my tear-gas-induced temporary retreats. Either way, I remember the crude, surreal scene. Despite the pleas for help, I was clearly looking at an already lifeless body, a corpse. I looked quickly away—too stark a reminder of our mortality will hinder the effectiveness of even the most fanatical revolutionary in combat, and I didn't want to dwell on it. But for a moment I thought of my parents, found a payphone, and took the time to tell them I loved them and that I was safe. They begged me to come home, to which I calmly responded that that was not an option and hung up the phone.

Swarms of police on motorbikes ride two per bike, the accompanying rider wielding an Itaka rifle. They, together with unmarked vehicles, drive around the area firing indiscriminately on the crowds. Outside an HSBC bank, a group is gathered. Suddenly a police car pulls up, somebody shatters the bank windows with a metal pole, and then "three or four security agents accompanied by a few policemen emerge from inside the bank and start shooting indiscriminately. People scatter, but one young person is left lying face down on the street. He has been shot in the head. He was Gustavo Benedetto."[5]

Gustavo is only twenty-three years old, the same age as Carlos "Pete" Almirón, who lost his life not far away from there, only one hour earlier. Almirón was a member of the piquetero organization 29 de Mayo as well as of the CORREPI (short for Coordinadora contra la Represión Policial e Institucional, or "Coordinating Committee Against Police and Institutional Repression") and probably walked the same route with us and the left-wing demonstration from Congress to the Plaza de Mayo. He was shot, seemingly at random, by the police in the midst of a tear-gas charge.

At almost the same spot as Diego Lamagna, Partido Justicialista (the mainstream Peronist party) member Alberto Márquez, fifty-seven-year-old father of three, has been shot in the back and lies dying. Héctor

REPRESION

GUSTAVO BENEDETTO,
OTRA MUERTE SIMBOLO

GUSTAVO CORREA

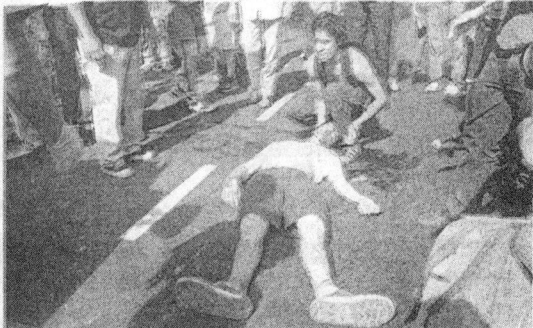

En plena calle. El jueves de la renuncia apenas después del mediodía.

Tenía 23 años y trabajaba en un súper de Tablada que fue saqueado. Se fue a la Plaza a protestar contra el Gobierno y terminó muerto de un tiro.

El pasado jueves 20 Gustavo Benedetto estaba como loco y le dijo a su amigo Arnaldo que había que ir a Plaza de Mayo, pero este no pudo acompañarlo. Apenas le alcanzó a decir: "Flaco, tené cuidado que la policía está dando duro". "Quedate tranquilo, a la noche nos vemos".

Gustavo, Flaco era su apodo más que usual, estaba por cumplir 24 años y era repositor de verdulería en el supermercado Día de su barrio, Tablada. "La noche del miércoles nos enteramos que estaban saqueando el súper, se puso re mal", cuenta Sergio Balmaceda, otro amigo. A la mañana siguiente el súper amaneció devastado y, cuando Gustavo se presentó a trabajar le dijeron que lo echaban porque era de los más nuevos y el local estaba en ruinas.

Desesperado, con bronca, harto de la situación económica, buscó a los pibes del barrio para ir a Plaza de Mayo a manifestar, pero terminó yendo solo. Y sí: la policía estaba dando duro, como le había dicho Arnaldo. La situación era muy distinta a la de la noche anterior, cuando el "cacerolazo espontáneo" desembocó en la Plaza y forzó la renuncia de Cavallo.

"La verdad, Gustavo era un pibe de barrio que ni siquiera iba a las marchas. Ahí fue a protestar, no a hacer quilombo", confiesa todavía sorprendido Sebastián Piacentini, otro de la barra de amigos, bajista de Baroja, la banda de su barrio que Gustavo iba a ver y que justo hoy presentará en medio del luto su disco autogestionado (ver agenda).

Por la tarde, Gustavo murió en una embestida policial. "La hermana creyó verlo por tele y nos llamó, pero nadie sabía nada", cuenta Sebastián. El viernes su foto estaba en el diario: tenía balas de goma en el rostro y una de plomo en el cuello, y era uno de los siete muertos cuya circunstancia se busca esclarecer entre la represión policial y las balas civiles de origen dudoso. Como se sabe, él no es el único: entre los muertos también había dos motoqueros que con ánimos más activistas, estuvieron a la vanguardia del enfrentamiento con la Policía. Unos 200 empleados de mensajerías, con sus motos, protagonizaron el momento más violento, ya de tarde y lejos de la Plaza en 9 de Julio y Avenida de Mayo.

Gustavo había sido baleado cerca del cruce con la calle Chacabuco. "Cuando Gustavo murió, se escucha que un pibe gritaba 'le dieron a mi amigo' ¡y se habían conocido recién! Es más estamos buscando a ese chabón para que nos ayude a saber qué pasó", dice Arnaldo.

Hoy los amigos buscan datos para encontrar a los culpables de su muerte. Pueden ser enviados a gusbenedetto@yahoo.com.ar (incluso se puede entrar con la clave "eliflaco" para chequearlos) o llamar por teléfono al 4699-7857.

EXPERIENCIA GENERACIONAL

Las distintas etapas de la protesta popular de la semana pasada tuvieron marcado protagonismo juvenil. Primero, en la espontaneidad de la protesta callejera: si el cacerolazo fue de las amas de casa, la marcha a la Plaza de miércoles tuvo la huella tanto de quienes enfrentaron los recortes en los presupuestos de Educación como de la Marchas por Bulacio contra el Gatillo Fácil. Pero también el jueves, ya sea por tele o en el lugar de los hechos, se pudo ver la cara joven. Para comprobarlo, solo basta mirar las edades de los muertos.

Twenty-three-year-old Gustavo Benedetto lies dying in the street in the vicinity of the Plaza de Mayo, murdered by a policeman's bullet.

García, one of the many ordinary people who displayed extraordinary solidarity and bravery on that December 20 afternoon, recalls the scene and the excruciating split-second decision he would have to make:

"They [the police] got out of their cars with short and long firearms, fanned out, and took aim. I yelled and threw myself to the ground. Paula Simonetti was there, she was shot in the lung.... She never really recovered and now lives in Spain."

There were others, a few meters from the Obelisco: "A young guy was shot, I don't remember his name, but he ended up committing suicide. When I get up I see Márquez with Marta, his wife, holding his head and crying out for help, and to his left I see Martín [Galli]," continues El Toba [García's nickname].

"The impact of the bullet spun Martín around.... In that moment I had to make a decision without thinking, instinctively, of who I could help. And maybe it's a generational thing: there was a kid with his whole life ahead of him, and Márquez, an older person who was with Marta, his wife."

The story is well known. Márquez died but for Martín the first aid received was decisive in pulling him through two cardiac arrests, just as much as the miraculous appearance of a taxi in the midst of the bullets and gas that rushed him to the Argerich hospital.[6]

The deaths are not limited to the clashes in Buenos Aires around the presidential palace:

On the 19th, in the city of Rosario, Racing fan and union delegate Claudio "Pocho" Lepratti was killed. The thirty-eight-year-old activist in social organizations fell from the roof of a people's school in the neighborhood of Las Flores, his throat penetrated by the lead of an Itaka rifle. His murderer was agent Esteban Velázquez, who had arrived in a patrol vehicle, together with other police officers from Arroyo Seco. El Pocho, who collaborated in the neighborhood with *murgas* [an Argentine equivalent of carnival], guitar sessions, and campouts—as well as working in the kitchen of the school—heard the shots ring out and climbed onto the roof to tell the cops to stop. "Sons of bitches, don't shoot! There's just kids eating here!" Velázquez shot him. He turned him into "The

Miraba desde el techo y la Policía le disparó

Estaba sobre el techo de la escuela en la que trabajaba como portera. Miraba lo que pasaba en el corazón del barrio Las Flores. Pasó un móvil con policías que intentaban evitar un corte en la avenida Circunvalación, a metros del lugar. Y un policía le disparó. La bala, una "posta" de escopeta Itaka, le entró por la tráquea.

Claudio Lepratti, de 35 años, soltero, que vivía en una villa en la otra punta de Rosario, en el barrio Ludueña, sirviendo a la gente como integrante de la comunidad salesiana, murió. Fue asesinado.

Claudio –Pocho para todos sus amigos– era "un pacífico, comprometido con el barrio; el sueldo que sacaba en la escuela lo ponía a disposición de la gente de la villa que lo necesitaba", cuenta, con marcada tristeza, el padre Néstor Gastaldi.

La villa, dentro de la cual tenía su humilde casa, es la de la Vicaría del Sagrado Corazón en el barrio Ludueña, en la zona norte de Rosario. La escuela donde trabajaba, la 756, está en el sur de la ciudad. Y

UN HOMBRE QUERIDO. EL SEPELIO DE CLAUDIO LEPRATTI, AYER, EN EL BARRIO DONDE TRABAJABA.

Pocho iba y venía todos los días.

"El ángel de la bicicleta, le decíamos, porque andaba en su bicicleta, estaba enterándose y buscando la ayuda para cada familia", recuerda el padre Gastaldi.

Es más: un día volvió a su casa y la computadora no estaba. "Le habían robado la compu; rápidamente se enteró quién se la

había llevado y le dijimos que la fuera a buscar. Pero no: prefirió dejar la cosa ahí. Esto habla de cómo era Pocho", sigue recordando Gastaldi.

Lepratti, criado y formado en una familia de buena posición social y económica de Concepción del Uruguay, Entre Ríos, llegó a Rosario hace unos quince años. Lo

hizo para estudiar de seminarista. Pero después de unos años dejó.

Igualmente, siguió ligado a lo religioso y como servidor de los salesianos optó por desarrollar una tarea de "animador pastoral" en uno de los sectores más desprotegidos de la ciudad. Además, estudió en un instituto terciario y se recibió de profesor de filosofía.

"No nos podremos olvidar de su actividad en el comedor escolar", cuenta el padre Gastaldi. Como tampoco podrá olvidar que "la Policía lo mató", mientras aguarda que en el Instituto Médico Legal entreguen su cuerpo.

El informe médico es contundente: hemorragia masiva de tórax por herida de arma de fuego. Y el doctor Víctor Frigerio precisa a Clarín: "Impacto una posta en la tráquea". La "posta" fue un proyectil de copeta con "bolitas metálicas de ocho milímetros". Fue disparado con Itaka.

Lo ocurrido con Lepratti tiene testigos. El director de la escuela, Carlos de la Torre, dijo: "El balazo vino de la Policía". Y varios compañeros se presentaron ya en los Tribunales para formalizar la denuncia, acompañados por miembros de entidades de derechos humanos. Adriana Hernández Larguía precisó: "Los policías venían en un móvil, le dispararon y se fueron".

JORGE BRISABADA ROSARIO, CORRESPONSAL

Mourners cry over the casket of Claudio Lepratti, "The Angel on the Bicycle," shot and killed by police while protecting kids at a neighborhood soup kitchen.

Angel on the Bicycle," as the León Gieco song remembers him. El Pocho used to travel the streets on two wheels, motivating the kids and promoting groups working for social change. The bullet multiplied him. "El Pocho Lives" proclaim the walls of the town.[7]

In all, thirty-nine people are killed across the country during the course of the uprising. Five people are killed in and around the clashes of the 20th for the Plaza de Mayo, while another fifty or so suffer gunshot wounds, and several hundred are injured. In the months and years that follow, those responsible for this murderous and savage repression will be brought to trial and indeed will try to justify their actions with our attempts to storm the presidential palace. A police chief stated to *Clarín*:

"The information we had was that the demonstrators wanted to enter the presidential palace. And that if they made it past the police, the last line of defense would have been the soldiers, armed with FAL assault rifles." According to the police official, "The leftist groups acted in a united and coordinated manner, despite belonging to different left-wing organizations. This way they advanced on the plaza on four fronts: Diagonal Norte, Avenida de Mayo, ... San Martin, and Bolivar."[8]

Much like in the case of the Dirty War of the '70s, it is important to affirm the agency of the thousands upon thousands, myself included, who threw themselves into battle with the distinct and conscious objective of toppling not only the current government but the entire structure of state power. But by and large, with the exception of Carlos Almirón, who it was eventually concluded was shot leading a column of demonstrators in an attempt to return toward the Plaza de Mayo, most of the dead and wounded were shot blocks away from the main points of conflict, often indiscriminately and usually from behind. Except for Carlos, none had any affiliations with left-wing or revolutionary organizing. Given the green light to carry out the repression, the security forces of the Argentine state immediately reverted to the tactics of the dictatorship: death squads and the shooting and killing of anybody who might somehow be associated with "subversives." On December 20, that meant anybody out on the streets of downtown. Police would later attempt to lay blame for the murders on the "excesses" of a few rogue officers. Yet, as *Clarín* would detail:

> The repression with firearms, automatic weapons, and shotguns (firing at times lead and at times rubber bullets) has at least three points in common that discredit the official version of "excesses" conducted by isolated officers, supposedly lacking in experience as a result of a decade without large protest mobilizations: it started at a concrete and specific time, around 3:30 p.m.; it began to include armed civilians acting independently or together with uniformed officers shooting at demonstrators; and finally, it relied on the support of unmarked vehicles from which both civilians and uniformed officers shot indiscriminately.[9]

We have transitioned directly, and relatively seamlessly, from some of the most inspiring acts of solidarity and revolutionary spirit that I've ever seen to a heartbreaking parade of death. But it would be dishonest to speak about the beauty, dignity, and inspiration of this day without speaking of the human cost. I make it a point to constantly remind myself that these days in general and this day in particular, which I remember so fondly as some of the most powerful and inspiring of my life, to many others are the same days in which loved ones disappeared forever. It's a reminder that if we want to reach the new world that we hope lies beyond the destruction of this one, we will have to walk through some painful places, and each of us needs to think about how willing they are to live through those experiences.

As night falls, I'm not yet aware of all of this—of the extent of the death that has taken place in the streets around me, not to mention

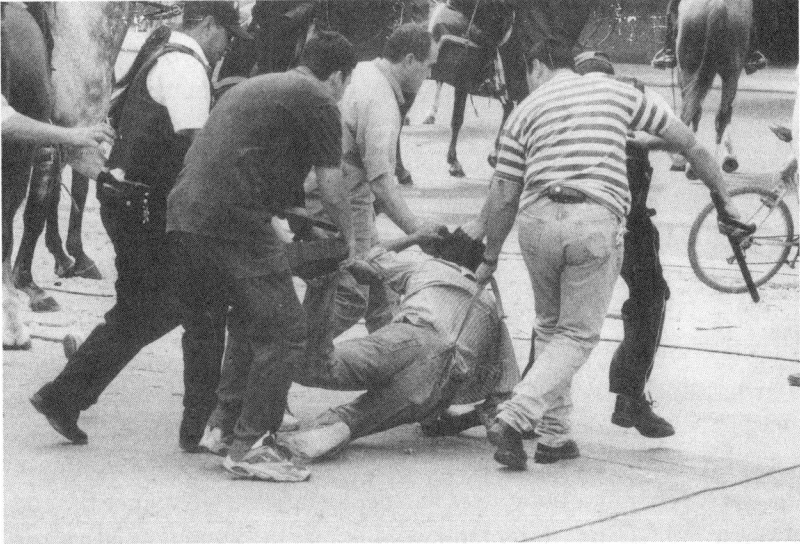

Above and below: Police sweeps in the downtown area during the evening and night of December 20.

around the rest of the city and the country. I know there have been casualties, as I saw at least one body and heard dire warnings of phantom death squads circling the area, but I also know not to believe every panicked rumor I hear on the street in the course of an uprising. But night is falling, I am alone, and I no longer have the relative safety of being surrounded by other people from similar political traditions. That has long since disappeared, and now there is just an eclectic mix of people, some looting, and the occasional sound of rifle fire in the distance. I don't feel I have just been in any kind of imminent danger. Although audacity, planning, and a strong affinity group have often kept me safe, I have to accept that sometimes, such as in Genoa outside the Diaz school, where a delay in checking my email kept me outside the building for just long enough to avoid being one of the victims of "the worst human rights abuses in a democratic country since the end of World War II," or again today, what is keeping me safe is either the guardian angels in which I don't believe or the purest, dumbest luck.[10] Either way, I feel it is time to leave.

For me, the final act of the day of revolution, after I decided it was time to make my way home, is to stroll into a record store and exit with all the records my heart desired, not just the ones my wallet could afford. As I stroll back out and calmly walk away from downtown, wondering what the next days might still bring, it hits me that this has been the day I have fantasized and dreamed about all of my short life. Much like anytime a dream becomes reality, it is rarely how one has imagined it.

For one, I never imagined that when the revolution came, I would find myself simultaneously utterly and completely alone, with not a person who knew my name anywhere in my vicinity, yet for most of the day would be safe in the knowledge that the spirit of mutual aid and solidarity was everywhere around me.

I also certainly never imagined myself living the revolution in Argentina. For one, we were soundly defeated decades earlier. And then there is the detail of … I don't even live here! Despite considering myself deeply internationalist, as both my politics and my nomadic upbringing demand it, living a revolutionary experience in my home was emotionally charged in ways I didn't expect. (To this day I don't know how to properly articulate it. These were streets I had walked a thousand times, and it was a society whose experiences and traumas I shared. Interpret this how you will, but regardless of how far away I was from this place, or for how long, this is apparently my home, and it made the whole experience significantly more emotional.)

In the end, and though I am not quite sure of it as I walk home that night, this wasn't a revolution. It was an insurrection, an uprising. A dress rehearsal. But now, not just me but thousands of us have seen it. We know that the other world exists, and not just in our dreams. There is no going back from this, and next time we will finish what we started. We will take the palaces and storm the skies. When you least expect it, everything is possible.

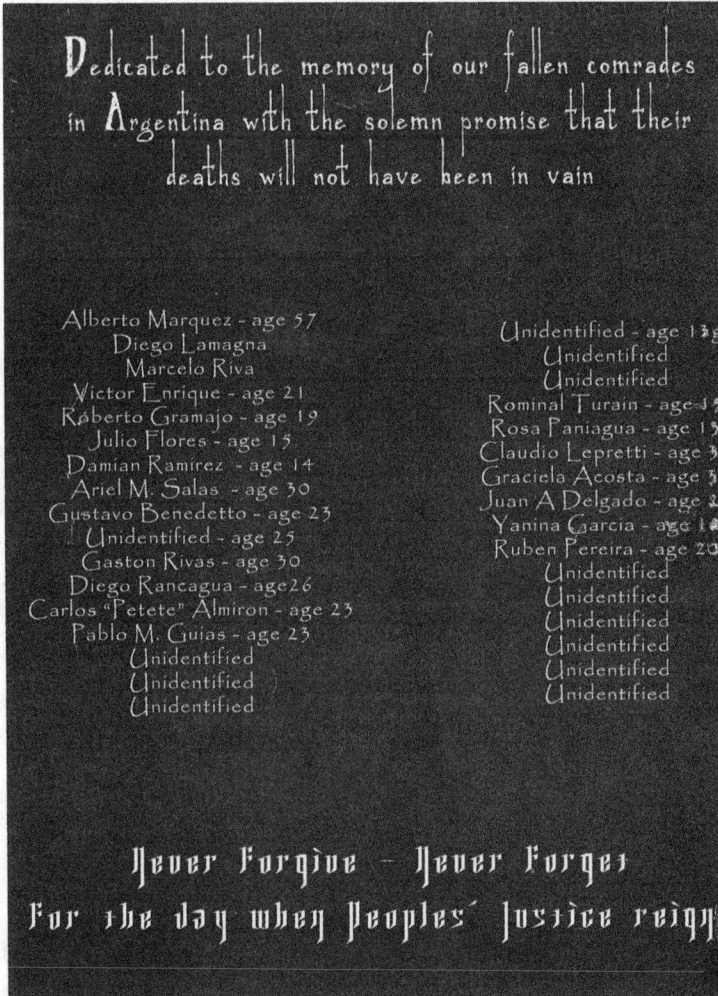

Dedicated to the memory of our fallen comrades in Argentina with the solemn promise that their deaths will not have been in vain

Alberto Marquez - age 57
Diego Lamagna
Marcelo Riva
Victor Enrique - age 21
Roberto Gramajo - age 19
Julio Flores - age 15
Damian Ramirez - age 14
Ariel M. Salas - age 30
Gustavo Benedetto - age 23
Unidentified - age 25
Gaston Rivas - age 30
Diego Rancagua - age 26
Carlos "Petete" Almiron - age 23
Pablo M. Guias - age 23
Unidentified
Unidentified
Unidentified

Unidentified - age 13
Unidentified
Unidentified
Rominal Turain - age 4
Rosa Paniagua - age 15
Claudio Lepretti - age 3
Graciela Acosta - age 3
Juan A Delgado - age 2
Yanina Garcia - age 14
Ruben Pereira - age 20
Unidentified
Unidentified
Unidentified
Unidentified
Unidentified
Unidentified

Never Forgive – Never Forget
For the day when Peoples' Justice reigns

Back cover of the January 2002 issue of *Barricada*.

enFoco

UNA FIESTA POPULAR EN UN PAIS DE DIAS TENSOS

Lo que el futbol
puede

▶ La consagración de Racing demostró cómo la gente logra reír inclusive en tiempos de desesperanza colectiva. Y que la pelota, tantas veces usada por intereses sectoriales, sigue siendo un camino para la felicidad.

Clarín, December 29, 2001: "What football makes possible: Racing's consecration demonstrates that people can smile even in times of collective desperation. And that a ball … can still be a road to joy."

14

After the Fall

El descontento toma las calles,   Discontent floods the streets,
agitadores en todas partes   agitators everywhere
                              —Los Subversivos, "Estallido social"

I remember the evening of December 27. Racing Club has secured its first championship in thirty-five years, and tens of thousands are again streaming to downtown Buenos Aires, to the Obelisco. To the same streets on which only one week ago many of those same people fought for—and sometimes with—their lives to change everything. Today, though, there are no barricades, no clouds of tear gas, no dead or dying comrades. There isn't even a cop in sight. There's just unbridled joy and celebration—again spread across generations, genders, and social conditions. I pop a flare and hand it to my little sister, who is on my shoulders. Joy reverberates through me, through her, and through every single soul around us. Even in that moment, I remember thinking that we deserve this explosion of unfiltered happiness that football has given us. That tomorrow we'll continue fighting, and that if maybe it is not another world that is yet on the horizon, at least another society or another Argentina might be.

Eventually, as the days, weeks, months, and years passed, my young anarchist heart began to understand something seemingly obvious, but lost to many of us in the hope of the moment. We toppled a government on that December 20, and while it is no small feat, it is not the same thing as making a revolution. Our militancy and the collective fury of large sectors of society succeeded in creating a power vacuum, but none of the revolutionary poles were anywhere near developed enough to be

Dos días que cambiaron la Argentina

Fueron 48 horas de frenesí, en las que cayó el gobierno de Fernando de la Rúa y el desborde social resultó incontenible

Los efectivos policiales chocaron con los manifestantes para desalojarlos de la Plaza de Mayo durante el estado de sitio

un camión hidrante; adelante, un manifestante que parece dispuesto a desafiar su avance por el centro porteño

Oficinistas que huyen de los disturbios

Las avenidas de la Capital, convertidas en un campo de batalla

En medio de los incidentes, el rezo

La Nación, December 22, 2001: "Two days that changed Argentina: It was 48 hours of frenzy, which toppled the government of Fernando de la Rúa and proved the social rage to be uncontainable."

in a position to fill it. Hunger and anger were the principal forces that created the conditions for the uprising, but while they may provide the material conditions that render society ripe for rebellion, they are not substitutes for popular self-organization, class consciousness, and the broad implantation and acceptance of revolutionary forces in society that are prerequisites for the successful completion of a revolutionary project.

This is not to say that these did not exist. To the contrary: many thousands of sincere and principled comrades, in the piqueteros movement, in their workplaces, and, yes, some anarchists in their political organizations as well as within broader structures, worked tirelessly for years and were instrumental in lighting the spark that turned hunger and anger into uprising and insurrection. To say otherwise would be to erase their tireless commitment and often sacrifice, both before December 2001 and after.

But because we failed to complete the revolution that day, or in the days and weeks that followed, the old world came roaring back. A reminder we didn't really need that the state, when wounded, becomes an even more vicious animal and must be put down mercilessly when the opportunity arises. We gave the capitalist system one hell of a scare, though, and we planted a lot of seeds. In the days, weeks, and months that followed, directly democratic neighborhood assemblies flourished. Diverse and deep networks of mutual aid emerged, and numerous workplaces were taken over by workers by way of collectivization and expropriation.

Some of these structures, networks, and worker-owned and -operated projects still exist. One of the largest, longest-lasting, and most emblematic of these is the former Zanon ceramics factory in the province of Neuquén, which still operates to this day, employs hundreds of people, and now goes by the name FaSinPat, short for Fábrica Sin Patrones (Factory Without Bosses).[1] Workers occupied the factory in October 2001 and held on for years before obtaining the formal legal recognition of the expropriation, even resisting an eviction attempt by the Gendarmería Nacional (essentially military police) in April 2003, with the support of a wide network of social organizations, unions, and left-wing groups.

Yet the most powerful seed of all was another: We put into the collective consciousness of a generation the practical knowledge of just

A workers' assembly at the self-managed former Zanon ceramics factory, 2015.

how uncontrollably powerful we are as individuals and as a people. It was an unmistakable message that reverberated among both friend and foe, serving as both warning and inspiration, not just in Argentina but across the world. In the fury of 2001 and the antiglobalization movement, we could be forgiven for thinking that the fall of the neoliberal economic order in Argentina was imminent, and apparently during those days I wasn't alone in thinking that a different world might be around the corner, or behind the next barricade.

One comrade, in an interview on the uprising for the Buenos Aires anarchist publication *Gatx Negrx*, states bluntly, "We thought there would be a revolutionary 2001.... We definitely believed that we were very close. Imagine, you could go to the corner of your house and participate in an assembly, who could have imagined that?!"[2] She references Ojo Obrero, a media project of the Trotskyist Partido Obrero (Workers' Party), which ran a video with the title "The Revolution Begins!," and highlights that it wasn't just militant youths smashing banks but also "old people" and the "insubordination not just of activists but of the old lady on the street corner."[3] Yet another comrade recalls, "Everything was popular assemblies, occupations, committees.... There was talk of self-management."[4] With all this happening around us, it was difficult not to believe that we were possibly one spark away from the one that might start the domino effect marking the end of the new capitalist normality and the end of the "end of history."

But capitalist normality did indeed eventually return. There are concrete reasons for this, but an in-depth analysis of them would require a book of its own. It would also be unfair for me to try to give lessons relating to what led up to the uprising or what followed. That is best left to those who did the work on the ground, which is not my case. For the Spanish speakers among us who wish to delve deeper into the matter, I would, however, recommend a couple of texts. The first, which I have quoted repeatedly in this work, is *En la Calle: Una*

El paro y la miseria no son un destino inevitable
Una fábrica argentina marca el camino ...

EN ZANON SE EXPROPIÓ A LOS CAPITALISTAS

"Unemployment and misery are not an inevitable fate. Zanon was expropriated from the capitalists!"

lectura anarquista de la crisis neoliberal en Argentina 1997–2007, which is a collection of writings from the *En la Calle* editorial group that gives an excellent glimpse into conditions leading to the uprising as they develop, as well as anarchist efforts within the piquetero and social movements both prior to the uprising and in the years immediately following. The other is *Anarquismo en el movimiento piquetero* (Anarchism in the piquetero movement) by Natalia Díaz, and as its title states, it is an excellent overview of anarchist participation in the piquetero movement, in many cases from the first-person perspective of those involved for years prior to and following the uprising.[5] None of which was my case. I simply had the privilege of being a participant in the moment, without having put in the work, and so I limit myself to sharing to the best of my abilities the experience, along with the thoughts and reflections it generated in me.

12 | CLARÍN | POLÍTICA | DOMINGO 30 DE DICIEMBRE DE 2001

EL TEMA DEL DOMINGO ▶ LA CRISIS DEL NUEVO GOBIERNO

EL CACEROLAZO Y LOS INCIDENTES

Imágenes de bronca y violencia

▶ Todo ocurrió en cinco horas de cacerolazo creciente e incidentes sobre el final. La protesta tranquila empezó en los barrios y llegó a Plaza de Mayo. Los incidentes, en la Plaza y el Congreso.

INVASION. EL HALL DE ENTRADA A LA CASA DE GOBIERNO POR BALCARCE 50, A LAS 2.00 DE AYER.

A LA INTEMPERIE. UN SILLON DEL CONGRESO, A LAS 5.00, EN LA AVENIDA ENTRE RIOS.

MANOS Y CACEROLAS. LA PROTESTA PACIFICA EN PLENO AUGE, EN LA MEDIANOCHE DEL VIERNES, FRENTE A LAS PERSIANAS CERRADAS DE LA CASA ROSADA. ENTRE LA MULTITUD, SOLO HABIA BANDERAS ARGENTINAS.

AGRESION. A UN POLICIA CAIDO, A LAS 3.00, EN LA PLAZA DE MAYO.

REACCION. MANIFESTANTES FRENTE A LA CASA ROSADA, A LAS 2.30.

A LAS PUERTAS. UN INTENTO DE ENTRAR A GOBIERNO.

DOMINGO 30 DE DICIEMBRE DE 2001 | DEPORTES | CLARIN | 51

CARLOS VILLOLDO

IMPONENTE. COMO A LO LARGO DE TODO EL CAMPEONATO, LOS SIMPATIZANTES OFRECIERON UN ESPECTACULO DESLUMBRANTE EN LAS TRIBUNAS.

Images from December 28 and 29, 2001. Late at night on the 28th and into the morning of the 29th, a new uprising against the government in front of Congress and another presidential resignation. The next evening, championship celebrations at Racing's stadium. Many of us went from the attack on Congress to bed, then straight to the stadium the next day.

An experience that inspired me, while at the same time challenging my anarchism, as uprisings and insurrections should. The inspiring parts are self-evident, but the challenging ones come in the aftermath, when you have the time and space eventually to observe how events unfolded from a distance. Neither popular self-organization nor the vanguardist parties of the authoritarian left were capable of filling the power vacuum we created. And so the Peronist Partido Justicialista reconstituted itself and returned us to "normality."

For a few years, I felt like this was a sign of an unmitigated defeat. The uprising was maybe a warning shot (another one) of the potential for anarchist ideas as a force for revolt and resistance, but it also revealed our shortcomings as far as being able to push situations of societal rupture definitively toward the antiauthoritarian, classless, and stateless world we envision. At the same time, it's probably important to not be overly critical and to recognize that, considering the small size and marginal implantation in society, or even social movements, of anarchism in Argentina, our ideas and methods of struggle were probably even overrepresented in the uprising, as well as in the months that preceded and followed it.

Yet another lesson that challenged not necessarily my anarchism, but more so my relation to a lot of First World so-called fellow revolutionaries and fellow travelers of the antiglobalization movement, was the cynical and hypocritical difference in reaction to the events in Gothenburg and Genoa: The shooting of one person in Sweden and the killing of another in Italy led to frantic calls to "reflect" and "back away from so much violence," while the uprising in Argentina, with its staggering body count of thirty-nine deaths, some of them even children, was cheered and applauded wildly. A clear sign that even for these people, whether consciously or unconsciously, First World white lives were apparently worth more than Third World lives. It was okay if we died for revolution, or if we employed and suffered great violence in its pursuit, but somehow terrible and tragic if it took place close to home.

To me, this hinted at a kind of tacit understanding between the state and some First World self-identified revolutionaries—one that remained unspoken and was even potentially subconsciously embedded in the psychology of many comrades to such an extent that, while it angered me, I couldn't necessarily fault them for it. It was a dynamic that even played out during the famed events of May 1968 in France a

A mural in Avellaneda at the onramp to the Pueyrredón Bridge, an access point to Buenos Aires often blockaded by piqueteros, portrays Maximiliano Kosteki and Darío Santillán, victims of the Massacre of Avellaneda in 2002.

Another part of the same mural, reading "Work, Dignity, and Social Change. Maxi and Darío ... Present!"

generation before us. The state, understanding the privileged positions of many of the students it faced on the barricades, shied away from the use of deadly force—despite the stock exchange being set on fire, endless barricades on the streets, and even the death of a police officer in the course of the clashes. In Mitchell Abidor's oral history *May Made Me*, he writes, "The state had all the means of repression at hand, yet they never fired into the crowds."[6] Some claim this was due to fear that "a few dead students would have set off a wave of revolutionary violence, outside student ranks and outside of Paris." Others believe that "such a suicidal tactic would have led to a quick end" to the uprising of May '68 and that the actual motivation was very much the opposite.[7]

Participant Jean-Michel Rabaté explained to Adibor, "The French cops had orders not to kill. . . . Why? Because they knew the people who'd be killed were children of ministers and judges." As such, "those on the streets, despite their rebellion against their parents' world, were still protected by their families."[8] And so, both sides effectively played out their parts under the tacit agreement often afforded First World revolutionaries so long as they have not yet been deemed a mortal danger to the state or capital. An unspoken agreement in which, while "the rebels imagined themselves in the midst of an insurrection and in this way fictionally fulfilled their dreams of revolution," as Pierre Goldman writes, the state took care in "maintaining the confrontation within peaceful limits, from which the use of arms was banned" and thus protected itself from a more serious challenge.[9]

Third World revolutionaries, or those in the First World who found themselves in open battle with the state, have historically been afforded no such considerations or restraint. For me, an understanding of the revolutionary's proximity to death is part and parcel of anarchist consciousness, and of the ensuing revolutionary militant struggle if one engages in it. If the state doesn't confront us with this consequence, chances are we are not a danger to it. For anarchists in Argentina, through their involvement in wider social struggles both before and after the uprising of 2001, proximity to the death of comrades and loved ones became inescapable as the state reconstituted capitalist normality. The comrade interviewed by *Gatx Negrx* says, "We realized that death was terrorizing us, so we had some meetings with psychologists. How do we continue? We set the goal of trying to maintain our mental health. These were years that eventually culminated with what happened to Kosteki

A CORREPI (Coordinating Committee Against Police and Institutional Repression) flyer stating, "Today, like yesterday, the only road is the road of struggle. Until victory always!" At bottom: "Carlos 'Petete' Almirón, murdered during the popular rebellion of the Plaza de Mayo, December 20, 2001."

and Santillán."[10] She is referencing a fierce anti-piquetero repression in July 2002 during which Maximiliano Kosteki and Darío Santillán, both in their early twenties, were murdered by cops in what came to be known as the Massacre of Avellaneda. A great rebellion, unfinished, will almost inevitably bring with it a great repression, and this time was no different. "My comrade went out one night to do political graffiti ... but by 3 a.m. he wasn't back, so I just assumed he had been killed. From 2001 forward, that's just how we lived."[11]

From *En la Calle*'s "Adios se dice 'hasta siempre,' compañero":

We can write about the dead, it seems easy to scrawl on paper that we know there will be death in order to birth true life. But when our dead have eyes on their face, a voice and a gaze—a kiss that dries as it becomes a memory, a hand that will touch you again only in your dreams, the word becomes a cheap recourse. Carlos Almirón, at age twenty-three, murdered by the government on December 20 during the popular revolt in the city of Buenos Aires, is not the first crime to haunt us. The certainty that it won't be the last hurts us. But each of these blows away a fragment of our humanity, wants to see us become machines.

The government wanted to cling to the privileges acquired through years of pillage by tooth and nail, bullet and tank, but the kingdom it governed has collapsed. To stop its own fall, it sends its troops to kill and imprison. But that crime and those prison bars are kindling for the fires of justice. Each blow against this system carries with it a name from the past emblazoned in blood. Petete [Almirón's nickname] gives new names to those blows. While searching for life, for a life with dignity, death set him a trap. But a rumor already runs through our neighborhoods. We are many who have risen up. We know that this crime has responsible parties, that all crimes carry the fingerprint of who thought them and who executed them. Our vengeance will be in learning, in never forgetting, and in arriving—despite obstacles, both of our own creation and of our enemies—at the free and liberated society that Petete fell fighting for.[12]

15

The Kirchnerist Era
April 27, 2003

Me imagino un tren,	I imagine a train,
recorriendo mi país,	traveling my country,
del norte hasta al sur,	from the north to the south,
cambiando la cabeza por vivir	opening my mind in order to live

—Los Gardelitos, "America del Sur"

O n April 27, 2003, barely sixteen months after the events of December 2001, Argentina headed to what was essentially a referendum by way of presidential election, the two main candidates representing clearly defined polar-opposite conceptions of the role of the state and economic policy in shaping society. One was none other than former President Carlos Menem—president from 1989 to 1999, architect of the country's wave of privatizations, and personified representative of the neoliberal reforms of the '90s. His primary opponent was Néstor Kirchner, an exponent of a center-left current within Peronism—at least in his rhetoric, a proponent of a clear break with the old economic model, in favor of a state and an economy at the service of the workers and masses and not the interests of capital. While Menem came in first place in the first round of voting, drawing 24.45 percent of the vote almost exclusively from the upper middle class, upper class, and those who identify with their interests versus 22.25 percent for Kirchner, it was clear that he would lose by an ample majority in the runoff election. Carlos Menem chose to withdraw his candidacy, beginning the era of *Kirchnerismo* in Argentina.

Kirchnerism skillfully identified the most influential social actors of the era. Shortly after being elected, Kirchner himself stated in an interview, "We've come to do what Perón did with the unions, which is

Then-President Néstor Kirchner and future President Cristina Fernández de Kirchner, his wife, on stage at a rally. The flags in the crowd include the red flags of the "Communist Party–Extraordinary Congress," one of several leftist organizations (eventually including the relatively large Maoist Revolutionary Communist Party) that became part of the Kirchnerist ruling coalition.

incorporate them into the state. We need to incorporate the piqueteros into the state."[1] And so, significant parts of the piquetero movement were indeed integrated into the state machinery, Kirchnerism succeeding in bringing into the fold many sectors of it, as well as the critical support and eventual participation of some of the country's left-wing organizations and parties, including for example the relatively large Maoist Revolutionary Communist Party (Partido Comunista Revolucionario) of Argentina (keyword: relatively).

In yet another challenging turn of events for my anarchist orthodoxy, some of the class struggle and platformist elements of anarchism—those with which I most identified and looked to for political reference from outside the country—apparently dissolved into the Peronist movement as it sought to integrate and tame what it could of the piquetero movement. AUCA, from La Plata and one of the three organizations coediting *En la Calle*, "continued its development efficiently based on the same strategy used by the left at the time: accumulation based on the management of the resources that the state was assigning in an attempt to contain social demands," with the idea being that they would continue to self-manage and develop poles of dual power, "with the intention of turning those palliative measures against the state that delivered them."[2] That growth brought with it "new discussions and an eventual questioning of their social political identity." The organization fractured, and "the minority who were incorporated into the government were absorbed into Peronism. The majority, who took refuge in social movements, eventually abandoned anarchist political practice."[3] With the Rosario group having already disbanded, just a few short years after the uprising, those agitating for a political anarchist organization in the streets and the struggles were either in disarray or explicitly moving away from anarchism as the practical and theoretical tool of choice to advance popular struggle. Only the Buenos Aires group was left, and by 2007 *En la Calle* was no longer being printed.

I know full well that the project of Kirchnerism has very little to do with that of a liberated society free from capitalism, classes, and state. I know that its politics are often little more than lip service to left-wing ideas, at best a left-leaning populism and at worst a new embodiment of the dangers of caudillismo and clientelism in left-wing movements, which often serve to cheapen and discredit left-wing and revolutionary ideas in society. I know that the Kirchner era was responsible for repressive projects against revolutionary dissidents, and worst of all, the appearance of such center-left movements following periods of revolutionary or prerevolutionary upheaval is often precisely the escape valve that capitalist normality and the state require to adapt and guarantee their survival, as would later be the case, for example, in Greece with Syriza, following social and economic processes that were shockingly similar to the ones experienced in Argentina a decade earlier. Finally, I know beyond doubt that when I was in Argentina, and if I were in Argentina, my place was not and would never be among the supporters of the ruling party, but with the radical left, the anarchists, and the social movements that never stopped fighting for a better alternative and a completely different model of society.

I'm also perfectly aware that Kirchnerism was the vessel through which "cold water was thrown onto the fires" of rebellion in Argentina.[4] What followed was capitalism with a human face, which today has left us with a 50 percent poverty rate and near triple-digit annual inflation, which hits society's most vulnerable hardest. Worse yet, although Kirchnerism governs at the will of the International Monetary Fund, which in 2022 the Kirchnerist government again struck a deal with and which imposes a brutal austerity regime on the population, mainstream society interprets Kirchnerism as a left-wing phenomenon, due to its lip service to left-wing ideas of social and economic justice. The consequence of this is a generalized disillusion with left-wing politics and, worse yet, a youth who see "leftism" as associated with state bureaucracy and the brutal social and economic conditions of the country—leaving the lane wide open for the growth of the right wing and far-right elements, much like the Bolsonaro and Trump phenomenons.

And yet, if in the years immediately following the uprising Kirchnerism was able to appease and integrate not just huge sectors of the youth and a significant portion of the left but even some anarchists, there was probably at least something to analyze there. I couldn't help but smile in the years that followed when Kirchner and his government spoke of "redistribution of wealth" and basically declared war on the farm- and land-owning oligarchy. How could we not be pleased when they pushed forward with the prosecutions and trials of the generals responsible for the Dirty War of the 1970s against the Argentine left? Who didn't feel joy when the picture of Jorge Rafael Videla, the hated and murderous military leader who in the 1990s used to walk free in the

"7,587 lives since 1983 [when the dictatorship ended]. All governments murder, torture, and disappear people." Anarchist anti-state propaganda, 2021.

President Néstor Kirchner (right) oversees the removal of the painting of ex-dictator Jorge Rafael Videla at the ESMA facility. The facility was then handed over to human rights organizations and is now a museum and memorial preserving the history of the crimes committed there.

streets of Buenos Aires, was taken down from the walls of the ESMA, a navy installation in Buenos Aires previously used as a concentration camp by the dictatorship, and the building handed over to the Mothers of Plaza de Mayo? When the press monopoly of the Clarín media group was challenged, for whatever reasons, and a law was passed to democratize mass communication in Argentina, was that not a positive step? When Indigenous languages and cultures were given space and recognition on public TV for the first time ever, I couldn't help nodding approvingly. When football television rights were stripped from private interests and matches began being broadcast free of charge on television as "football for all," it may have been bread and circus (and certainly was, particularly as the ad space between halves was used to air state propaganda), but was there anything to criticize with the principle of the idea? Is it not, for better or for worse, a part of our popular culture, and as such should it not be accessible to all regardless of income? The legalization of same-sex marriage, the universal monthly benefit for Argentine children—the list goes on and on. It is these politics that have enraged the old, the privileged, and the reactionary in Argentina and brought a generation who not ten years ago was chanting "Que se vayan todos" out in the thousands to proclaim their will that Cristina Fernández de Kirchner continue the *proyecto nacional y popular* (national and popular project) after Néstor Kirchner's sudden death in 2010. Fernández de Kirchner, who had been elected president in 2007, won reelection by a landslide a year after her husband's passing.

The Argentina of *Kirchnerismo* is still without doubt an Argentina of capitalism, inequality, and poverty. But the fact remains that when Kirchnerism was temporarily displaced from 2015 to 2019, it was not by a better and revolutionary alternative but by another proponent of the most brutal form of free market capitalism and the reactionary, nostalgic, and coup-sympathizing adherents of the old Argentina who stood behind him. A spectrum of people who, much like Republicans in the US, see any sort of social progress or economic equality as a curtailment of their God-given freedoms and a socialist barbarism to be combated at all costs.

If nothing else, the uprising of 2001 gave Argentine society a forceful push away from the worst excesses of capitalism, and while the political space it created may have been filled by the deeply imperfect Kirchnerism, it also moved us toward a more generalized acceptance of concepts of social justice, not to mention the growth of workers' self-organization and autonomous and combative popular organizations. It proved the power and effectiveness of direct action and massive militant resistance in the face of fierce and indiscriminate state repression, as well as the actuality and viability of anarchist principles of self-organization and direct democracy, such as those seen in the numerous neighborhood assemblies that sprang up in its aftermath.

We didn't make the revolution that day, but I like to think that we both shifted society leftward and contributed our grain of sand to the birthing of an entire generation who now knows that social revolution is possible. The success or failure of revolutionary struggle is not always to be measured in black-and-white terms of "the dawn of the new world" or total failure. Progress can, and does, exist even without the possibly unattainable "final and glorious victory." It's not an argument against tireless, uncompromising war against capital and the state. To the contrary, it's an appeal to continue it, but at the same time to recognize that our struggles of the past have possibly already moved us closer to that goal. And so next time—and there will be a next time—the road still to be traveled might be shorter, and the result will hopefully be more than a rehearsal.

A mural in the Villa Crespo neighborhood of Buenos Aires reading "Bohemian Territory" and "Villa Crespo Antifa."

16

Las Balas No Podrán Frenar el Viento
(Bullets Can't Stop the Wind)
Club Social y Deportivo La Cultura del Barrio, Villa Crespo, Buenos Aires, November 15, 2018

Disculpá yo me quedo aquí,   *Sorry, but I'm not moving from here*
las pieles ya curtidas por   *my skin toughened through vast*
vastos inviernos,   *winters*
la convicción intacta de todos   *the conviction in my dreams still*
mis sueños   *intact*

—Eterna Inocencia,[1] "Vivan mis caminos"

Yesterday the hated Colonel Falcón was again the target of an anarchist bomb. Two anarchists were arrested in the vicinity of the explosion, one gravely injured as the artifact they carried detonated prematurely. Nearby, police found a metal plaque reading "Simón Lives On in the Hearts of All Insurrectionaries!"[2]

Once again the government beats the drum of anti-anarchist hysteria, and the looming danger of anarchist terrorism, real or imagined, is projected dramatically and obediently by the mainstream media. Again, the armed forces of the state are dispatched to raid anarchist spaces across the city. But this is neither 1909, 1919, nor any of the numerous subsequent periods of military dictatorship between then and the present day. This is happening on November 18, 2018.

The colonel has been dead for 109 years to the day, and the note is a reference to the legacy of the anarchist who took his life, Simón Radowitzky. The bomb has exploded in the vicinity of Falcón's tomb, in the elegant Recoleta Cemetery in central Buenos Aires. We also happen to find ourselves in the immediate run-up to the summit of G20 leaders taking place in the city at the end of the month.

The tomb of the infamous anti-anarchist Colonel Ramón Falcón, killed by Simón Radowitzky's bomb. His tomb lies in the elegant neighborhood of Recoleta, at the same cemetery as Eva Perón.

One of the spaces raided is the Ateneo Libertario de Constitución, formerly the home of the Federación Libertaria Argentina.[3] The other is a social and boxing club in the neighborhood of Villa Crespo:

> There's a raised fence and a yellow gate.... The gate is halfway open and sports an endless array of stickers, a sign reading "Cops Out of Our Neighborhoods!" and another proclaiming the May 1 as a day of struggle "against austerity, precarity, and unemployment." The hallway has two large photo printouts, facing each other, on each side of it.
>
> "When are these photos from?"
>
> "From the day we were raided." ...
>
> One of the images shows police securing a perimeter while a crowd of people gathers facing them in the street. The other, an image from later that same day, is of a public boxing lesson, held in the street, improvised, with dozens of neighbors watching the scene....
>
> The neighbors responded to the attack with their bodies, with and for them. Eventually the officers withdrew, and in an emotional moment, they were able to reenter their place in the world.[4]

We are not outside the Biblioteca Popular José Ingenieros, which does indeed still exist, but rather one short kilometer's distance away.

The anarchist spaces in Villa Crespo have multiplied, and we are at the space of the Club Social y Deportivo La Cultura del Barrio (The Culture of the Neighborhood Social and Sporting Club), the first anarchist and antifascist social club to be born in Argentina in almost ninety years.

> The neighborhood club focuses primarily on boxing, although it also offers other disciplines such as muay thai, yoga, and functional training. Their doors open between 8:30 and 9:00 a.m. and close around 11:00 p.m., every day.
>
> Aside from sports, the club offers cultural alternatives as well as events on Fridays, Saturdays, and Sundays. It is self-financed through these activities and through the membership fees.[5]

Needless to say, no one is ever turned away from the club and its activities due to lack of funds. Aside from the economic factor, it's a sporting space within which "without caring about your gender identity, or whatever body you have, nobody will ask you anything or demand anything from you," according to Gastón Marin, director of a documentary film about the club titled simply *LCDB*. "The freedom in the air in that place I don't think exists anywhere else in sport."[6]

Aside from its numerous and growing activities in the neighborhood of Villa Crespo, LCDB also runs the Boxeo Popular project in the Isla Maciel, located on the other side of the city and one of its most impoverished and marginalized neighborhoods, under the motto "Without prejudice or discrimination, another sport is possible." This "social and sporting project, one of a kind in Argentina, is aimed at youths and adolescents. Popular boxing appears as a pathway to access rights, learn to protect them, and foster the cohesion of a working-class identity. Faced with the state and its indifference, an antifascist organization restores the social bonds and achieves concrete transformations in the community." About 150 youths participate every weekend in the program's classes, during which the "antifascist organization coordinates the training sessions, distributes food and school supplies, and stimulates a space where active listening is an absolute priority."[7]

While the club itself was founded in 2011, its very existence is the result of the seeds planted during the crisis and revolt of 2001. Further evidence that the desperate bullets of the state cannot stop the wind. "We are the result of that 19th and 20th of December, we are part of an organization that was born during those days, we were participants

Police stand guard during the 2018 raid of La Cultura del Barrio.

A public boxing class held in the street during the police raid of the club.

A multi-club boxing exhibition day at La Cultura del Barrio.

in that historic moment and we continued to be so in the times that followed, generating alternatives from below," the club states in a social media post.[8] Luis Tabera, one of LCDB's founding members, says, "We're part of an organization called Antifascist Action," which was itself created in 2001 by several of the current actors in LCDB. "We come from the unemployed workers' movement in Avellaneda, from the times of 2001. Then we started exploring other methods. We started a workers' cooperative. We had a bakery, a textile store. Ten years later the Club Social y Deportivo La Cultura del Barrio was born."[9]

The club is not necessarily explicitly anarchist, as is often the case with spaces or organizations coming from, among other things, antifascist youth culture and subcultural scenes. (The LCDB space is and has always been deeply connected to Buenos Aires's SHARP and RASH skinhead scenes.) LCDB members represent a plurality of people who identify with positions from the broader revolutionary left. But its deep implantation in anarchist praxis is inescapable, from its roots and ongoing active participation in the militant and revolutionary antifascist tradition of Antifascist Action, to the red-and-black flag reading "Against All Oppression," to the club's stated pillars of "generating alternatives, mutual aid, and grassroots organization."[10]

"We always move across these three axes," says Tabera. "Grassroots organization because we continue working in a neighborhood, in this

The front entrance to La Cultura del Barrio.

An antifascist panel at LCDB. The club is regularly used as a meeting space by various collectives and organizations, as a debate space, and as a concert space.

case Villa Crespo, which we have taken as our home. Mutual aid means that everybody collaborates. At the beginning, for example, many of us would finish our workday and then come work here. We installed floors, walls, built a rehearsal space, all kinds of things. From zero. We saw the practical implementation of our ideals. Generating a sporting and cultural alternative was key." Tabera, who defines the club conceptually as anticapitalist and against the "commodification of sport," continues, "Today … almost all the people here live from this. This is what we call generating alternatives that are real and can be sustained over time.… We don't exploit anybody.… We believe in class struggle, and we know which side we are on."[11]

The club's firm alignment with the anarchist space and ideas is best illustrated by its day-to-day practices of self-management and the initiatives of popular power that it drives—but it is also illustrated in the club members' active participation in the anarchist and antifascist bloc at demonstrations, the organization of which often takes place at the club itself, as is often the case with the yearly March 24 demonstrations marking the anniversary of the military coup of 1976.

Three days after the police raid on La Cultura del Barrio, five hundred meters away, Club Atlético Atlanta has a home game at its stadium. Gone are the romantic but dangerous wooden stands. The once

Above and below: Antifascist Action Buenos Aires members doing propaganda work during a demo, March 24, 2021.

Facing page: The Antifascist Action Buenos Aires and LCDB bloc at the demonstration on the anniversary of the military coup d'état, March 24, 2024.

Atlanta's once decrepit and abandoned social center, now again in the hands of the club and its members. It has been fully remodeled and is used by hundreds of people of all ages every day for a variety of sporting activities.

decrepit stadium has now been largely rebuilt, a process that sent the club and its "Bohemian" fans on a three-year-long semipermanent away-game exile. But the club currently sits in the third division of Argentine football, itself a decade-long exile that seems eternal but will end with a promotion that is six short months away from today.

While success on the pitch may still be elusive, Atlanta has already won its most important battle. In 2006, after a decade of struggle that included road blockades and numerous demonstrations in front of Buenos Aires's city hall, an expropriation law was passed that returned the social center to the club. I walk past the once abandoned and shuttered social center a few hundred meters beyond the stadium. The walls of the building are painted in vibrant tones of yellow and blue. Beyond its doors, hundreds of kids from the neighborhood participate in any one of the twenty-seven sporting activities the club now offers—from chess to table tennis, from handball to martial arts, and everything in between. In the years to come, the pool will be reinaugurated and a space for barbecue will open, as well as a restaurant. The area will explode with the sights, smells, and sounds of neighborhood families collectively enjoying the space. The club, which by 2022 will have reached several

Flyer for a popular market at Atlanta in May 2024, as ultraliberal reforms stagnate wages while the prices of goods soar: "Bohemian Market. Affordable prices for the neighborhood. With the participation of workers' cooperatives and producers."

thousand dues-paying members, becomes a pivotal space during the pandemic as a vaccine center, while its fans organize a popular food kitchen for neighbors economically affected by the pandemic shutdown.

All that is still to come. But today, as Atlanta's players take the pitch, they carry a banner with them. A gesture of solidarity with the other neighborhood club. As the players line up for the traditional starting lineup pictures, the banner they carry reads proudly, "La Cultura del Barrio."

Atlanta fans at the remodeled Estadio León Kolbowski.

No Te lo Puedo Explicar, Porque No Vas a Entender

(I Can't Explain It to You, Because You Wouldn't Understand)

Downtown Buenos Aires, December 20, 2022, 3:00 p.m.

Moriré con la paz, porque al mundo lo intente cambiar, como ves sigue igual, pero no me resigne a soñar	*I'll die at peace, because I attempted to change the world, as you can see, it's still the same— but I haven't given up on dreaming*

—Cadena Perpetua, "Si me ves"

December 20 is a scorching-hot early summer's weekday in Buenos Aires. The streets of downtown have been flooded by a human sea of people. This river of people—young and old, rich and poor, of all sexes and genders—has transformed the urban landscape in the way we anarchists often dream: from a gray concrete jungle at the service of cars, commerce, and routine to an open space filled with joy. A blank canvas that this outpouring of humanity paints and shapes as they see fit.

The area around the Avenida 9 de Julio is normally a cauldron of stressed and hurried people going about their day. Motorists yell at pedestrians and at each other at red lights, almost without exception making colorful mention of the other driver's mother's private parts or supposed participation in the "world's oldest profession." They merge with some of our most marginalized, who are hoping to clean their windshields in order to secure today's subsistence, while pickpockets, cops, and unsuspecting tourists play their daily game of cat and mouse. It's a microcosm of class struggle, inequality, social cannibalism, and just generally urban capitalist hysteria.

Today, though, class divisions and their inevitable consequences seem to have disappeared. The violence and social cannibalism of class society is nowhere to be seen on these streets. Instead there's solidarity.

Fans celebrate in downtown Buenos Aires. Over five million people took to the streets in what is believed to be the largest sports celebration in human history.

Strangers embracing each other. People share beer, water, and food with others they've never met before. Chants break out constantly among the crowd. Shopkeepers, at least of those shops still open, offer people space to sit and rest without forcing them to consume anything, while old ladies help the crowd cool down by hosing them from their balconies or dumping buckets of cold water.

The scene is repeated and multiplied countless times over, in neighborhoods, on street corners, and even on highways, across all of Buenos Aires. And again, the appeal of it to our little anarchist hearts isn't hard to grasp. The structure of society, in this case class society, seems to have disappeared, the constraints of time and routine suspended and removed. The general constraints of the architecture and structure of class society are gone, and the state is next to nowhere to be seen. Today it feels like anything is possible, like the norms of the old world might have been swept away. Speaking of sweeping away, if I sweep away from the scene the sea of Argentine flags, if I suspend my critical thinking as to why this is all happening, it feels prerevolutionary.

In reality, though, it's the illusion of what revolution could look like. In fact, if I try to analyze it calmly, while there is an undeniably positive aspect to seeing so much human joy and happiness and a collective sense of unity, it probably doesn't hold up to even the most superficial analysis. If anything, it's very likely class collaborationism and the strengthening of myths of national unity. It's a distraction that will, of course, change absolutely nothing in society. Sooner rather than later, the dispossessed of society will return to their daily struggle for survival, our near triple-digit inflation will continue to eat away at the wages of those fortunate enough to have jobs, and the middle and upper classes of Argentina will continue to place the blame for our economic ills and growing levels of violence on those poorest and most vulnerable rather than on the landowners, corporations, and politicians who govern and trade in exclusive defense of their class interests.

Because today there is not joy and solidarity confronted by tear gas, bullets, and a brutal repression that claims dozens of lives. There are no red (or black) flags in the streets, no barricades, no presidents fleeing the presidential palace from a rooftop helicopter, no delusional mob of young communists (among whom I find myself) chanting about seizing power as they fight their way meter by meter, inch by inch, and rock by rock toward the Plaza de Mayo and the presidential palace. Today is not

December 20, 2001, when the streets filled with all of the above, to the sound of "¡Que se vayan todos!" (Out with all of them!).

Today is, astoundingly, exactly twenty-one years later to the day, December 20, 2022, and the chant reverberating on the streets— the same streets that were the epicenter of the uprising on this day twenty-one years ago—goes, in part, "No te lo puedo explicar, porque no vas a entender" (I can't explain it to you, because you wouldn't understand). Which is strikingly accurate, as how on earth can I, or anybody for that matter, pretend to possibly explain to you that what has sparked this mobilization of dimensions never before seen in modern human history—with over four million people spilling into the streets of Buenos Aires—is a football match. It is because, thanks to two Leo Messi goals, thanks to Dibu Martínez making the greatest save in the history of the sport, and thanks to, as the chant goes, "el Diego [Maradona] … from the heavens" cheering us on, Argentina has claimed its third World Cup title. It's the culminating moment of what I can only describe as a collective obsession—with the sport in general, with our local clubs, and every four years with the World Cup—of dimensions unimaginable elsewhere (no, not Brazil, not England, nowhere). A force so powerful that I sincerely believe it's taking on elements of the beginnings of a religion. A phenomenon bringing thousands of people, of all genders and ages, to tears. And one that even transforms many an anarchist, for a month every four years, into a rabid fan.

★

I can't explain it to you, because you would indeed not understand. Therefore, I've refrained from any attempt at sociological or academic analysis of the events or dynamics. First because I would fail, and second because I'm not interested in them. So I've limited myself to drawing the picture. To attempting to bring you as close to the place where football, passion, and radical politics sometimes intersect in our society. To the joy it brings, the lives it touches. And maybe to highlight some of the historical elements both cultural and political that have exacerbated this phenomenon to levels rarely if ever seen elsewhere.

In December 2022, "No te lo puedo explicar, porque no vas a entender" was the song heard around the world, the battle cry of millions of Argentines. Not "Argentine football fans," but simply Argentines. At this point, there seemed to be next to no distinction between one and

Scenes on the streets from December 20, 2022.

the other. And so the chant rang out in the most unexpected of places across the landscape of Argentine society. When Harry Styles played in Argentina, at every single concert or nightclub for that matter, in schoolyards, in retirement homes, in packed subway cars, even at a church during a Mass.

And, of course, in and around the stadiums of Qatar, a place to which some forty thousand Argentines pilgrimaged from all corners of the world. From an impoverished country in a far-flung corner of the other side of the world, an improbable mobilization sprang up that dwarfed the amount of fans from anywhere else. Because Argentines don't care about the plight of the thousands of migrant workers exploited and killed to build the blood-drenched stadiums that hosted the World Cup? Because our society is deaf to the glaring issues of homophobia, lack of women's rights, and the generally almost feudal society that is Qatar? Of course not, and the argument could be made that as a whole Argentine society is just as, if not more, acutely aware of these issues as many others. We have, after all, been governed by a center-left coalition almost without interruption since the uprising of December 2001, one that is at least in discourse if not always in form acutely progressive on social issues.[1] Over the course of the last decade, Argentina has made significant strides on social issues for a Latin American country, first legalizing gay marriage, and most recently fresh off the "green tide" of the abortion rights movement, which mobilized a wide swath of society and culminated in the passage of legislation putting Argentina on the forefront of reproductive rights in South America.

This mass mobilization seems to stand in direct contradiction to the generalized calls to boycott the Qatar World Cup that, completely understandably, rang out almost unanimously from sensible and socially conscious people from all corners of the world. Instead of boycotting, Argentines of all social classes, ages, and backgrounds flocked to Qatar. Young, old, women, men. They sold their cars, emptied their savings, proclaimed loudly on banners that "money and fear are two things we've never had," and ate once a day for weeks if not months—and some even managed to be taken in by wealthy Qataris who financed their stay in the country. Whatever the cost, whatever the context, we felt the need to be there.

I can't explain; you wouldn't understand. Maybe in large part because it's just generally inexplicable. Passion, at the end of the day,

Scenes from downtown Buenos Aires, December 20, 2022.

is difficult to put into words. Not to mention why it sometimes matters so much to an apparently otherwise reasonable anarchist cadre if a little ball kicked by millionaire young men passes a white line on a grass field. If I want to grasp at a justification, if I want to romanticize what is also (or, if we're being honest, mainly) a ruthless business like any other, I could potentially make the argument that fandom for a club (not a franchise!), passion for a game, is in and of itself a small act of rebellion against capitalism. It serves no purpose, can't be quantified or qualified. Like anything in capitalist society, it of course can and is commercialized and traded, but the collective experience as we here live and understand it exists outside of that. It advances no productivity, serves no spreadsheet. It simply brings people together (when not ripping them apart). I like to think of love and passion as inherently revolutionary.

In the end, it's completely possible that I'm trying to reconcile a glaring contradiction. I'm well aware. Decades of radical left politics have made me adept at debating just about any position, and the constant drive toward anarchist purity makes me instinctively wary of being caught in a contradiction. Which is why I tried my hardest not to go to Qatar, not to partake in what was clearly the most grotesque of FIFA's sportswashing of reprehensible regimes. I resented that my passion was being held hostage in this manner, and I promised to restrict myself to watching on TV. A kind of compromise in which I limited myself to passive and money-free participation.

However, maybe unsurprisingly in hindsight, because I am apparently human first and anarchist second (and because I am fortunate enough to more or less be able to afford it—less so than more, to be honest, but as the chant goes, "We might have no money but we're here anyway"), when Argentina dramatically defeated the Netherlands on penalties in the quarterfinals, I snapped . . . and two days later magically found myself in a far-off land, surrounded by friends I hadn't seen for years and perfect strangers who might as well have been my best of friends. Because with my passion—in football, as in anarchism, and as in life—I've always felt the need to be there. To be if not a protagonist, at least a participant, and most certainly never merely a witness. Argentine footballs fans, myself included, are convinced that we too are active participants in the game. And if you've ever been to a stadium in Argentina, or heard the forty thousand Argentines during the most recent World Cup broadcast, you'll know that this isn't as delusional as it might at first sound.

When "we" won and the country again erupted, I couldn't help but be moved and constantly reminded of the scenes on that same day, on those same streets, of 2001. Argentine society is again wracked by an almost 50 percent poverty rate, and the old specter of hyperinflation is eating away at the salaries of those fortunate enough to have employment, with an inflation rate for 2022 of almost three digits. The false "leftism" of the nearly two decades of "progressive" Kirchnerism has opened the door to the homegrown incarnations of the radical right, in the vein of US Trumpism and Brazilian Bolsonarism. Worse yet, these modern-day fascists brand themselves "libertarians," defaming the history of our anarchist movement, and, because "leftism" seems institutionalized, they are capturing a frightening amount of young minds. More and more, the capitalist cultural hegemony has succeeded at installing its warped logic as unavoidable common sense, and it terrifies me.

Staring at the exact spot where our barricades once stood and red flags flew against all odds, it dawned on me that in 2001 I only happened to find myself here because my twin passions, my club and social revolution, incredibly converged after decades-long parallel processes into one momentous week in late December. As I watch this mass, I have to remind myself that while passion may have again brought me here, and that it is incredible that I get to witness this twice in my life despite living almost all of it outside Argentina, the similarities end here. But as I take it all in, I have to once again remind myself that these are not those days of 2001, although on the surface they certainly do look like them.

Surrounded by boundless solidarity and joy, I can't help but hope that in the future as in the past, I'll again be surprised by the strength of popular power and anger. That when we least expect it, a spark will again start a prairie fire. Maybe then the memory of December 2001 and the energy of December 2022 will merge toward a third December. A red December that will be neither rehearsal nor illusion.

Repression, not clashes: April 2024, as the "libertarian" government criminalizes all street protests.

Back to the Future: The Return of the Ultraliberal Right in Argentina

November 26, 2023

El desvalije está latente,	*The looting is latent,*
lo sabe hasta el presidente,	*even the president knows it,*
en un avión se llevó el dineral	*on a plane he funneled out the fortune*

—Hermética,[1] "Olvidalo y volverá por más"

Javier Milei, the newly elected president of Argentina, ran a presidential campaign in which he proposed abolishing the Argentine peso and adopting the US dollar as national currency, eliminating the central bank, privatizing health care and education, privatizing or shutting down all public media outlets, and privatizing most aspects of the country's economic and strategic infrastructure.

Milei's character and politics would make him perfect for the role of supervillain in an overly dramatic anarchist work of fiction. Until recently, he was running around in a black-and-yellow superhero costume as General AnCap (short for "anarcho-capitalist"). He could be found calmly pontificating about how the free market should regulate all aspects of society—including the sale of children and bodily organs, or one's freedom to sell an arm in order to survive—and stating that a person forced to choose between starving or working eighteen hours per day is "of course" free, since that would be his choice. When not engaging in such philosophical delights, he would appear on talk shows, frothing at the mouth and yelling about "piece-of-shit leftists," "cultural Marxism," the hoax of global warming, and so on.

Milei's vice president, Victoria Villarruel, is known for her virulent defense of the military leaders who were jailed for their role in the torture

and disappearance of thousands during Argentina's last military dictatorship in the 1970s. Both she and Milei dispute the long-established
figure of thirty thousand dead or disappeared. Milei publicly denies that
the dictatorship carried out systematic genocide at all, referring to the
acts of the dictatorship simply as "excesses." Those "excesses" included
a network of hundreds of clandestine detention centers, the throwing of
drugged but still-living victims from helicopters into the Río de La Plata,
and the handing off to military families of several hundred newborn
babies abducted from prisoners accused of being "subversive." His entou-
rage is not much better. It includes "men's rights activists," flat-earthers,
a so-called philosopher who called for privatizing the oceans, and the like.

So his politics are a nightmare for anarchists. They are also diametrically opposed to the politics of large swaths of the Argentine populace.
We are talking about a society that has a strong sense of social justice, in
which the dominant political current of the last two decades has been
Kirchnerism, a sort of progressive center-left Peronist tendency that
grew out of the uprising of 2001. With the exception of Mauricio Macri's
presidency from 2015 to 2019, Kirchnerist governments ruled Argentina
uninterrupted from 2003 right up to Milei's victory. The first decade of
Kirchnerist rule brought significant improvements in many Argentines'
quality of life, reducing both unemployment and poverty rates and
bringing inflation under control (at least by Argentine standards). It
represented a leftward shift in both public discourse and government
policy, a significant departure from the neoliberal hegemony of the 1990s.

But the second decade of Kirchnerist government was less successful, plagued by corruption scandals as well as one of the world's
longest-lasting COVID-19 lockdowns. Despite a battery of economically protectionist measures—limiting imports, taxing exports, and
establishing currency controls and a host of different exchange rates for
the Argentine peso—the last decade has seen a continuous devaluation
of the peso. This led to a sharp increase in inflation—over 100 percent
in the last twelve months—which has plunged millions beneath the
poverty line. By the election, over 55 percent of minors and 40 percent
of all Argentines were officially living in poverty.

Against this backdrop, Milei garnered almost 56 percent of the vote
in the runoff election, after netting just 30 percent in the first round,
on October 22.

How did we get here? Where are we going? And what is to be done?

"Death to the Enemies of the People."

"¡Viva la Libertad!": Freedom to Work or Starve, to Submit or be Shot

At first, most people saw Milei as an exotic novelty—an obscure economist who became a regular guest on political talk shows and news channels, driving ratings by ranting against the "political caste," yelling about "draining the swamp," turning blood red as he vented about "gender ideology."

His television appearances won him a fan base of politically alienated young middle-class men. For them, he offered an outlet through which to channel their resentment against the welfare state, which they saw as supporting hordes of lazy bums with the tax money of hardworking Argentines. Against immigrants, who they imagined came to Argentina to mooch off free public education and health care. Against political correctness, the globalist agenda, the COVID-19 vaccine, and quarantines. Incredibly, against "socialist rule" in Argentina, despite Argentina being a capitalist country with a government that was mildly left of center at best.

Coalescing online, largely through TikTok clips of Javier Milei and alt-right content from Brazil and the US, these young men became the activist wing of the budding La Libertad Avanza party when Javier Milei announced his intention to run for Congress in 2021. Yellow Gadsden flags and "Make Argentina Great Again" caps began appearing at his campaign rallies.

Milei was elected to Congress by tapping a latent river of resentment coursing through a specific sector of the Argentine population: young, urban, middle-class, downwardly mobile men. But as their ecosystem, influence, and reach grew, these young men became instrumental in the far right's success at channeling popular discontent with Argentina's economic and political crisis.

This succeeded because, at the same time that life is miserable, entrepreneur and hustler logic is creeping ever further into society, especially among young people. The logic of capitalism is more and more widely held to be common sense. If you're poor, there's no systemic reason for it—you simply must not be working hard enough. If you don't make enough money, it's not that your wages are too low—you simply need to work more. If you want to change your circumstances, if you want to be "free," you shouldn't join and organize with others—you should start your own business, selling some commodity, aiming not only to escape wage slavery but also to acquire some wage slaves of your own one day. Freedom is understood as a wholly individual pursuit, a zero-sum game in which you must exploit others if you wish to be free.

As capitalist hegemony advances, collectivism and socialism are blamed for the failures of capitalism. Progressive rainbow capitalism, ideologically if not practically, addresses the struggles of some oppressed sectors of society while reducing large numbers of people to grinding poverty. This makes it easy to channel the rage of the unemployed and working poor away from the capitalist class into resentment against whichever scapegoats the pseudo-libertarian far right concocts.

There's a good chance you're thinking you've seen this movie before. It doesn't take the most acute analysis of world events to see the parallels to Trump in the United States or Bolsonaro in Brazil. The similarities are all drawn directly from the handbook of the new fascist right. The politics of grievance, the culture wars, the racist dog whistles, the characteristically fascist obsession with a humiliated nation needing a strongman to lead it against its many enemies, both foreign and domestic. There's also the hallucination of socialism everywhere, even among political actors who are the furthest thing from socialists. In Argentina, the actual left, which is dominated by the Trotskyist Frente de Izquierda (or "Left Front," an electoral alliance composed of four separate Trotskyist parties), garnered less than 3 percent of the vote in these elections. This shows the extent to which the left has failed to position itself as a viable alternative even amid massive popular discontent and mistrust of the political class.

Milei and his "libertarians" succeeded in painting the radical left social movements and the center-left Kirchnerist government as a single entity, much as Trump was able to conflate "antifa" with Democrats in the eyes of his supporters. From there, the culture war propaganda was simple: Socialists want a Big Brother state to control and oppress the good, upstanding working people of the country; lazy, violent hordes live off of welfare programs while good workers struggle under the burden of taxes; and all this serves an entrenched and corrupt political class.

This segment of society alone represented 30 percent of the vote in the first round of elections in October. That was significantly more than the 15 percent or so that was originally believed to be the upper estimate of Milei's support, but still not nearly enough to get him into power. This is where we encounter another striking similarity with US Trumpism. Former President Mauricio Macri and his former minister of defense, Patricia Bullrich (who came in third in the general election with 23 percent of the vote), immediately declared their support for Javier Milei in the runoff election. Their constituents were not the youth vote, nor voters seeking to radically change the system, but rather the classic anti-Peronist and anti-Kirchnerist vote of the Argentine upper middle class and oligarchy. Just as traditional conservative Republicans did in the United States in response to Trump's election success, they immediately dropped their scathing criticism of Javier Milei and pounced on the opportunity to wield power with and behind him.

While people like Mauricio Macri and Patricia Bullrich might frown on Milei's extravagance and clutch their pearls in horror at the manners of a man who ran around rallies with a chainsaw to dramatize his intent to cut government spending, Milei's politics undoubtedly represent their wildest dreams. This part of the electorate has always dreamed of privatizing industry, of streamlining the state to serve the interests of capital, reducing it to purely repressive functions to discipline society. They simply lacked the political capital to insinuate that they had those intentions without condemning themselves to political irrelevance.

Now, in the immediate aftermath of the election, the key posts of the upcoming Milei administration have gone to the former ministers and economists of the disastrous government of Macri. After Néstor Kirchner finally released Argentina from the weight of debt to the International Monetary Fund, Macri took on the largest loan in the IMF's history in 2018—much of which was used not to fund infrastructure projects or strengthen the economy but rather to distribute payments to finance capitalists. Some of it was illegally siphoned out of the country.

The campaign promises to drain the swamp have already been forgotten before Milei has even been sworn in. The names of the newly appointed ministers and consultants are a who's who of a quarter of a century of discredited right-wing politicians.

There are differences between Trumpism and the ultraliberal phenomenon in Argentina. Trump was somewhat economically protectionist, while Milei is a fervent and dogmatic champion of the free market. Trump is clearly an opportunist, a sort of empty vessel. Milei is a true believer in the most reactionary, vile, and outdated model of capitalism imaginable today. This ideology has led him to declare— openly, clearly, and repeatedly—that there is no right to education or health care, that if something is not profitable in the market, there is no need for it and it should not exist. Roads should be privatized, and bodily organs should be a market commodity. For all Milei's talk of "anarchism," his second-in-command is a staunch defender of the Argentine military and its criminal past, whose plan to deal with social movements is naked violence.

The key difference between Trumpism and the Milei phenomenon is the age of their supporters. While promoting an economic model that would return Argentina to the nineteenth century, Milei has somehow managed to position himself and these ideas as new and rebellious. With the exception of small pockets of radicalized youth, the Trump base is generally older, rural, and isolated, while the majority of people

Cover of position paper by anarcho-communist Federación Anarquista de Rosario: "Argentina, you wouldn't understand it: Devaluation, chainsaw, batons, and warplanes."

under thirty staunchly oppose him. By contrast, Javier Milei has made significant inroads into popular neighborhoods and the working poor and has established a base among young people thanks to his agitated speeches, his imagery of his followers being "not sheep to herd, but lions to awaken," and his dominance of TikTok and new social media platforms.

As a result, the most widespread interpretation of freedom and rebellion among teenagers and twentysomethings in Argentina today not only is diametrically opposed to our values of solidarity and mutual aid, it even co-opts our language, openly appropriating the terms *anarchist* and *libertarian*. What they mean by these words is a carbon copy of the most rancid elements of "libertarianism" and ultraliberal capitalism. It's the entrepreneurial TikTok influencer vision of society.

Despite their differences, Bolsonaro, Trump, and Milei are staunch allies, with Bolsonaro expected to attend Milei's inauguration and Trump recently announcing his intention to visit him in Argentina. Together, the three are the vanguard of a budding proto-fascist international. Despite proposing the tired old model of xenophobia, repression, and capitalist austerity, this right-wing resurgence has successfully positioned itself as a new alternative to politics as usual, at least in Argentina. As a consequence of the failure of the center-left to improve people's everyday lives and the way that many social movement actors of the post-2001 period have been gradually incorporated into the state apparatus, the ultraliberal alternative has managed to position itself as the representation of youthful rebellion.

In the words of a post-election statement titled "Y Ahora Qué Pasa?" (And now what?) released by especifist anarchist organizations in Argentina:

> For a far-right political option to grow this way, the defeat is cultural and ideological and has been ongoing for many years—mainly starting with the "retreat" of many of the emancipatory projects, not to mention the progressive ones, from the majority of the popular neighborhoods and unions, the absence of a concrete vision of how to confront this capitalist system, and that of a revolutionary project that is unwavering in opposing the machine of impoverishing society that is neoliberalism. A process in which the state progressively incorporated and institutionalized numerous tools and practices of the people, taking all political action into its camp and transforming the ballot box into the only possible horizon of political action. That vacuum of rebellion, of an antagonist presence, of social struggle, was filled with the pseudo-fascist and ultraliberal rhetoric of a handful of economists and reactionary elements.[2]

History Repeats Itself ... Again

Although repackaged and with improved marketing, Milei's ideas are little more than the classic formula of ultraliberalism. Ironically, if there were one place in the world where such experiments in ultraliberalism have already been tried, it would be Argentina.

The Peronist movement emerged in the 1940s around General Juan Domingo Perón, combining an economically protectionist capitalist

Anarchists and antifascists attack an office of Milei's party, La Libertad Avanza, in the city of La Plata.

project with a strong welfare state and rhetoric about "social justice." Decades of antagonism between Peronism, which was often allied with left-wing forces, and the Argentine oligarchy and military eventually culminated in the military coup of 1976. It was the sixth coup in Argentina in the twentieth century.

The military junta launched the infamous Dirty War against the remnants of the country's armed guerrilla organizations—the left-wing Peronist Montoneros and the Trotskyist ERP, both of which had been largely defeated and dismantled by late 1975, along with anyone else deemed remotely "subversive." Hand in hand with the IMF, which provided what was at that time the largest loan ever to a Latin American country and demanded a series of market reforms in return, the junta imposed the first wave of neoliberal economic reforms on the country. They dismantled the protectionist policies of Peronism, eliminating tariffs on imports and decimating the national industry, while simultaneously eliminating all taxes or restrictions on exports. At the same time, they eliminated rent control, canceled all subsidies to public transportation, and attacked unions and collective bargaining rights.

The results were disastrous for the majority of Argentine society. Workers bore the brunt of years of triple-digit annual inflation triggered by the country's ever-increasing foreign debt. By 1982, an unpopular military junta drove the country into war with Great Britain over the Islas Malvinas in a desperate bid to deflect from its domestic problems, taking another thousand or so lives with it before the return to capitalist democracy in 1983.

The burden of crushing debt to the IMF proved impossible to shake. The 1980s saw astronomical rates of annual inflation, regularly in the 400 to 600 percent range. By 1989, inflation had put 47 percent of the country below the poverty line. Then a wave of hyperinflation—200 percent in one month—led to widespread looting and clashes that left over forty people dead.

Enter 1991, hot on the heels of the fall of the Berlin Wall and the collapse of the Eastern bloc. Francis Fukuyama proclaimed "the end of history," the triumph of neoliberal capitalism as the best and only possible world. Argentina put an end to inflation through "convertibility," which artificially tied the Argentine peso to the US dollar at a one-to-one exchange rate. This was financed by yet another IMF loan, this time to the tune of one billion US dollars—one of several IMF loans to Argentina over the course of the 1990s. At the same time, newly elected President Carlos Menem launched an unprecedented new wave of neoliberal reforms centered on the privatization of industry, loosening or eliminating import controls, restructuring the state, and economic deregulation. Private enterprise and market forces were the order of the day—and indeed, the first few years saw relative stability and prosperity. For the first time in decades, inflation was brought under control, the influx of fresh cash into state coffers allowed for some tax breaks, and the initial improvements in commerce and infrastructure through foreign investment coupled with the lack of import tariffs brought jobs, wage growth, and cheap goods to the country.

A postcard of the return to the politics, and struggles, of the 1990s: "We'll defend our public universities in the streets. Always." Acción Socialista Libertaria, April 2024.

But it was a bubble. Unable to compete internationally, small businesses and factories began closing. The foreign investors who gobbled up public infrastructure began aiming to secure their profits and failed to reinvest. Unsurprisingly, this led to the rapid deterioration of public services, especially transportation. The trade imbalance in which more dollars were leaving the country than entering it made the one-to-one exchange rate increasingly unsustainable. As more and more people lost their jobs, open resistance to factory closures began to emerge in the mid to late '90s, giving rise to the unemployed workers' movement, which came to be known as the *piqueteros*—famous for using militant road blockades as a practical show of force and a symbolic tool to draw attention to their struggle.

All this came to a head in December 2001. Following a bank rush driven by rumors of an impending devaluation of the Argentine peso, the minister of economy, Domingo Cavallo, imposed what came to be known as the *corralito*, limiting cash withdrawals from banks to $250 per week. This created a crisis among the middle class, which converged with the wave of discontent among Argentina's popular classes, hardest hit by an unemployment rate of over 20 percent and a poverty rate of over 40 percent. On December 19, 2001, widespread looting erupted in several cities across the country, particularly in the greater Buenos Aires region. In response, that night, President de la Rúa declared a state of emergency—the first in the country since 1989. Tens of thousands of people immediately converged on the Plaza de Mayo in front of the presidential palace as hundreds of thousands more took to their balconies in solidarity to bang pots and pans in an endless cacophony of rebellion. Police unleashed a fierce wave of repression; after hours of pitched battles, they succeeded in clearing the plaza and dispersing the demonstrators.

It might have ended there, if the night of the state of emergency did not happen to fall on a Wednesday, the night before the Mothers of Plaza de Mayo come together in protest in front of the presidential palace.

And so, at around 10 a.m. the Mothers of Plaza de Mayo began gathering. Shortly thereafter, the state apparatus began its repression, and images of little old ladies being beaten with whips by police on horseback beamed into thousands and thousands of households across the city and the country. Little old ladies who already carried with them the weight of not knowing the fates of their children. I don't know if another

"Freedom."

spark was needed or if the flames were already destined to spiral out of control. We'll never know.

But the fact remains that that day, December 20, 2001—only a few short hours after the repression against the *madres*—the youth, working class, and unemployed of Argentina laid siege to the presidential palace, with tens of thousands of people "young and old, thrusting themselves straight into the gas and the bullets, not knowing if the one they shot at you would be rubber or lead."[3]

By the end of the day, despite a murderous repression that claimed thirty-nine lives over the course of those two days, we had forced the president to resign and watched as he fled the presidential palace in a helicopter. It seemed, at the time, that it was the definitive end of the neoliberal experiment in Argentina, and a lesson about the intrinsic relationship between ultraliberal politics and repression, illustrating the enormous cost in human life of both neoliberal experiments.

We thought that would serve to inoculate Argentina against the return of neoliberalism for generations. The passage of time has proved us wrong.

Ultraliberals, the Military, and Repression: A Love Story

Even before the start of Milei's presidency, the bait and switch of the Milei campaign was already obvious. The promise that the austerity and budget cuts would be paid for "by the political class" almost immediately pivoted to "It's going to be six incredibly difficult months for everybody." In December 2023, even before his formal inauguration, he had already announced the possibility of not paying year-end bonuses to public workers. His reassurances of an immediate solution to inflation gave way to "It will take eighteen to twenty-four months." Finally, in a nod to Trump's promise to "drain the swamp," the political caste he railed against now surrounds him and fills government posts, including many of the people responsible for the economic and social disasters of the 1990s and the Macri government.

In other aspects, however, Milei has made it clear that he will govern as close to his ideology as the balance of power in the branches of government and on the streets permits him to. The first day after his election, he announced his intention to go through with the sale or closure of all public media outlets and the halting of all public infrastructure projects. Unsurprisingly, we are already seeing a propaganda campaign in the corporate media to pit private sector workers and society as a whole against state employees and those who work for public media channels; corporate media have been publishing false and inflated salary numbers and framing state employees as wanting to preserve "their privileges at the expense of society." Not content with the insecurity of poor-against-poor conflict that we experience in our neighborhoods, these reactionaries are now making a concerted attempt to provoke a social cannibalism in which workers who still have access to job security and benefits are portrayed as privileged at the expense of everyone else.

As resistance is already stirring against the upcoming layoffs, privatizations, and austerity—with workers, unions, and social organizations calling for open assemblies to discuss the situation and begin organizing their resistance—the symbiotic relationship between ultraliberal reforms, corporate media, and the repressive apparatus of the state is coming into view. Many in the media are warning of the danger of a "coup," in reference to potential unrest that might eventually topple the Milei government. This rhetoric is intended to conflate popular revolt with a military seizure of power.

An image repeated across every social mobilization under Milei's "law-and-order" government.

At the same time, former President Mauricio Macri went on television to encourage young Milei supporters to attack those who might take to the streets to oppose layoffs and budget cuts. Dripping with racism and classism, he suggested that "the orcs," as he refers to unemployed workers and other piqueteros, "should think very carefully about what they do on the streets, as the young people won't stand to have them rob them of the opportunity to change the country." The language, with Macri calling us "orcs" and Milei calling us "piece-of-shit leftists" who stand in the way of change and a "better future for upstanding Argentines," isn't just a reflection of the classism and racism of the Argentine upper middle class and oligarchy. It's a consciously crafted and wielded tool to begin stigmatizing and ostracizing popular resistance in order to immunize as broad a swath of society as possible against solidarity with social movements when clashes inevitably begin.

Less than a week after election day, the first public appearance of Milei's vice president, Victoria Villarruel, was a visit to a police facility, where she appeared flanked by officers as she spoke about the need to grant them more funds and equipment. Simultaneously, Milei's camp is already announcing that they will try to modify the national defense law in order to allow the use of the military for purposes of interior security once more, including against "terrorists." The message is clear for anarchists, the left, and anyone else considering taking to the streets to oppose this new government: We will be branded terrorists. From there, it's one short step before the infamous Argentine military is once again unleashed against anything and anyone unfortunate enough to be considered "subversive."

It's no coincidence that Milei's vice president is Villarruel, a fanatical defender of members of the military who have been convicted of crimes against humanity during the last dictatorship. The military and the repressive apparatus of the state as a whole are essential elements in the ultraliberal project, especially in countries with well-developed networks of resistance like Argentina. For all their talk about "anarcho-capitalism," a ridiculous oxymoron, ultraliberalism represents a streamlining of the state to enable it to better defend the interests of property and the capitalist class. It is the state ridding itself of the baggage of the welfare system, social programs, and any responsibility toward the mass of society. It's the transformation of the capitalist state into its crudest and rawest form: an instrument to preserve class society and discipline all who oppose it.

It's no coincidence that Milei refused to answer when an interviewer asked plainly if he believes in democracy. The ultraliberal project places the market above all, seeing the rights to property, capital, and exploitation as the only inalienable rights. From that perspective, the "immaturity" and "whims" of society—even something as squarely within the framework of capitalist representative democracy as voting politicians out of power or rejecting their policies in the legislature— are only an obstacle to be overcome. This mindset is best summarized by Henry Kissinger's statement about Chile in the 1970s: "The issues are much too important for the Chilean voters to be left to decide for themselves."

It's also no coincidence that it was precisely in Chile, hand in hand with the dictatorship of Pinochet and with the material support of the United States, that the other major ultraliberal experiment in Latin America took place. In Chile, the "Chicago Boys," a group of Chilean economists educated at the University of Chicago and adhering to the ideas of Milton Friedman (whom Javier Milei reveres), were able to implement a battery of neoliberal reforms. The necessary precondition for

Antifascist and autonomous bloc, March 24, 2024, on the anniversary of the 1976 military coup d'état.

implementing those reforms was a military junta that killed and disappeared dissidents by the thousands, just as in Argentina. The lasting consequences of several of these reforms (such as privatizing pension plans, creating school and university voucher systems, and privatizing public transport) were the catalysts behind the Chilean uprising of 2019.

Freedom for the market necessarily means exploitation for workers and misery for the majority of society. The history of this country shows this. Eventually, when this state of affairs generates enough popular resistance, the only way to maintain it is via the brute force of the state. Despite the empty rhetoric of freedom, Milei and Villarruel are the political heirs of the policies of Pinochet and the Chicago Boys, of José Martínez de Hoz during the Argentine dictatorship, and of the neoliberalism of the 1990s that took thirty-eight lives in one week before ceding power. Coddling state security forces and dismissing the crimes of the Argentine dictatorship are not just culture war maneuvers. They know as well as we do that sooner or later, ultraliberalism can only be imposed via repression and violence—and they intend to do it again.

The "Forces of Heaven" Against the Orcs

Today many of us are afraid. There's no use trying to hide it. Many of us are not eager for battle. Maybe it's because now, for the first time in decades, we find ourselves squarely on the defensive. We are fighting some battles, such as the battle for the collective memory of what the last dictatorship represented, that we thought were definitively won twenty years ago. We are fighting other battles that we thought had been won a full century ago, such as the struggle for public education and health care.

I used to smile beneath the mask, reveling at the prospect of facing the guardians of the state head-on. Now, I play my part in an assembly or a clash reluctantly, acutely aware of how many lives we lost to repression the last time around. Maybe it's because those of my generation are older now. We have more to lose. Life has taught us the fear that was absent in the clashes of our youth.

Or maybe we are frightened because in 2001, when the last neoliberal experiment in Argentina reached its disastrous climax with a 50 percent poverty rate and the fury of the dispossessed culminating in widespread looting and the siege of the presidential palace, it was us—the youth—who were at the forefront of those clashes. Today, in a turn of events that has many of us feeling significantly older than we actually are, a large segment of the youth are the ones behind Milei and the new ultraliberal government.

This is yet another example of the failure of progressivism and the statist left, who fail to attack capitalism at its root. In Argentina, after the uprising of 2001, they failed to strike the final blow when the beast was wounded, discredited, and at its weakest. Instead, they attempted to tame and rule it. This process integrated hundreds if not thousands of the militants and fighters of the 1990s and the uprising of 2001 into the machinery of the state. Yes, the state took on a progressive appearance, legalizing gay marriage, taking on the rural oligarchy, challenging corporate media monopolies, finally freeing the country from the IMF debt, and even putting "redistribution of wealth" into mainstream discourse. But associating the left with the state and the disastrous financial situation paved the way for the victory that the ultraliberal far right has won today.

Maybe we're doomed to an endless cycle in which each generation must relearn the painful lessons of the past. Considering that this generation has known little more than 40 percent poverty, triple-digit annual inflation, the erosion of the quality of public health care and education, and the grotesque corruption of a political class that preaches social justice and redistribution of wealth while vacationing on yachts in the Mediterranean, can we blame them for desperately turning to a man who promises them "freedom" from this? It makes no sense to warn the Uber driver or Rappi (the local version of DoorDash) delivery kid that they will lose their benefits or right to a paid vacation when they already have neither. But the alternative they are embracing is even worse.

How the coming months will play out will depend on a variety of factors. Will the mainstream bureaucratic unions withdraw and try to ride out the storm, or will they support their workers facing layoffs? Will they mobilize in solidarity with unemployed workers, will they call for a general strike if Milei attempts labor law reform or tries to change collective bargaining laws? Will people mobilize in defense of public institutions and publicly owned enterprises? Will the far right successfully leverage culture war politics to discourage solidarity with the country's most oppressed and most vulnerable?

While Milei has the solid support of his base of young fanatics and the virulently anti-Kirchnerist and anti-Peronist middle and upper

A mural in the city of La Plata for "an anarchist and antifascist May 1," by the Unión de Organizaciones Antifascistas (Union of Antifascist Organizations).

Antifascist and autonomous bloc, March 24, 2024, on the anniversary of the 1976 military coup d'état.

classes, a significant portion of his voters are unemployed and working poor. These people voted for him out of a misplaced but genuine hope that he could actually change their lives for the better. They are not ideologically bound to his ultraliberalism, and they are in no condition to wait patiently for six months as things "get worse before they get better." If inflation spirals out of control and the weight of austerity and budget cuts falls squarely on Argentina's most vulnerable, social conflict could spread once again.

Social movements in Argentina are demoralized right now. As far as the anarchist camp is concerned, the sad reality is that despite the commendable efforts of generations of anarchists, the movement is currently small in numbers and the presence of anarchists in social movements is marginal. While the movement maintains certain physical spaces and there are attempts to begin to pull together a more cohesive and visible anarchist presence, we are little more than a remnant of what was once one of the world's most powerful anarchist movements.

We should all be acutely aware that history does not magically trend toward liberation. Just because we defeated the forces of neoliberalism before doesn't mean that they are destined to fall again this time. History will be what we make of it. Nothing more, nothing less. The defeat of the politics of ultraliberalism—whether in the nineteenth century, or under Pinochet, or during the latest dictatorship, or in the uprising of 2001—has always come at the expense of immense struggle, sacrifice, and loss of life.

The last neoliberal experiment in Argentina generated the worst economic and social crisis in the history of this country. Before the uprising of December 2001, revolutionaries, organizers, and, yes, anarchists—despite being few and far between then too—put in years of work. That meant generating networks of solidarity and mutual aid in neighborhoods. Building grassroots organizations of unemployed workers that were independent of mainstream unions or political parties. Holding assemblies in workplaces, schools, and universities. Standing in practical solidarity wherever we were needed. All of this will have to take place once again today.

Again from the "Y Ahora Qué Pasa?" statement:

> Comrades, the times ahead will require us to redouble our efforts
> and strive for the broadest unity of the popular organizations, in

the context of a strategy of popular struggle in the streets.... We need to undo the fragmentation and individualism that created the context that brought this character to power. There's no use to preach to the converted. It's our task to talk to each colleague at work, to each neighbor, always from the perspective of struggle and grassroots organization.[4]

Eventually, just as in 2001, the time will come to take to the streets—as young people and old people, as workers, as students, as various elements of society in solidarity with each other and fed up with the capitalist class and its politicians. With the cry of "Que se vayan todos," our collective rage defeated them in just forty-eight hours in December 2001.

Hopefully, when the time comes, we'll do it again.

Six Months in a Neoliberal Dystopia: Social Cannibalism Versus Mutual Aid in Argentina

June 17, 2024

El mundo hipnotizado	*The world hypnotized*
cansado y agotado sin poder	*Tired and exhausted and*
reaccionar . . .	*unable to react . . .*
justicia sobornada	*bribed justice*
hospitales sin nada que poder	*hospitals with nothing to*
brindar . . .	*provide . . .*
Que mundo inmundo	*What a vile world we inhabit*
habitamos	*that confuses fashion with*
que asocia la moda con la	*crude truth*
cruda verdad	*there's girls dying for lack of*
hay chicas que mueren por	*hunger*
falta de hambre	*there's boys dying for lack of*
y hay gente que muere por	*bread*
falta de pan	*and the rage accumulates with*
y se acumula la bronca en cada	*every step*
paso	

—Cadena Perpetua, "Mundo inmundo"

Snapshots

Social movements, neighborhood assemblies, and leftist organizations mobilize to protest against the massive package of neoliberal reforms being debated in Congress. The mobilization is met with an enormous police apparatus and constant provocations on the side of the forces of "order." One officer can be seen strolling around wearing a "Don't Tread on Me" Gadsen flag patch on his vest. By the end of the evening, although nothing much has happened, the repression is in

NO PASARÁN
¡Salud, Socialismo y Libertad!

Acción Socialista Libertaria

"No Pasarán (They shall not pass). Health, socialism, and freedom." Image from the spontaneous mobilization of thousands on December 21, 2023, after Milei announced a mega executive order massively deregulating the Argentine economy.

full swing and police are riding two abreast on motorbikes, shooting rubber bullets indiscriminately into the crowd.

★

Sandra Pettovello, minister of "Human Capital," refuses to meet with social organizations to discuss the delivery of food aid to thousands of *comedores populares* (essentially neighborhood soup kitchens). In finest Marie Antoinette style, she states that "if there is anybody who is hungry, I will meet with them one on one"—but without the intermediation of social organizations. The next day, thousands take her up on her offer and line up in front of her ministry. She refuses to meet with them.

★

Telam, the public news agency, has been shut down and shuttered. So has the INADI, the national institute against discrimination. There is talk of privatizing the national bank, while waves of layoffs decimate almost all public institutions, including the national library. As workers mobilize to defend public institutions and their workplaces, they find the buildings barricaded off and surrounded by riot police. Meanwhile, "libertarian" activists stage a photo op celebrating the closings and firings.

★

Ursula is interviewed on live TV by a reporter from one of the pro-government channels. "I'm a widower, I receive a government subsidy, and I live with my mother who is retired." She mentions that she has three children, one of whom is standing on the street in the cold next to her as she's being interviewed, and that she recently lost her job. As she explains that they try to make ends meet by selling packs of stickers on the street, she breaks down in tears as her teenage daughter watches. Minutes before Ursula's interview, another woman was interviewed on the street. "I work three jobs to make ends meet," she said. Neither of them make mention of the political and economic decisions that have led them to these situations.

★

The cost of living has exploded. Inflation is kept "under control" (if one can call a 9 percent monthly inflation rate "under control") because consumer demand has collapsed. Utilities, medicine, and basic food items have exploded with well over 100 percent price increases in all of these areas, while rent contracts have been completely deregulated.

The result is unsurprising: As the real value of wages collapses, sales plummet. It's not just public workers, whom the ultraliberals have stigmatized as "parasites living off of society," who are losing their jobs. Small businesses as well as factories are closing one after the other. Just this month, three hundred thousand "salary accounts" (bank accounts used exclusively to receive monthly wages) have been closed.

In one factory in the province of Catamarca, workers have not taken the loss of their workplace lying down. The 134 workers of the Textilcom textile factory, suspecting an imminent closing of the plant, proceeded to occupy it as an act of resistance against the closure and as leverage to ensure that they are not robbed of back pay and compensation owed.

Yet even here, workers who are taking collective action, occupying a factory, and suffering the practical consequences of capitalist market logic make it a point to state that "we don't depend on state aid, we don't want aid, we aren't like the piqueteros," in reference to the unemployed, informally employed, and most marginalized who make up the bulk of the social movements.

★

President Milei is confronted by a random person on the street who yells at him that "people can't make ends meet" or "can't make it to the end of the month." Milei responds that "if people weren't making ends meet, they would be dying in the streets, so that's false." Even the pro-government and right-wing press describe his statement as "despicable."[1]

★

Almost parallel to the above, news breaks thanks to a report by social organizations that the "Ministry of Human Capital" (Ministerio de Capital Humano), accusing the vast network of comedores populares run by social organizations of everything from extortion to stating that an audit revealed half of the comedores populares to be nonexistent, has been refusing to distribute over five thousand tons of food and goods that sit, close to expiring and rotting, in their warehouses. The government even appeals a judicial order to begin distributing the food. Meanwhile,

49 percent of the country lives in poverty, with 11.9 percent in extreme poverty, defined as "those unable to meet their basic food needs."[2]

★

The dates of these snapshots are almost irrelevant, although the last four are all from just this past week. They are simply illustrative moments, a few out of innumerably many, of the massive economic and social tragedy that is unfolding in Argentina since the government of Javier Milei has come to power. A government in which, to the surprise of nobody, the neoliberal political class of the past has not only not been exiled but has been once again readily welcomed back into the halls of power, with a cabinet representing a who's who of neoliberal ideologues responsible for Argentina's last crash in the early 2000s.

Of course, spiraling poverty rates and out-of-control inflation didn't begin with Milei's government. In fact, their preexistence is very much one of the determining factors to understanding his appeal and electoral triumph. But the difference is that if the prior center-left government's failures had more to do with a misconception as to the fundamental nature of capital (namely the impossibility of reaching a lasting truce between market interests and the general interest of society), it was a government that at least in principle, if not in practice, held up the vision of society as a collective whole and freedom as a commonly constructed concept. And while, again, it is in large part this disconnect between the words and deeds of the past center-left Kirchnerist governments that opened the road for the "anarcho-capitalist" experiment of today, Argentine society is now in the hands of the most fanatical adherents of obscure Austrian school ultracapitalist economists—people who believe firmly that the invisible hand of the market will resolve all of society's ills and problems and that freedom is an individual good, constructed by every man, woman, and child for themselves.

The consequences as the theories and fantasies of the ultraliberal capitalists meet the real world are almost immediate—as is the explosive growth of collective suffering and misery they are bringing with them.

The Ultraliberal Capitalist Fantasy Meets the Real World

It was like watching a child learning in real time during their first economics class. Esteban Trebucq, one of the most pro-Milei journalists on the right-wing news channel La Nacion+, was discussing the recent skyrocketing increases in monthly premiums of private insurance companies. In a span of five months, private insurers have raised their premiums by over 150 percent, one of the many consequences of Milei's massive executive order deregulating large sectors of the Argentine economy, including, of course, the insurance "industry." "There's old people, retired people on fixed budgets, people who have preexisting conditions, families who can no longer afford the premiums and fall back into the public system." A public health system that, needless to say, is already feeling the strain from "the greatest austerity project in history," as Milei himself likes to boast, and is ill-equipped to handle the influx of tens of thousands of extra patients from the private sector.

"With inelastic goods and services, things that people need in order to survive, there's a power imbalance between the one who needs the good or service and the provider." I'm paraphrasing because I can't find the segment and can't recall his exact words. But I do remember myself blinking blankly at the screen, wondering how he could be getting so close and yet still be so far. Milei's massive December executive order, an abuse of presidential authority to begin with, as these executive orders were meant for emergency purposes, was announced on live TV and led to immediate and spontaneous mobilizations in many neighborhoods of Buenos Aires as well as in front of Congress. Milei essentially wielded the tool of the Decreto de Necesidad y Urgencia ("Executive Order of Need and Emergency," roughly) as something close to a constitutional reform while bypassing Congress. In it, he abolished over 40 regulations and modified another approximately 250 to liberalize or loosen them. (The executive order has since been rejected by the lower house of Congress, but it is still in effect as, due to a Kirchnerist modification in 2005, executive orders must be rejected by both houses of Congress in order to be repealed.)

Many of the deregulatory changes were in the most naked neoliberal and Austrian school of economics spirit: that social, and commercial, relations in society are always taking place between two equals, and that any intervention by the state (or, in anarchist language, by the whole of society in its interest and not those of the capitalist class) only leads to distortions, inefficiency, and poor service, hinders competition and therefore growth and productivity, and thus is the eventual driver of a society's poverty.

In their eyes, the tenants who need a roof over their heads and the landlords who own the homes are simply two equals, free to come to a common agreement. Freedom to either pay your entire salary in order to have a roof over your head or choose, freely, to sleep under the stars. The worker who needs a job in order to feed her family or not be reduced to scavenging for scraps out of a dumpster to put food in her mouth is not being coerced in any way by the capitalist who owns the means of production.

And yet, here is this right-wing "libertarian" journalist conceding that in capitalism there is no position of equality between those who own and control the resources needed to survive and those who have no choice other than to sell their labor in order to acquire them.

Of course, there was no moment of realization. There was eventually the accusation, which has turned into a judicial affair, that the insurance companies constituted themselves into a de facto cartel, conspiring to uniformly raise prices. Which, of course, they did—because that's exactly what happens when an industry reaches the late-stage-capitalism phase of development (the monopoly stage) and is left to its own devices.

Meanwhile, deregulation has led to an explosion in the cost of utilities and basic living expenses: increases in the 300 to 400 percent range on public transportation, increases of over 100 percent in gas and electricity bills, an increase of over 100 percent in the cost of fuel, and an increase of well over 100 percent even in the cost of basic foodstuffs, like rice and bread.[3] This, coupled with austerity measures, has powered a brutal recession, best illustrated by drastic drops in consumption in two areas with inelastic demand: basic foodstuffs and medicine.

Within six months of the capitalist fantasy economy meeting the real world, the consequences are that people in Argentina are going without their medicine and skipping meals in order to survive. In a country that is "the wheat field of the world," a loaf of bread costs the same as it does in Paris. In a country where average wages are a tenth of what they are in Europe, a cup of coffee costs the same in Buenos Aires as it does in Madrid. And in a country that processes its own oil and has a public oil company, fuel now costs the same as it does in the US. Argentina is now, literally and statistically, simultaneously the country in Latin America with both the highest cost of living and the lowest minimum wage.[4]

The brunt of austerity is not being borne, as promised, by the political class but rather by the country's workers, both employed and unemployed, and middle class. The capitalist class, given free rein, is quickly proving that their program is nothing more than one of maximum extraction of wealth from the producing class to them. To us anarchists who warned of the bait and switch from the beginning, who yelled to anybody who would listen that it was no coincidence that all the oligarchs of Argentina were behind this supposed "rebel," this comes as no surprise. No malfunction. It's the eternal dream of the capitalist class: to strip the state raw of any elements not purely in the interest of their accumulation of wealth, and to maximize profits by returning us to the conditions of the late nineteenth century.

Their dream is our nightmare, and larger and larger sectors of society are realizing it as they experience it in the flesh. European prices, African wages, Southeast Asian labor conditions.

The Battle of Ideas

If people can see, feel, and experience that they are objectively materially worse off, how do you contain and prevent disturbances, unrest, and general upheaval? Or an even better question currently is: Why is there, aside from isolated or specific flashpoints of conflict, no general mass movement of resistance or uprising against this political project? Even more incredibly, how can we explain that Milei still maintains a popularity rate of around 50 percent?

The answer, principally: ideology.

Ideology, paired with resentment, distraction, and the leveraging of poor against very poor.

As I write, Milei is yet again abroad, where he constantly is seen with the likes of Donald Trump, Spain's far-right Vox leader Santiago Abascal, and extremely poorly thinly veiled white supremacist Elon Musk. In a few days, he will also be meeting with El Salvador's president, Nayib Bukele. To his fanatical hard core, a burgeoning sect that I can spare myself explaining by simply stating that his diehard base is shockingly similar to that of Donald Trump—overwhelmingly male, open to conspiracy theories, frustrated with their position in life, and virulently convinced that "socialism, foreigners, and the woke agenda" are responsible for both their personal plight and Argentina's general socioeconomic crisis—this is all proof of Milei's incredible popularity and his undeniable position as a worldwide beacon in defense of capitalism, freedom, and Western values. A role that, also just like Trump, Milei is constantly presenting himself in—in the most obnoxious and self-absorbed way imaginable—in his many Twitter posts and reposts. This will contain and motivate his hard core, who zealously believe that "we need to suffer now in order to be better off tomorrow" and that a V-shaped economic recovery is inevitable and imminent.

Likewise, the discourse about abortion being murder and sooner or later trying to once again criminalize it in Argentina—as well as the positive references to the military and the last dictatorship—are meat for the more classic, older, relatively well-to-do right-wing voter who feels the economic pressure somewhat less than other sectors of society and has accepted Milei—first grudgingly and now somewhat more eagerly—after the political marginalization of a more moderate and classic right-wing option. Again a phenomenon very similar to how Trumpism consumed large segments of the traditional conservative base in the US.

But there is a broader ideological battle at hand. Milei and the ultraliberals are extremely conscious that it is being waged, and they reference it constantly. For the true believers among them, it's a matter of transforming the core mentality of Argentines, Argentine politics, and thus the country. For the pragmatically minded among the far right and the capitalist class, it's the understanding of a latent reality: that their best protection against a social uprising, against solidarity spreading between struggles and across sectors of society, is to continually drive wedges not just among the working class but also among those suffering the social and economic crises to different extents and in different forms.

The public worker has to be pitted against the worker in the private sector of the formal economy. The worker in the formal economy has to be pitted against the worker in the informal economy. Those with work, formal or not, have to look with disdain and contempt at those unemployed who are either trying to survive on their own or organizing collectively to demand at the very least to not go hungry. Those who happen to be unemployed, active in social organizations, and also foreign are to be particularly demonized.

We see the results of these divisions daily, gleefully reproduced, normalized, and multiplied by the right-wing media outlets. The small shopkeeper rages on camera against the street vendors who don't pay taxes and often "aren't even from this country." The office worker states on camera that he's glad public employees are being fired and institutions shut down, since he has been convinced that there apparently exists a high tax burden on private enterprise in Argentina, created by the need to finance the state—and this, not capitalist greed or maximization of profits, is what keeps his wages from going up. The taxi driver interviewed while stuck in traffic as a protest of unemployed workers is being blocked from advancing toward the president's residence fumes against the lazy moochers who don't provide anything to the economy and don't let others work. He is outraged that they expect to live from handouts and that the "culture of work" has been lost. Later, the same journalist will go store by store, talking to shopkeepers about how severe the losses created by the demonstration were to their daily revenue. We are to believe that the unemployed and the social organizations, the most vulnerable and poor of Argentina, are the demons keeping the Argentine economy from booming.

The recession is reducing the inflation rates, while unemployment is now what's booming. For the last few years, job "opportunities" were abundant in the country, yet they were very poorly paid and, more often than not, one job was not enough to live off of—and the real value of salaries was constantly losing against inflation. And while inflation hits the lowest earners hardest and is almost always a de facto tax on the poor, it is still an inarguably collective phenomenon. One that no advocate of the market economy can possibly blame on the personal failures of individuals.

As the recession advances and we trade one crisis for another, the ideological battle of ideas waged by the capitalist class comes into poignant focus. Unemployment unfolds as a personal drama. A death by a thousand cuts taking place in thousands of homes across the country, as somebody sits alone thinking how they will make ends meet next month, or arrives home to tell their partner that they'll have to turn to odd jobs to somehow keep the kids fed. It is, as we saw last week, the recently laid off bus driver desperately throwing himself under a bus in protest. Or a family heading for the first time, shy, timid, and embarrassed, to a comedor popular because the fridge is empty that day. Each unemployed person is bombarded with propaganda implying, or outright stating, that it is their fault. You should work more, if you really look you'll find something, hustle more, start a small business. Capitalism sells us the idea that unemployment is a personal failure, for which you and only you are responsible. And that position is no coincidence: It's yet another containment dam against the spread of resistance and solidarity.

And because to a large extent they are winning, we see examples like the snapshot above of the Textilcom workers. Workers involved in the most classic of workers' struggles: While occupying factories to defend their interests against bosses firing them as a response to economic and political decisions of this government and its economic policies, about to become unemployed workers themselves, they still find it necessary to differentiate and separate themselves from the currently unemployed. Though many of them might be, quite literally, soon in exactly the same position, they still feel it a priority to clarify that they are not like the ones on social plans, the piqueteros, etc., in order to appeal to the solidarity and goodwill of society. And when asked about this government and its policies, the answer is that they are "not interested in politics."

The battle of ideas against capitalist common sense is, of course, not lost forever. But we are clearly not currently on the winning side. The wedge to avoid a convergence of struggle from those whose interests are aligned in their conflict with the capitalist class, the protective dam against a generalization of revolt and uprising, is still holding strong. But for how long?

It's the afternoon of May 30, and again my attention turns to La Nacion+, which I inexplicably keep turned on in the background as I write (nothing like a good "rage listening" as one tries to concentrate). They have a correspondent on the Roca train, one of Buenos Aires's main train lines, which is traveling at a reduced maximum speed of thirty kilometers per hour as a protest by railway workers in demand of wage increases—a partial measure as prelude to a twenty-four-hour strike on June 4 if no agreement is reached.

The journalist is interviewing commuters, clearly hoping for the habitual "They should protest but without complicating the lives of other workers," "I make half of what they make and you don't see me out here blocking roads," "This is the problem in this country, people always protesting and not working," or one of the many other typical reactionary platitudes. Instead, when he asks for opinions about the action, a woman in her mid-thirties replies calmly, "I'm fine with it. Everything that is done in defense of the workers is perfect. Of course it will affect us all, but I'm in favor of all protests against injustices against workers." He pushes her about the "inconvenience of the delays," and she says, "It's part of what we have to go through. If we aren't all united in the situation we're going through . . . there's no way out. We're all workers, and if one day I was in their position I would like others to support me too." The next person interviewed, a young guy in a hoodie, flatly states, "They need to negotiate wages, this is all Milei's fault. He's a son of a bitch." The next to be interviewed, a machinist wearing a Boca Juniors jersey, responds, "Of course it's annoying, I'm taking over an hour to get home. But Milei needs to resign, everybody needs to take to the streets."

Four or five more people are interviewed, and all respond in the same vein before the reporter sends it back to the studio, where once again de facto government spokesperson Esteban Trebucq has been listening live. His only response: "Seems to be a lot of leftists on the train today."

Maybe. Or maybe, while the tide isn't necessarily already turning, at least the cracks in the dam seem to be multiplying.

The Construction of the Internal Enemy: The Journalists Point the Gun . . .

So it has to be, again, the good Argentines against the "orcs," as ex-president Mauricio Macri recently referred to leftists and social organizations—the glaring classism and racism becoming ever more normalized. Just last week, and of course again on La Nacion+, a teenage Milei fanatic at the president's book release and concert (yes, he sang . . . no, I don't care to explain) stated flatly, "Milei has a tough job ahead of him, but I believe he can get this country of *negros* going again." In Argentina, *negros*, which literally means "blacks," is a term that while being based in and stemming from racism is more classist than racist. It is used to refer more to a socioeconomic condition than a skin color. It's basically slang for "lazy, ignorant poors." Either way, it's a scandalous thing to say on national TV—or anywhere, really. But the journalist on La Nacion+ doesn't bat an eyelid. The process of stigmatization is in full swing.

And public enemy number one, the embodiment of the *negros*, the orcs acting collectively to make the lives of the good Argentines impossible, are the social organizations.

There is in Argentina an incredible quilt of solidarity, keeping capitalism's most exposed, forgotten, and marginalized protected from the elements as best it can. Over decades of chronic poverty, unemployment, and poverty wages, the social organizations, which are better known as piqueteros and which essentially grew as a response to and resistance against the neoliberal policies of the 1990s, have woven a network of comedores populares that is essentially the Red Cross of Argentina. They are spaces—sometimes as small as the kitchen of the woman who lends it for that purpose, and sometimes as large as a rented space—where anybody can find a warm plate of food or, at the very least, a mother or father who has chosen to go hungry so that their kids can eat can have some maté, the traditional Argentine drink, to silence the rumblings of hunger in their stomach. But these spaces are also much more than that.

They often provide the local youth with a space where they have access to free cultural activities, much in the same way a neighborhood sports club might. Where they can sit and draw or see a free puppet show. Or, very simply, find a space of containment that is off the streets. Streets that are often overrun with petty crime, drug gangs, and drug addiction—all things to which many of these kids can and do fall victim, as participant, user, or prey, without the networks of support built by the comedores populares and the social organizations.

But if the government and mainstream media are to be believed, the comedores and social organizations are the dregs of society, criminals who have made it their business to leech off of the poor for economic and political gain. For weeks now, a stigmatization and criminalization campaign has been raging, spearheaded by the Ministry of Human Capital and gleefully amplified by the press. The accusations coming from the ministry are as serious as they are varied. That a government audit revealed approximately half of the comedores to be *comedores fantasmas* (phantom comedores)—as in they don't actually exist. That leftist and Peronist organizations, who manage access to the comedores and the government-subsidized jobs that exist there, were forcing people to attend marches and demonstrations under threat of being expelled from the comedor or not receiving food. In other cases, that the food aid delivered by the government was being sold in the neighborhoods rather than distributed at the comedores. Finally, the accusation that organizations were providing fake expense reports to the government in order to divert funds intended for the comedores to their political organizations. And here is where it gets complicated, and where a grain of possible truth is instrumentalized by the right wing and its media for a vile political campaign of stigmatization and criminalization.

There are approximately 35,000 comedores populares in Argentina, at which over 130,000 people work, and who knows how many hundreds of thousands are fed.[5] Many of the comedores populares are run by the mass organizations of traditional leftist parties, the largest being the Polo Obrero, which is the unemployed workers' front of the Trotskyist Partido Obrero.[6] Others are extensions of left-wing Peronist organizations, while still others are truly independent and simply neighborhood based. As a result of a Kirchnerist strategy in the early 2000s—which understood that the social organizations had a revolutionary or at least antagonist potential and posed a potential threat to governability—they are incorporated into a system of interdependence with the state. It's the social organizations who manage and act as intermediaries of the subsidized work plans that many people who aren't strictly volunteers at the comedores depend on to subsist. Likewise, the comedores depend greatly on food aid that comes directly from the federal government. And, given the enormity of the structure of the comedores, the dire conditions that many around them exist in, the endemic corruption in Argentina, and the extreme clientelism, verticalism, and authoritarianism that permeates Peronist political organizations, nobody would be surprised that there are indeed cases of abuse, corruption, and extortion. Indeed, as anarchists, we need to be—and are—critical of the dynamics of *clientelismo político*, which can essentially be described as welfarism or political clientelism. It may look on the surface like mutual aid, but it is in fact a tool by which authoritarian organizations, as well as corrupt elements within them, leverage the needs and urgencies of poor communities for political influence and financial gain.

But this in no way diminishes or takes away from the reality that the overwhelmingly vast majority of the comedores, their workers, and their volunteers are an essential—and collectively generated and run— bulwark of solidarity and community defense against the consequences of capitalism in the country's popular neighborhoods. It is simply an attempt by an ultra-right-wing government to advance the construction of a dark and dangerous "other," to stigmatize the social organizations in order to preemptively discourage solidarity with them when they are criminalized in the courts or repressed on the streets.

It's a joint state and media campaign with the objective of destroying the network of comedores and social organizations, again on the premise of abuses, but with the true motivation of them simply not believing in the concept. As their economic policies deepen the river of misery and desperation running through the country, they seek to atomize and isolate society. They do so by discrediting and stigmatizing collective struggle. Worse yet, they refuse to distribute food to the comedores populares. They are trying to simultaneously dismantle or weaken collective bastions of resistance while building the social consensus for the upcoming, and inevitable, repression.

As they do so, weakening the comedores by criminally even refusing to distribute thousands of tons of food, they either don't realize or don't care that by attacking the concept of collective survival through solidarity they are contributing to the gradual eroding of the social safety nets of Argentina's most marginalized neighborhoods. Where the comedores populares and social organizations cease to be present, people will look to escape poverty and hunger through other means. Thus, this paves the way for the advance of social cannibalism and the narco-state—which is nothing more than free market capitalism in its purest of forms.

... The Cops Pull the Trigger

It's already happening, on both fronts.

Rosario, March 5

The popular neighborhoods and slums of Rosario, Argentina's third-largest city, are already largely dominated by rival narco gangs. That Rosario is a port city, and that its ports are privatized, make it a particularly attractive and lucrative strategic hub for the drug trade. Many of the local youths, hopeless and faced with a choice between twelve hours a day of exploitation at a dead-end, low-paying job and the relatively lucrative—and "glamorous"—"job" of low-level narco soldier, take the latter option.

Pablo Coccocioni, who is the minister of security of the province in which Rosario is located and who answers to national Minister of Security Patricia Bullrich (yet another recycled figurehead of the neoliberal era of the '90s), emboldened by the "law-and-order" line of the new government, posts an image to his Instagram account. Under the headline "They're Going to Have a Worse and Worse Time," dozens of prisoners can be seen lined up in rows, sitting cross-legged, shirtless, heads down. It's a carbon copy of the photos of captured gang members that we regularly see coming from Bukele's El Salvador.

On March 9, a fifteen-year-old narco foot soldier walks into a gas station and murders twenty-five-year-old Bruno Bussanich, who was working there as an attendant. It's the fourth in a string of random murders of workers across the city of Rosario since Coccocioni posted the image. In the past few days, taxi drivers Héctor Figueroa and Diego Celentano, ages forty-three and thirty-two respectively, along with bus driver Marco Daloia, age thirty-nine, have been murdered in cold blood while on the job. The city has become a ghost town, with people afraid to leave their homes.

While the images may have been almost identical, there is a critical difference. As Bukele himself put it, "The picture was a grave mistake; you can only do that when the gangs are neutralized and you have control of the street." Which is in no way the case in Rosario, and the consequences of the swift and brutal response were borne not by the political class, not by the police or armed forces, but by innocent workers going about their day. While this was a strategic mistake by the government, a failure to differentiate between campaigning and the potential consequences of campaign slogans when carelessly implemented while actually governing, it nevertheless laid the foundation, understandably, for yet another rightward shift in society. We live in a jungle, we are faced with animals and murderers, law-and-order politics are the only way out of this jungle.

Western Suburbs of Buenos Aires, May 26

Like countless young (and now also not so young) people in Argentina, musician Manuel López Ledesma, age thirty, is working as a Rappi delivery driver to make ends meet. As he waits outside a pizzeria for his order, he's intercepted by two teenagers—nineteen and seventeen—who, in an attempt to steal his motorcycle, shoot and kill him. It's a classic example of the kind of social cannibalism, bred by poverty and the cycles of violence it generates, that now permeates the greater Buenos Aires region.

The next day, a militant protest of Rappi delivery drivers in front of the local police precinct results in the arson of five vehicles, including one police cruiser.[7] It's a small and contained explosion of anger and fury. Righteous, yet again fertile ground for a potential ultra-right-wing law-and-order outcome when the current social, political, and economic crisis inevitably leads to an explosion of social upheaval.

As the social crisis deepens, except for spectacular crimes, it overwhelmingly isn't the rich and ultra-rich who are exposed as crime rates explode. They are protected behind walls, by private security, in closed neighborhoods. They travel in private vehicles and have never set foot on a bus or train. It's workers and people from working-class neighborhoods who suffer the social cannibalism. Being beaten and maybe killed for your cell phone or backpack while riding the train or waiting for the bus, or while walking the streets of greater Buenos Aires in the early morning following a night shift. And this only deepens the social resentment and ideological rift. It lays the groundwork for reactionary uprisings.

Each passing day, each passing week, actual labor, economic, and social conflicts both multiply and intensify—and are constantly met with state repression on the streets. In the face of this, the parallel phenomenons of narco gangs gaining territory and the normalization of social cannibalism are functional to the protective architecture of repression that the program to completely deregulate and liberalize the Argentine economy and society will eventually depend on.

The police apparatus and a repressive consensus are critical to this economic and social program. Society needs to be conditioned to tolerate repression. If we live in a jungle, if anybody on the street could rob me as I wait for the bus on a cold Monday morning, if every hooded figure on the street could be my murderer as I wait to make a delivery for a few pesos, if the cost of ending insecurity is a war of law and order directed against those who have successfully been lumped together as an amorphous and terrifying horde of petty criminals, cold-blooded murderers, orcs, dirty leftists, corrupt social organizations who prey on the poor and vulnerable and who have been scapegoated as those holding us back from a future of shining capitalist prosperity ... how can we be anything but supportive of whatever measures might need to be taken to stop them? In the capitalist world, in the eyes of a terrified population and a society decimated by the propaganda of resentment and individualism, there is no alternative.

Their World Versus Ours: Solidarity and Mutual Aid Versus Hustle Culture and the Narco State

Isla Maciel, Any Given Saturday Morning

In the middle of the "famous Isla Maciel," an actual island near the internationally recognized neighborhood of La Boca, famous for being notoriously poor and dangerous even by Buenos Aires standards, a couple dozen teenagers are gathered. A closer look at them will reveal that, in this most unexpected of places, they wear T-shirts sporting the internationally recognized emblem of the twin flags of antifascism. The kids are taking part in one of several free boxing sessions being held in the neighborhood today, and every Saturday, for local kids and teenagers by Boxeo Popular, or People's Boxing, a project started and run by Antifascist Action Buenos Aires (Acción Antifascista Buenos Aires) and antifascist sporting and social club La Cultura del Barrio. Laura, one of the founders of the project, explains that "thirty-three families participate in the project, through which we support and empower about eighty-five kids." AFA and the club provide the kids with everything from uniforms and equipment, as well as the participation of a licensed coach and a post-training snack.

"We understand this project, which is now in its sixth year, through the logic of mutual aid, not of welfarism. We provide a framework and an initiative, while the kids and the families help make it possible every week by providing the necessary infrastructure and participating actively in its realization," explains Laura. As the project defines itself, "It's a means and not an end in and of itself. Guaranteeing access to sport and recreation at no cost, without prejudices or discrimination, through physical, sporting, and play activities that are oriented toward fostering values opposed to all forms of oppression—without losing sight of the different psychosocial situations of vulnerability that the youths participating in the project might be going through.... It's a means through which we foster working-class sport, organization and self-management through mutual aid, active participation, and education—reappropriating our strength as a class and collectively building spaces of real alternatives and spaces of social resistance."

Villa Crespo, Central Buenos Aires, Every Day, 8:00 a.m.

La Cultura del Barrio, Latin America's (and probably the world's) only explicitly antifascist sporting and social club, opens its doors for the day. The first participants in some of the morning activities begin strolling through its doors. They might be here for a functional training class, yoga, boxing, or muay thai. If it's in the evening, they could be here for more sporting activities, just as much as for a straight edge hardcore show, a debate, or any one of the myriad of activities spread out through the club's two stories. But either way, they're always a mix of young and old, all genders, subculture types and regular folks from the neighborhood. No matter who they are or what they're here for, there's no escaping the political culture of the space—which is covered in antifascist and queer flags, posters and stickers from anarchist organizations across the world, and a large banner reading "Contra la Violencia Estatal—Autodefensa Popular" (Against State Violence—Popular Self-Defense).

The club, which was founded in 2011 and is also an outgrowth of Antifascist Action Buenos Aires, is unique in that without at all hiding its political convictions, it has become a space used by the local community as a whole, with hundreds of dues-paying members participating regularly in its activities, while needless to say nobody is ever turned away due to lack of funds and the club strives to maintain accessible prices. The club's central values are an illustration of the generally anarchist and antiauthoritarian leanings of its active members: mutual aid, generating alternatives outside of the logic of profit and capital, and grassroots organization.

★

These are but two examples, honestly minuscule in the grand scheme of things, that I highlight because of the particular social and political affinity with them. But they are representative of a much more important general point. Social organizations, neighborhood assemblies, neighborhood sports clubs (which the current government also wants to privatize), mutual aid and solidarity groups, rank-and-file unions—they are all representations of our concept of society. They are, in Argentina in their current state, wildly imperfect. This is not surprising, as they too—like all of us—can't help but in part be a representation of the society that creates them. But the attacks by the state and its press aren't based on an ethical crusade against corruption or abuse. Corruption and abuse are endemic to Argentine society, and in fact if that were the concern we would all be agreeing about the urgent need to dismantle the police apparatus, which is wildly corrupt, abusive, and in many neighborhoods the hand that organizes crime and drug gangs. Or we would be talking about the church, with its history of subservience to military repression and numerous child abuse scandals. And yet, to nobody's surprise, there is no breathless outrage targeted toward those institutions.

Social organizations, trade unions, and neighborhood social and sports clubs are attacked on principle, because they are tangible and material representations of the interactions we want to build—interactions truly between equals in pursuit of a collective interest, which defy the logic of neoliberal capitalism.

They want us isolated, atomized, each of us a temporarily embarrassed millionaire with three jobs hustling until the inevitable day we become rich, if only we wake up early enough and work diligently enough. Failing that, foot soldiers of the narco-state. Every volunteer at a comedor popular, every militant of a social organization, every rank-and-file worker at a workplace assembly, and every kid taking part in a free activity at their neighborhood club is a brick in the wall of resistance to the capitalist project of society.

But just as the barricade simultaneously blocks the street but opens the road, our projects of mutual aid and solidarity are much more than just collective acts of resistance to capitalism. They are also spaces that enable others—friends, comrades, new acquaintances—to live experiences outside of the logic of capital. They allow you to see that you can participate in activities without necessarily having to spend money, that you can be welcomed in a traditionally macho space despite your appearance or gender, that you can get together with your friends and start a band or organize a demo. That you are much more than how much your labor is worth and how much you can consume. In a time when a future outside of capitalism is unimaginable to so many, they are glimpses, however small or fleeting, into what a different world could look like.

Resistance

The current objective reality is sobering. There is no convergence of struggles, no feeling of an imminent uprising. The large Peronist movement, including its left wing, is largely absent from the streets and protests—banking on letting the ultraliberals crash on their own, in order to then present themselves again as the only viable alternative providing governability to this country. The mainstream unions refuse to execute a plan of struggle, limiting themselves to periodic measures as a means of negotiating in the background to protect themselves against changes in labor law that would weaken their influence. And while it was nice to see the right-wing press cry about the huge losses generated by a twenty-four-hour general strike (which raises the question of who actually creates wealth), the traditional industrial strike can only get us so far in an economy in which half of the workforce is in the informal sector and can't participate, or at least can't do so with any kind of labor protections. Meanwhile, the Marxist left can be commended for being present on the streets and in the struggles, but their influence—both qualitatively and quantitatively—is marginal.

History does not inevitably tend toward "progress," nor is this Hollywood and the good side is inevitably bound to win. As poverty and hunger advance, and the capitalists attack the social fabric carefully woven by the popular, neighborhood, and social organizations over the decades since the last neoliberal experiment here failed, what awaits us if they succeed is the future of the anarcho-capitalist dystopia: poverty, isolation, extreme exploitation, and, finally, the narco-state.

Resistance is stirring, and flashpoints of conflict are becoming both more frequent and more intense. On March 24, hundreds of thousands took part in the traditional demonstration to remember the military coup and reject Milei's banalizing of the last dictatorship. Just a few weeks ago, probably close to a million people took to the streets in defense of free and public universities. The bureaucrat unions, led by the CGT, have held two general strikes, one of which was strongly felt due to the high levels of participation in the transportation sector. In the province of Misiones, education workers have been camping in protest for almost two weeks now. Even on the streets, hostility toward ultra-liberals is growing—as could be seen during Milei's last public event in Buenos Aires last week, during which ultraliberal militants were attacked and flags stolen.

The Final Snapshot

One of the deposits where thousands of tons of food are being held is now guarded from demonstrators by police vehicles and a water cannon. Meanwhile, Milei is giving a speech abroad. Not unironically, in the

United States. In true Austrian school fanatic fashion, he bluntly states, "A moment will come where people are starving to death. So somehow, they'll figure something out in order to not die. There doesn't need to be an intervention to resolve the external question of consumption, because somebody will resolve it."

As he says about those who would try to avoid dying of hunger in the streets, "You think people are so stupid that they won't do something?" For once, he and I agree—and I have no doubt that I and thousands and thousands who heard him had the same thought. In 2001, the "something" collectively done to put an end to the regime of hunger and misery was a popular uprising that forced the president to resign and flee the fury of the people from a rooftop helicopter. This time, the solution might end up not being much different.

Acknowledgments

There are individuals and organizations without whose practical support this project would have been impossible to realize. Or at least it wouldn't have achieved the deeply visual form that I envisioned and that I believed was the only way to meaningfully convey to a non-Argentine audience the spirit of the times, places, people, and ideas reflected in this book.

First is the Biblioteca Nacional, Argentina's national library—now under siege from neoliberal budget cuts—where I spent countless hours going through decades-old newspapers.

Several of the football clubs discussed within these pages—Defensores de Belgrano, Club Atlético Atlanta, Colegiales, and Racing Club—gave me access to their facilities and put their press departments at my disposal in order for me to obtain many of the images in this book.

I owe deep thanks to individuals either from within the actual club structures or who independently have also spent large parts of their lives documenting the ecosystem around Argentine football clubs—or passionately reporting on the happenings at the club they carry in their hearts. Such is the case with Club Atlético Atlanta's Edgardo Imas, himself an archivist of the history of Atlanta, a photojournalist, and a longtime activist within the Argentine left.

This is likewise the case with Alejandro Wall, whose book ¡Academia, Carajo! deals exclusively with Racing Club's championship and the parallel turmoil and uprising of 2001, which I devoured in one sitting when it was first published in 2011. Wall is today a prominent journalist and best-selling author—yet he too did not hesitate to find the time to support my endeavors toward this book, despite us sharing no previous bond beyond our mutual condition as Racing Club fans. Thanks is like-wise owed to my fellow Racing fan Flavio Nardini, who despite us not having seen or spoken to each over in over two decades also did not hesitate to give a fellow traveler of the Racing Club (mis)adventures of the '90s a helping hand.

There are then of course those whom I find myself—happily—having to constantly thank. Everybody at PM Press, but especially the editors Charlie and Wade, who patiently hold my hand through the process and are instrumental in crafting the final written product. Also Gabriel Kuhn, whom I've adopted as essentially my go-to person for whatever random even mildly remotely book- or author-related question under the sun that might cross my mind.

There is my family—the family I have chosen. My sister, who fortunately survived the more than one very sketchy and dangerous situation I recklessly exposed her to in and around soccer stadiums in my youthful exuberance. Despite me having to at times carry her in my arms like a small, precious package as we fled from the hail of stones of a visiting-fan ambush—among other "highlights"—or maybe indeed precisely thanks to these wildly age-inappropriate thrills, I somehow managed to infect her with the same fervor and love for all that happens in and around Argentine football stadiums that so shaped my life. And now shapes hers. My mother, to whom I probably owe deep apologies for never letting get a good night's sleep—knowing as she did that if there was trouble of essentially any kind and anywhere, I was in it. My kids, who have, sometimes enthusiastically and sometimes much less so, seen the insides of more football stadiums in more countries during their childhoods than most people see in their lifetimes. It's unclear if I should be thanking them or they should be thanking me. Maybe both. My partner—no stranger to the world of football herself, but who regardless of whether my obsession of the moment is changing the world or watching the stupid ball being kicked over the stupid line by the people wearing the correctly colored jerseys—is enthusiastic about things by simple virtue of me being enthusiastic about them. Which is, after all, probably the quintessential essence of love—and something I hope to be always reciprocating, in words and much more so in deeds.

My friends, those specifically who happened to share the passion for the same clubs as I, and accompanied me on the terraces wherever Atlanta and Racing played—and on the many often hostile streets and

neighborhoods those weekends took us to. The amount of simultaneously memorable, terrible, exhilarating, and frightening experiences
we were fortunate enough to live through unscathed are impossible
to count, but there's no doubt we lived spectacular childhoods and
adolescences. Their names have of course been changed to protect the
very guilty, but we'll call them Rodolfo, Juan, Carlos, José, Ivan, and
Pedro—and they'll know who they are as they read this text.

As is so often the case, aside from the strategic importance of
certain individuals, it is the collectives—the plurals organized into one
based on shared interests, convictions, and aspirations—to whom the
most thanks is owed. Those who with the force of their time, energy,
dedication, and commitment have given life to the collective phenomenons—of social movements and political resistance, as well as of
grassroots fan culture—that have so deeply shaped the character of
the popular classes of Argentina. They have provided the most solid
defense of the social fabric that protects us against the social disintegra-
tion provoked by the constant neoliberal attacks on Argentine society.

Once per generation, the newest iteration of neoliberalism's foot
soldiers descends on us, telling us that every person is an island unto
him or herself and that happiness and freedom are concepts only
meaningful in relation to your earnings, your job, and your consumption. But in every generation we find numerous pockets of resistance
where the common sense of the collective life experience clashes with
the propaganda of capital. In our neighborhoods, in the time spent at
the hundreds of sporting and social clubs that dot our landscape and
that exist outside of the logic of capital—spaces where one can exist,
be creative, and enjoy leisure with others without the expectation of
consumption or productivity. They are the antibodies that strengthen
our capacity to resist.

And finally, if we are talking about resistance, the biggest thanks of
all is owed to the people from La Cultura del Barrio: Luis, Gabi, Lau, Eze,
Nikoi, Mauri, and everybody else. A group of people whom I incredibly
only first crossed paths with recently but whose lives are largely carbon
copies of what I imagine my life trajectory would have been like if I had
stayed in Argentina, and mine likewise what theirs might have been if
they had left. But while I indeed left, they were the motor behind what
is now over two decades of Antifascist Action Buenos Aires—the reason
that in this city it is the fascists who fear us and not vice versa, and the

origin of a thousand DIY concerts, hundreds of solidarity campaigns, and dozens of actions. Most of all, a group of people who with their efforts and audacity have brought back to life the anarchist social and sporting club of a century ago. Who have forged in the middle of one of the world's largest metropolises—and, incredibly, less than a kilometer away from the Biblioteca Popular José Ingenieros, which likewise continues to exist and resist, and to which I likewise owe a debt of gratitude—an explicitly antifascist and antiauthoritarian space that the neighborhood has adopted as its own. They are living, breathing proof that we can work, relax, exercise, and resist collectively, no matter the circumstances.

Que vivan nuestros caminos.

Notes

All translations by the author.

Prologue: Racing Club vs. Vélez Sarsfield

1   Ten years later, I would learn in Alejandro Wall's excellent book *¡Academia, Carajo!* that the goal, scored by Gabriel Loeschbor, was scored from an offside position. As it turns out, the linesman that day, Alberto Barrientos, decided that both Racing Club and the country in general had gone through enough—and chose not to raise his banner. Incidentally, he was also a fan of Racing Club. Alejandro Wall, *¡Academia, Carajo!* (Editorial Sudamericana, 2011), 15.

Introduction: The Twin Utopias

1   The band Callejeros was a budding icon of the Argentine rock 'n' roll youth subculture in the early 2000s. Their fans were known for their fervor, setting off large amounts of flares and pyrotechnics in the crowd during the shows—something not uncommon in the Argentine rock scene at the time. During one of their shows, on December 30, 2004, at the Republica Cromañon club in downtown Buenos Aires, the pyrotechnics ignited a fire inside the club. With the emergency exits locked by the promoter, the lights out, and the rapidly expanding fire and fumes, the flames would claim 194 lives.

2   Peter Kropotkin, "'Anarchism,' from *The Encyclopaedia Britannica*, 1910," Anarchy Archives, accessed May 29, 2025, http://dwardmac.pitzer.edu/Anarchist_Archives/kropotkin/britanniaanarchy.html.

3   Karl Marx, *Critique of the Gotha Program* (PM Press, 2022).

4   G.P. Maximoff, ed., *The Political Philosophy of Bakunin: Scientific Anarchism* (Free Press, 1953), 269.

1: The Tides of Anarchy: The Anarchist Mass Movement of Late Nineteenth-Century Argentina

1   As well as "subversive" activists of all left-wing stripes. The law was eventually repealed in 1958.

2   Juan Suriano, *Paradoxes of Utopia: Anarchist Culture and Politics in Buenos Aires, 1890–1910*, trans. Chuck Morse (AK Press, 2010), 225.

3   Diego Abad de Santillán, *La FORA: Ideología y trayectoria del movimiento obrero revolutionario en la Argentina* (Libros de Anarres, 2005). The subtitle translates as "Ideology and trajectory of the revolutionary workers' movement in Argentina."

4   Jacinto Cerdá, "Negras tormentas: La FORA anarquista en Buenos Aires, 1930–1943" (master's thesis, Universidad de San Andrés, Graduate Program in

History, 2021), 33, https://dspaceapi.live.udesa.edu.ar/server/api/core/bitstreams/7955c3c7-57b3-4b4f-954b-2257fabbc0e2/content.

5   Suriano, *Paradoxes of Utopia*, 16.

6   Suriano, *Paradoxes of Utopia*, 225.

7   Suriano, *Paradoxes of Utopia*, 225.

8   Errico Malatesta, "Majorities and Minorities," Anarchist Library, accessed June 6, 2025, https://theanarchistlibrary.org/library/errico-malatesta-majorities-and-minorities.

9   Osvaldo Bayer, "El bondadoso ajusticiador," *Pagina 12*, November 7, 2009, https://www.pagina12.com.ar/diario/contratapa/13-134856-2009-11-07.html.

10   Bayer, "El bondadoso ajusticiador."

11   Originally sentenced to death, Radowitzky was eventually sentenced to life in prison and banished to a prison colony in Ushuaia, the world's southernmost city, once it was confirmed that he was underage. He was briefly able to escape the penal colony in a daring action organized jointly by Chilean and Argentine anarchists. Recaptured only a few days later, he remained in prison until 1930, when President Hipólito Yrigoyen both pardoned and exiled him, at which point he relocated to Uruguay. In 1936, he joined the ranks of anarchists fighting in the Spanish Revolution, escaping to Mexico through France after the defeat at the hands of the fascist forces. He lived in Mexico until his death in 1954.

12   Francisco N. Juárez, "El atentado contra Figueroa Alcorta y la gran fuga," *La Nación*, April 14, 2002, https://www.lanacion.com.ar/opinion/el-atentado-contra-figueroa-alcorta-y-la-gran-fuga-nid210319.

13   "Atentado a Manuel Quintana: La causa del anarquista sin esperanza," Asociación Pensamiento Penal, March 12, 2013, https://www.pensamientopenal.org/atentado-a-manuel-quintana-la-causa-del-anarquista-sin-esperanza.

14   Facundo Sinatra Soukoyan, "Francisco Solano Regis, el anarquista salteño que atentó contra Figueroa Alcorta," *Pagina 12*, May 1, 2022, https://www.pagina12.com.ar/418641-francisco-solano-regis-el-anarquista-salteno-que-atento-cont.

15   Sinatra Soukoyan, "Francisco Solano Regis."

16   Sinatra Soukoyan, "Francisco Solano Regis."

17   Suriano, *Paradoxes of Utopia*, 32.

18   *The Libertarian*, no. 7, April 1, 1911.

19   Suriano, *Paradoxes of Utopia*, 226.

20   Suriano, *Paradoxes of Utopia*, 226.

21   Horacio Ricardo Silva, *Días rojos, verano negro: Enero de 1919, la semana trágica de Buenos Aires* (Libros de Anarres, 2011), 239, 243.

22   Silva, *Días rojos*, 133.

23   Silva, *Días rojos*, 138.

24   Silva, *Días rojos*, 169.

25   Silva, *Días rojos*, 179.

26   Edgardo J. Bilsky, *La Semana Trágica* (Biblioteca Política Argentina, 1984).

27   "Semana Trágica: Buenos Aires bajo el terror y la muerte," Mágicas Ruinas, accessed June 9, 2025, https://www.magicasruinas.com.ar/revdesto036.htm.

28   Silva, *Días rojos*, 169.

29   Herman Schiller, "El primer pogrom," *Pagina 12*, January 3, 1999, https://www.pagina12.com.ar/1999/99-01/99-01-03/pag16.htm.

30   Poalei Sion was a socialist Zionist movement of Russian origin.

31   José Mendelson, *Di Idische Tzaitung*, January 10, 1919. In Schiller, "El primer pogrom."

32   John Raymond Hébert, *The Tragic Week of January, 1919, in Buenos Aires: Background, Events, Aftermath* (Georgetown University Press, 1972), 159.

33   Bilsky, *Semana Trágica*.

2: The Biblioteca Popular José Ingenieros

1   Los Violadores were one of the emblematic bands of the first wave of Argentine punk rock. Their controversial-sounding name is a play on words, born out of the need to evade the government censors during the last military dictatorship in Argentina. *Violadores* in Spanish means "violators," which would roughly translate to "lawbreakers" or "transgressors." But it is also unfortunately synonymous with "rapists," an association the band attempted to break with their 1987 song explicitly titled "Violadores de la ley" (Violators of the law).

2   Eduardo Colombo, "La Biblioteca Popular 'José Ingenieros,'" Biblioteca Popular José Ingenieros, accessed June 9, 2025, archived at https://web.archive.org/web/20080815090824/http://www.nodo50.org/bpji/historia.htm.

3   Colombo, "Biblioteca Popular 'José Ingenieros.'"

4   Peter Larsen lived in Argentina and remained a regular at the BPJI until 2016, when he returned to the United States. Sadly, he passed away in November 2021.

5   Natalia Díaz, *Anarquismo en el movimiento piquetero* (Kuruf Editorial, 2019), 39, https://ithanarquista.files.wordpress.com/2020/08/natalia-diaz-anarquismo-en-el-movimiento-piquetero.pdf.

6   *En la Calle: Una lectura anarquista de la crisis neoliberal en Argentina 1997–2007* (Editorial Madreselva, 2011), 6.

7   Díaz, *Anarquismo*, 50.

8   Díaz, *Anarquismo*, 39.

9   *En la Calle*, 6.

10 *Urubu* (La Turba Ediciones, n.d.), https://laturbaediciones.files.wordpress.com/2012/09/urubu.pdf.

11 "El Urubú: El que murió peleando," *El Muerto* (blog), August 29, 2012, https://elmuertoquehabla.blogspot.com/2012/08/el-urubu-el-que-murio-peleando.html.

12 I am paraphrasing, of course, and wary of it at that, since this beloved comrade, who remained a fixture in the anarchist movement and at the Biblioteca Popular José Ingenieros until his very last breath, passed away a few years ago and is no longer here to confirm that these words reflect his exact sentiment.

3: "We're Going to Kill Jews to Make Soap"

1   Guardia Negra was a self-described "Latinoi internationalist Redskin band" based in Boston. The band's members were from Chile, Venezuela, France, and Argentina—hence the song about the Atlanta club from Villa Crespo. The band was also closely linked to the Northeastern Federation of Anarcho-Communists.

4: El Barrio No Se Quiebra

1   *La Vanguardia*, January 12, 1919. In Leonardo Senkman, "El pogromo de la Semana Trágica: ¿Un olvidado de la esfera pública?," *Nueva Sion*, February 24, 2019, https://nuevasion.org/archivos/27176.

2   Tom Wichter, "Atlanta: Pasión futbolera en el corazón del judaísmo de Buenos Aires," *Ynet Español*, August 18, 2019, https://www.ynetespanol.com/global/america/article/Bycu8BvEB.

3   Anibal A. Parera, "Rescatando a los clubes de barrio," *El Cronista*, May 12, 2017, https://www.cronista.com/impresa-general/Rescatando-a-los-clubes-de-barrio-20170512-0014.html.

4   Parera, "Rescatando a los clubes de barrio."

5   Gustavo Veiga, "Los clubes de barrio siguen haciendo obra por deporte," *Pagina 12*, February 27, 2006, https://www.pagina12.com.ar/diario/suplementos/libero/9-2784-2006-02-27.html.

5: An Unlikely Heritage: The Immigrant, Radical, and Anarchist Origins of Argentine Football Clubs

1   I use the term *workingmen* in this case because it is the historically accurate description, women not being participants in the sporting clubs at that time.

2   Cristian Grosso, "Nadie puede hacerse el distraído," *La Nación*, March 12, 2009, https://www.lanacion.com.ar/deportes/nadie-puede-hacerse-el-distraido-nid1107855.

3   Juan Suriano, *Paradoxes of Utopia: Anarchist Culture and Politics in Buenos Aires, 1890–1910*, trans. Chuck Morse (AK Press, 2010), 16. Sadly, Juan Suriano passed away in 2018 at the age of seventy.

4   Suriano, *Paradoxes of Utopia*, 2.

5   Suriano, *Paradoxes of Utopia*, 26.

6   *La Protesta Humana*, April 20, 1901.

7   Nancy Méndez, "Osvaldo Bayer y el fútbol que llego con los barcos," *La Izquierda Diario*, December 24, 2019, https://www.laizquierdadiario.com/Osvaldo-Bayer-y-el-futbol-que-llego-con-los-barcos.

8   Suriano, *Paradoxes of Utopia*, 99.

9   *La Protesta*, October 15, 1904.

10   Suriano, *Paradoxes of Utopia*, 91.

11   Suriano, *Paradoxes of Utopia*, 92.

12   Suriano, *Paradoxes of Utopia*, 93.

13   Méndez, "Osvaldo Bayer."

14   Matías Mustafá, "Salta: Rechazan cierre de Libertad, histórico club de origen anarquista y comunista," *La Izquierda Diario*, August 31, 2016, https://www.laizquierdadiario.com/Salta-rechazan-cierre-de-Libertad-historico-club-de-origen-anarquista-y-comunista.

15   Mustafá, "Salta."

16   This is controversial, as many accounts state that the founding meeting was actually in offices of the Socialist Party, yet the choice of colors clearly indicates anarchist sympathies. It's possible that while the founders were anarchists, the actual meeting might indeed have been in a Socialist Party space.

17   Javier Bava, "Historia del Club," Club Atlético Defensores de Belgrano, accessed June 9, 2025, https://www.defeweb.com.ar/historiadelclub.

18   Juan Ignacio Provéndola, "Homenaje a hincha desaparecido: La tarde en la que Defensores de Belgrano perdió un partido, pero le ganó al olvido," *La Izquierda Diario*, March 3, 2020, https://www.laizquierdadiario.com/La-tarde-en-la-que-Defensores-de-Belgrano-perdio-un-partido-pero-le-gano-al-olvido.

19   Cristino Nicolaides, commander of the Third Army Corps, was eventually convicted of his murder.

20   Eduardo N. Carboni, "Colegiales, el club de los libertarios unidos," *De Hoy*, April 6, 2020, archived at https://web.archive.org/web/20230929004152/https://dehoy.com.ar/entrada/colegiales-el-club-de-los-libertarios-unidos-33375/.

21   Miguel Fernández Ubiría, *Fútbol y anarquismo* (Catarata, 2020).

22   Juan Ignacio Provéndola, host, *Micro Nacional*, podcast, "En Gerli: Anarquista Porvenir," Radio Nacional Argentina, October 10, 2017, https://soundcloud.com/juan-ignacio-provendola/sets/micro-nacional-recorriendo-el.

23   Hernan Bravo, "El Porvenir: Un club de Piñeiro entre el deporte y el anarquismo," *La Voz de Piñeiro*, October 5, 2020, archived at https://web.archive.org/web/20240305125941/https://lavozdepineiro.com/2020/10/05/el-porvenir-un-club-de-pineiro-entre-el-deporte-y-el-anarquismo/.

24   Suriano, *Paradoxes of Utopia*, 21.

25   F., "Entre la patronal y el sindicato: La historia del origen de Florentino Ameghino," *Pasta de Campeon*, May 3, 2020, archived at https://web.archive.org/web/

20200507073829/https://pastadecampeon.com/entre-la-patronal-y-el-sindicato-la-historia-del-origen-de-florentino-ameghino/.

26   "Petroleros, obreros y futbolistas," *El Patagónico*, December 13, 2007, https://www.elpatagonico.com/petroleros-obreros-y-futbolistas-n1315049.

27   F., "Entre la patronal y el sindicato."

28   "Club Atlético Germinal: 3 de septiembre de 1922," Copa Argentina, accessed June 9, 2025, https://www.copaargentina.org/es/news/9766_Club-Atletico-Germinal-3-de-septiembre-de-1922.html.

29   Ubiría, *Fútbol y anarquismo.*

30   "Argentinos Juniors: Anarquistas, socialistas, y solidarios," *Radio Gráfica*, April 15, 2020, https://radiografica.org.ar/2020/04/15/argentinos-juniors-anarquistas-socialistas-y-solidarios.

6: Solo Entiende Mi Locura Quien Comparte Mi Pasión

1   You can see and hear Racing fans rendering their version of this song in the stadium here: https://www.youtube.com/watch?v=Wht5eRjXkgs. Recommended viewing. In 2016, the English football website We Speak Football released a list of their top ten football chants ever, placing this one at number eight, as the Argentine daily newspaper *Clarín* reported. The piece conveniently includes a video of the top ten chants. "Las 10 mejores canciones de cancha, según el sitio We Speak Football," *Clarín*, November 11, 2016, https://www.clarin.com/deportes/futbol/10-mejores-canciones-cancha-sitio-we-speak-football_3_ByIU7LheM.html?srsltid=AfmBOorhKgOXOOGVWo_4q6Zkomuiysq2GH89deX3L_cD_LyMDO3atXz6.

2   This space, the Predio Tita Mattiussi, exists to this day and has become an integral part of the club's sporting infrastructure.

3   I am here again glossing over some aspects of the dark side of the world of Argentine football and its clubs. In 2013, thirty-two-year-old Nicolas Pacheco, a club member and journalist, was beaten by three people and left to drown in that same pool. The motives for the beating were never clarified, despite three people being sentenced for the crime.

7: The Golden Ticket

1   There have been numerous mass deaths due to stampedes in and around football stadiums in the course of the last century. One of the most notorious of these tragic human stampedes is the Heysel Stadium tragedy of 1985 in Belgium, where a panicked crush of Juventus fans attempting to escape advancing Liverpool hooligans caused the collapse of a wall, which resulted in thirty-nine deaths, but it is sadly by far not the most deadly. In Argentina, the "Puerta 12" tragedy in 1968 claimed seventy-one lives after panicked fans tried to exit through what turned out to be a locked gate, with those at the front being crushed by those behind them. Just a few years earlier, in what is still believed to be the greatest such tragedy, an estimated 328 people died in Peru's national stadium under similar circumstances.

2   The concentration of clubs with professional soccer teams in the greater Buenos Aires area is unimaginable to most people. First division alone is currently composed of fourteen teams from the area, and there are another seventeen in second division, eighteen in third division, and nineteen in fourth. Sixty-eight in total, all of which have some degree of hooligan/ultra factions whose game-day movements crisscrossing the city the police used to have to coordinate in order to avoid confrontations. This is no longer the case, only because there are essentially, with few exceptions, no visiting fans allowed at Argentine football matches since 2013, precisely because of the constant outbreaks of violence.

3   A "pastime" that on February 17, 2002, claimed the life of Independiente supporter Gustavo Rivero, in the hours prior to an Avellaneda derby, during an armed confrontation between barrabravas of both clubs in the vicinity of the stadiums.

4   "Argentina Erupts," *Barricada*, no. 13 (January 2002).

5   "Hubo incidentes en Avellaneda," *La Nación*, December 19, 2001.

8: Sleeping Through the Uprising

1   Salta la Banca was a band with explicit left-wing lyrics, whose singer was also a fervent Racing Club fan, that reached mainstream popularity in the mid-2010s. In 2017, however, a group of women accused front man Santi Aysine of sexual abuse, leading the band to suspend activities and disband, with Aysine stating that he was guilty of "exhibiting macho pathologies for which I am so ashamed that I'll be apologizing as many times as necessary," before withdrawing from the public sphere for several years.

2   Level of fanaticism: No matter what was happening in my life or where I lived in the world, I always forced myself to have a bare minimum of $900 in savings. This was the cost of a ticket to Argentina from just about anywhere, and I needed to always be prepared should this glorious moment ever come.

3   *En la Calle: Una lectura anarquista de la crisis neoliberal en Argentina 1997–2007* (Editorial Madreselva, 2011), 161.

4   Moira Birrs, "The Piquetero Movement: Organizing for Democracy and Social Change in Argentina's Informal Sector," *Journal of the International Institute* 12, no. 2 (Winter 2005).

5   *En la Calle*, 125. Ellipsis in original.

9: While You Were Sleeping

1   This quote is actually misattributed to Lenin and seems to be a modification of a comment written by Karl Marx in a letter to Friedrich Engels, which reads as follows: "Only your small-minded German philistine who measures world history by the ell and by what he happens to think are 'interesting news items' could regard twenty years as more than a day where major developments of this kind are concerned, though these may be again succeeded by days into which twenty years are compressed."

2   Fernando de la Rúa, "Cadena nacional: De la Rúa decreta el estado de sitio," public address, December 19, 2001, from Archivo Histórico RTA, 4 min., 32 sec., https://www.archivorta.com.ar/asset/cadena-nacional-de-la-rua-decreta-el-estado-de-sitio-19-12-2001/.

3   "Argentina Erupts," *Barricada*, no. 13 (January 2002).

4   "Argentina Erupts."

5   Alejandro Wall, *¡Academia, Carajo!* (Editorial Sudamericana, 2011), 47.

6   Wall, *¡Academia, Carajo!*, 51.

7   Wall, *¡Academia, Carajo!*, 51.

11: The Long Shadow of the Past

1   Los Olimareños was a Uruguayan folk duo. Due to the political content of their music, they were exiled from Uruguay to Argentina in 1973 at the onset of the Uruguayan military dictatorship. In early 1976, one of the two members of the band went into exile in Argentina, where in March of that same year, he would be arrested by the Argentine dictatorship following the military coup d'état in Argentina. He was released in March 1977. The duo eventually returned to Uruguay in 1984, where they were met by almost a thousand people at the airport,

before performing in Montevideo's mythical Estadio Centenario, host venue of the first FIFA World Cup, in front of fifty thousand spectators during a torrential downpour.

2   The description comes from an event held in 2005 to commemorate twenty-nine years since the disappearance of Resistencia Libertaria militants. "Argentina: La resistencia anarquista a la dictadura," Nodo50, accessed June 17, 2025, https://www.nodo50.org/fau/revista/lucha_50_aniv/46.htm.

3   Hugo Montero and Walter Marini, "Resistencia Libertaria: El anarquismo armado en los 70," *Sudestada*, no. 63 (October 2007), https://revistasudestada.com.ar/articulo/435/resistencia-libertaria-el-anarquismo-armado-en-los-70.

4   Fernando López, "Resistencia Libertaria: Anarchist Opposition to the Last Argentine Dictatorship," interview by Chuck Morse, on Morse's blog, July 15, 2018, translated by Morse, http://www.cwmorse.org/resistencia-libertaria-anarchist-opposition-to-the-last-argentine-dictatorship/#more-639. This excellent interview first appeared in *The New Formulation: An Anti-Authoritarian Review of Books* 2, no. 1 (February 2003).

5   María later became a Mother of Plaza de Mayo, and she remained a tireless fighter not only in defense of the memory of those who fell fighting the dictatorship but for social justice globally, until her death on April 1, 2015.

6   Acción Socialista Libertaria, "La Resistencia Libertaria," Izquierdos Humanos, June 1, 2018, https://izquierdoshumanos.wixsite.com/izquierdoshumanos/single-post/2018/05/31/La-Resistencia-Libertaria.

7   López, "Resistencia Libertaria."

8   "The Invisible Dictatorship: Organization or Irrelevance, Revolutionary Organization and Objectives," *Barricada*, no. 12 (December 2001).

9   López, "Resistencia Libertaria."

10   "Trotskyism vs. Anarchism: Barricada: Which Side of the Barricades Are You On?," *Workers Vanguard*, no. 769 (November 23, 2001): 6, https://www.marxists.org/history/etol/newspape/workersvanguard/2001/0769_23_11_2001.pdf. It is a wonderfully entertaining read and I strongly recommend it.

11   *En la Calle: Una lectura anarquista de la crisis neoliberal en Argentina 1997–2007* (Editorial Madreselva, 2011), 155, 188.

12   "Argentina Erupts," *Barricada*, no. 13 (January 2002).

12: The Day of Revolution, Part 1—Rage: We Are the Children of Those You Killed

1   "Argentina Erupts," *Barricada*, no. 13 (January 2002).

2   "Argentina Erupts."

3   "Argentina Erupts."

4   "Argentina Erupts."

5   The display of the red flag was banned in 1905, having been declared a symbol of "war and disassociation": "Some assert that the red flag represents their demands and rights, while their children need simply to recognize the flag of the Fatherland." Juan Suriano, *Paradoxes of Utopia: Anarchist Culture and Politics in Buenos Aires, 1890–1910*, trans. Chuck Morse (AK Press, 2010), 5.

6   "Argentina Erupts."

7   *En la Calle: Una lectura anarquista de la crisis neoliberal en Argentina 1997–2007* (Editorial Madreselva, 2011), 155, 158.

13: The Day of Revolution, Part 2—At the Intersection of Life and Death

1   In Argentina, *negros* is a racist insult that literally means "blacks," but it is also a prime example of the class character of the construction of racial identity. Argentina has an extremely small Black population, and *negro* is usually used

as a derogatory term to refer to working- or lower-class Argentines who are, as far as skin tone is concerned, usually identical to those aiming the term at them. Many Argentines, unwilling to recognize their racism, will argue that they mean *negro* not as a racist insult but as a reference to the perceived negative, lazy, confrontational attitudes of the people to whom they are referring.

2　*En la Calle: Una lectura anarquista de la crisis neoliberal en Argentina 1997–2007* (Editorial Madreselva, 2011), 191.

3　"El día que la Plaza se volvió a cubrir de sangre," *Clarín*, January 19, 2002, https://www.clarin.com/politica/dia-plaza-volvio-cubrir-sangre_0_S1LlReUeoKl.html.

4　Walter Rodriguez, "Los '90: El sueño trunco de Diego Lamagna," *10 de Diciembre*, October 12, 2019, archived at https://web.archive.org/web/20211019085808/https://rededitorial.com.ar/27/los-90-el-sueno-trunco-de-diego-lamagna-walter-rodriguez/.

5　"El día que la Plaza se volvió a cubrir de sangre."

6　"Las víctimas no olvidan el 20 de diciembre del 2001," *Telam*, October 28, 2020, https://www.telam.com.ar/notas/201310/38432-las-victimas-no-olvidan-el--20-de-diciembre-del-2001.php (archive not available).

7　Alejandro Wall, ¡*Academia, Carajo!* (Editorial Sudamericana, 2011), 64. Esteban Velázquez, as well as his partner, Ernesto Genesio, would eventually be sentenced to a fourteen-year prison sentence for the murder of Claudio Lepratti. Velázquez would be released on parole after serving little more than nine years. He is now an activist in the right-wing political party of ex-president Mauricio Macri, PRO.

8　"El día que la Plaza se volvió a cubrir de sangre."

9　"El día que la Plaza se volvió a cubrir de sangre."

10　"Al G8 la più grave violazione dei diritti umani," *Il Secolo XIX*, October 30, 2008, https://www.ilsecoloxix.it/genova/2008/10/30/news/al-g8-la-piu-grave-violazione-dei-diritti-umani-1.33367778.

14: After the Fall

1　As an interesting aside, all three ceramics factories in the province of Nequén are self-managed and operated by their workers: the aforementioned FaSinPat and Confluencia in the capital city of the province, as well as CerSinPat (short for Cerámica Sin Patrones, or "Ceramics Without Bosses") in the city of Cutral Có, site of one of the first anti-neoliberal piquetero-style uprisings in Argentina, in 1997.

2　"A 20 años del 2001, charla con compañerxs anarquistas presentes en la crisis," *Periódico Gatx Negrx*, November 2021, republished by Revista Adynata, https://www.revistaadynata.com/post/a-20-a%C3%B1os-del-2001-charla-con-compa%C3%B1erxs-anarquistas-presentes-en-la-crisis---peri%C3%B3dico-gatx-negrx.

3　"A 20 años del 2001."

4　Mariana Gabriela Calandra, "El movimiento anarquista en Buenos Aires y La Plata entre 1996 y 2013: Tendencias y devenir durante la crisis y restauración del sistema," paper presented at the Segundo Congreso sobre Anarquismos (Second Congress of Researchers on Anarchism), 2019.

5　The full text of *Anarquismo en el movimiento piquetero* is available at: https://ithanarquista.files.wordpress.com/2020/08/natalia-diaz-anarquismo-en-el-movimiento-piquetero.pdf.

6　Mitchell Abidor, *May Made Me: An Oral History of the 1968 Uprising in France* (AK Press, 2018), 17.

7　Abidor, *May Made Me*, 17.

8　Abidor, *May Made Me*, 17.

9   Pierre Goldman, *Souvenirs d'un Juif polonais né en France* (Seuil, 1975; repr., Editions Points, 2005), 70–71.
10 "A 20 años del 2001."
11 "A 20 años del 2001."
12 *En la Calle: Una lectura anarquista de la crisis neoliberal en Argentina 1997–2007* (Editorial Madreselva, 2011), 192.

15: The Kirchnerist Era

1   "A 20 años del 2001, charla con compañerxs anarquistas presentes en la crisis," *Periódico Gatx Negrx*, November 2021, republished by Revista Adynata, https://www.revistaadynata.com/post/a-20-a%C3%B1os-del-2001-charla-con-compa%C3%B1erxs-anarquistas-presentes-en-la-crisis---peri%C3%B3dico-gatx-negrx.
2   *En la Calle: Una lectura anarquista de la crisis neoliberal en Argentina 1997–2007* (Editorial Madreselva, 2011), 9.
3   *En la Calle*, 9.
4   "A 20 años del 2001."

16: Las Balas No Podrán Frenar el Viento

1   Started in 1995, Eterna Inocencia has become a figurehead of independent, DIY, antifascist, and politically engaged punk rock in Argentina. The popularity of the band allows them to regularly sell out clubs with capacities of over a thousand spectators, but the band continues to manage itself independently of commercial record labels. They maintain strong ties to La Cultura del Barrio, where they last played on October 7, 2023. The five hundred tickets to the show were only available physically at the club and sold out within twenty-four hours.
2   "Argentina: Represión estatal asalta Ateneo Anarquista de Constitución en Buenos Aires," *El Libertario*, accessed June 19, 2025, http://periodicoellibertario.blogspot.com/2018/11/argentina-represion-estatal-asalta.html.
3   *Ateneo* is a common Spanish designation for an anarchist social space that is neither library, nor bookstore, nor social club, nor meeting space but serves as a combination of some or all of these functions. The literal translation to English is "atheneum," a word I'm pretty sure no human has used in conversation in decades, if ever. The most appropriate common-use translation would probably be "social center."
4   Santiago Nuñez, "La Cultura del Barrio: Antifascismo, arte y deporte," *El Grito del Sur*, May 10, 2022, https://elgritodelsur.com.ar/2022/05/la-cultura-del-barrio-antifascismo-arte-y-deporte.html.
5   Nuñez, "La Cultura del Barrio."
6   Julieta Galiano, "Rock y deporte contra el fascismo: La Cultura del Barrio ya tiene su propio documental," *Rolling Stone en Español*, February 15, 2023, https://es.rollingstone.com/la-cultura-del-barrio-documental-arg.
7   Gastón Lippi, "Boxeo popular en la Isla Maciel: Lecciones sobre cómo hacerle frente a todo," *La Tinta*, May 11, 2022, https://latinta.com.ar/2022/05/boxeo-popular-frente-todo.
8   La Cultura del Barrio Official (@laculturadelbarrio.official), "Somos el resultado de ese 19 y 20, somos parte de una organización que nació en esas fechas, fuimos parte de ese momento histórico y lo seguimos siendo después, organizando alternativas desde las bases," Instagram, December 20, 2020, https://www.instagram.com/p/CJCeAoMgJU-/.
9   Nuñez, "La Cultura del Barrio."
10 Gerónimo Kenner, "Una piña al fascismo," Agencia de Noticias Ciencias de

la Comunicación, August 22, 2022, http://anccom.sociales.uba.ar/2022/08/16/una-pina-al-fascismo.

11   Nuñez, "La Cultura del Barrio."

Epilogue: No Te lo Puedo Explicar, Porque No Vas a Entender

1   The exception to this is the 2015 to 2019 mandate of the center-right or right-wing President Mauricio Macri, from the Juntos por el Cambio (Together for Change) coalition.

Appendix 1—Back to the Future: The Return of the Ultraliberal Right in Argentina

1   Hermética was probably inarguably the most important and popular band of the Argentina heavy metal scene. The band split in 1994 due to internal differences, notably political disagreements between lead singer Ricardo Iorio, who was developing right-wing, ultranationalist, and anti-Semitic political positions, and the rest of the band, who continued to hold left-wing, pro-worker, and pro-Indigenous positions. Iorio went on to start the band Almafuerte, while the rest of the ex-Hermética members started Malón. While the vast majority of each band's fans were not overtly political, and there was indeed significant overlap between both groups of fans, there were at times physical conflicts between the rival bands' fan bases.

2   "Y Ahora Qué Pasa? Posición del anarquismo organizado frente a lo que se viene en Argentina," November 21, 2023, statement published jointly by Federación Anarquista Rosario, Organización Anarquista Tucumán, Organización Anarquista Cordoba, Organización Anarquista Cordoba, and Organización Anarquista de Santa Cruz; available at https://www.federacionanarquista.net/y-ahora-que-pasa-posicion-del-anarquismo-organizado-frente-a-lo-que-se-viene-en-argentina/.

3   "Argentina Erupts," *Barricada*, no. 13 (January 2002).

4   "Y Ahora Qué Pasa?"

Appendix 2—Six Months in a Neoliberal Dystopia: Social Cannibalism Versus Mutual Aid in Argentina

1   "La repudiable frase de Javier Milei: 'Si la gente no llegara a fin de mes ya se hubiera muerto,'" *Ámbito*, May 24, 2024, https://www.ambito.com/politica/la-repudiable-frase-javier-milei-si-la-gente-no-llegara-fin-mes-ya-se-hubiera-muerto-n6004357#.

2   "Casi la mitad de la población en Argentina vive en la pobreza, según medición académica," *EFE*, May 16, 2024, https://efe.com/economia/2024-05-16/casi-la-mitad-de-la-poblacion-en-argentina-vive-en-la-pobreza-segun-medicion-academica.

3   For a government in theory so concerned with liberty and "personal freedom," this detail is incredible: If you don't register your public transportation card and continue to travel "anonymously," you pay double the fare.

4   "Argentina tiene uno de los salarios mínimos más bajos de América Latina y la inflación más alta del mundo," *Perfil*, April 2, 2024, https://www.perfil.com/noticias/economia/argentina-tiene-uno-de-los-salarios-minimos-mas-bajos-de-america-latina-y-la-inflacion-mas-alta-del-mundo.phtml.

5   Fernando Brovelli, "Comedores en Argentina: Filas más largas, raciones más pequeñas y ausencia del Estado," *Ámbito*, June 1, 2024, https://www.ambito.com/politica/comedores-argentina-filas-mas-largas-raciones-mas-pequenas-y-ausencia-del-estado-n6008227#.

6   Please remember that Argentina is the world mecca of Trotskyism, which

completely dominates the Marxist left and is even organized into an electoral front of five separate Trotskyist parties, the largest being Partido Obrero and Partido de los Trabajadores Socialistas. The coalition garners around 3 percent of the vote in national elections.

7   "Repartidores atacaron una comisaría y quemaron autos y un patrullero tras el asesinato de un colega," *La Nación*, May 28, 2024, https://www.lanacion.com.ar/seguridad/violenta-protesta-de-deliverys-tras-el-crimen-de-un-repartidor-en-loma-hermosa-nid27052024.

Image Credits

Page 74: Tomas Rothaus
Page 75: (left & right) Tomas Rothaus
Page 76: (top left & top right) Tomas Rothaus; (bottom) *Clarín*, March 3, 1999
Page 78: *Olé*
Page 81: Sergio Goya, *Clarín*
Page 82: Néstor Sieira, *Clarín*
Page 83: (top & bottom) *Clarín*, March 5, 1999
Page 84: (top) *Olé*; (bottom) Mario Quinteros, *Olé*
Page 86: *Olé*
Page 87: (left) *Clarín*; (right) *Olé*
Page 88: (top & bottom) Tomas Rothaus
Page 89: Tomas Rothaus
Page 91: N. Pisarenko, *La Nación*, December 3, 2001
Page 92: *La Nación*
Page 94: *Clarín*
Page 96: *Diario Popular*
Page 97: (top & bottom) Gustavo Garello, *Clarín*
Page 99: Claudia Conteris, *Diario Popular*
Page 101: *Clarín*
Page 102: (left) *Clarín*, December 2, 2001; (right) *La Nación*, December 2, 2001
Page 103: Tomas Rothaus
Page 104: Tomas Rothaus
Page 106: *Clarín*
Page 112: Gustavo Fidanza and Hernán España, *Diario Popular*
Page 114: *Barricada*, no. 13
Page 116: (top) *Clarín*; (bottom) Sergio Goya, *Clarín*
Page 120: Tomas Varnagy
Page 121: Tomas Varnagy
Page 122: (top) Archivo General de la Nación / Martin Lucesole; (bottom) Tomas
    Varnagy
Page 124: Acción Socialista Libertaria
Page 128: Tomas Rothaus
Page 130: Seba Delacruz
Page 132: Editorial Madreselva
Page 134: Acción Socialista Libertaria
Page 139: (top) Tomas Rothaus; (bottom) Acción Socialista Libertaria
Page 142: *Workers Vanguard*
Page 146: Carlos Barria, *La Nación*
Page 147: Tomas Varnagy
Page 148: (top) *Diario Popular*, December 21, 2001; (bottom) Tomas Varnagy
Page 150: (left) *Diario Popular*, December 21, 2001; (right) *Prensa Obrera*, no. 735,
    December 28, 2001
Page 151: (top & bottom) Tomas Varnagy
Page 152: Hernan Zenteno, *La Nación*
Page 153: (left) *Clarín*; (right) *La Nación*
Page 155: *Diario Popular*
Page 156: *La Nación*
Page 161: Gustavo Correa, *Clarín*, December 28, 2001
Page 163: Agencia Rosario, *Clarín*, December 21, 2001
Page 165: (top & bottom) Tomas Varnagy
Page 167: *Barricada*, no. 13
Page 168: *Clarín*

Page 170: *La Nación*
Page 172: Prensa Obrera
Page 173: *Contracorriente*
Page 174: *Clarín*, December 29, 2001
Page 175: Carlos Villoldo, *Clarín*, December 29, 2001
Page 177: (top & bottom) Tomas Rothaus
Page 179: CORREPI
Page 182: Presidencia de la Nación Argentina (Creative Commons)
Page 185: Tomas Rothaus
Page 186: Presidencia de la Nación Argentina
Page 188: Tomas Rothaus
Page 190: Tomas Rothaus
Page 192: (top & bottom) Gastón Marin
Page 193: Gastón Marin
Page 194: Gastón Marin
Page 195: Gastón Marin
Page 196: (top & bottom) Juan Lijtmaer
Page 197: Nicolás Bondarenko
Page 198: Federico Ernesto Imas
Page 199: Prensa CA Atlanta
Page 200: Federico Ernesto Imas
Page 201: Federico Ernesto Imas
Page 202: Lucas Agustín (Creative Commons)
Page 204: Federico Imas
Page 207: (top) Federico Imas; (bottom) Enzo Ariel Castillo (Creative Commons)
Page 209: Alvaro Camacho (Creative Commons)
Page 212: Federico Imas
Page 215: Tomas Rothaus
Page 219: Federación Anarquista de Rosario
Page 221: Nicolás Bondarenko
Page 223: Acción Socialista Libertaria
Page 225: Federico Imas
Page 227: Federico Imas
Page 229: Nicolás Bondarenko
Page 232: (top) Nicolás Bondarenko; (bottom) Juan Lijtmaer
Page 236: Acción Socialista Libertaria

Index

Page numbers in *italic* refer to illustrations. "Passim" (literally "scattered") indicates intermittent discussion of a topic over a cluster of pages.

About the Contributors

Tomas Rothaus is a lifelong anarchist and antifascist as well as an athlete and a father. He was born in Buenos Aires, Argentina, and has led a nomadic life with stops in Athens, Boston, Buenos Aires, and Paris, followed by longer stints in Germany and, more recently, a return to Argentina. He has been involved with a broad range of organizations including the CNT-Vignoles, Collectif Anti-Expulsions (Anti-Deportation Collective), Barricada Collective, Northeastern Federation of Anarcho-Communists, Antifaschistische Linke International, and Acción Antifascista Buenos Aires. Over the past twenty-plus years, he has been an active participant in militant demonstrations and antifascist mobilizations including the 2001 Bush inauguration, the FTAA summit in Quebec, the 2007 G8 summit in Rostock, and the 2011 mobilization to stop the march of several thousand neo-Nazis in the city of Dresden. PM Press published his first book, *Another War Is Possible*, in 2025.

Gabriel Kuhn is an Austrian-born writer and translator living in Sweden. His numerous authored and edited books include *From Hash Rebels to Urban Guerrillas: A Documentary History of the 2nd of June Movement*; *All Power to the Councils! A Documentary History of the German Revolution of 1918–1919*; *Turning Money into Rebellion: The Unlikely Story of Denmark's Revolutionary Bank Robbers*; *Liberating Sápmi: Indigenous Resistance in Europe's Far North*; and *Soccer vs. the State: Tackling Football and Radical Politics*.

ABOUT PM PRESS

PM Press is an independent, radical publisher of critically necessary books for our tumultuous times. Our aim is to deliver bold political ideas and vital stories to all walks of life and arm the dreamers to demand the impossible. Founded in 2007 by a small group of people with decades of publishing, media, and organizing experience, we have sold millions of copies of our books, most often one at a time, face to face. We're old enough to know what we're doing and young enough to know what's at stake. Join us to create a better world.

PM Press
PO Box 23912
Oakland, CA 94623
www.pmpress.org

PM Press in Europe
europe@pmpress.org
www.pmpress.org.uk

FRIENDS OF PM PRESS

These are indisputably momentous times—the financial system is melting down globally and the Empire is stumbling. Now more than ever there is a vital need for radical ideas.

In the many years since its founding—and on a mere shoestring—PM Press has risen to the formidable challenge of publishing and distributing knowledge and entertainment for the struggles ahead. With hundreds of releases to date, we have published an impressive and stimulating array of literature, art, music, politics, and culture. Using every available medium, we've succeeded in connecting those hungry for ideas and information to those putting them into practice.

Friends of PM allows you to directly help impact, amplify, and revitalize the discourse and actions of radical writers, filmmakers, and artists. It provides us with a stable foundation from which we can build upon our early successes and provides a much-needed subsidy for the materials that can't necessarily pay their own way. You can help make that happen—and receive every new title automatically delivered to your door once a month—by joining as a Friend of PM Press. And, we'll throw in a free T-shirt when you sign up.

Here are your options:

- **$30 a month** Get all books and pamphlets plus a 50% discount on all webstore purchases

- **$40 a month** Get all PM Press releases (including CDs and DVDs) plus a 50% discount on all webstore purchases

- **$100 a month** Superstar—Everything plus PM merchandise, free downloads, and a 50% discount on all webstore purchases

For those who can't afford $30 or more a month, we have **Sustainer Rates** at $15, $10, and $5. Sustainers get a free PM Press T-shirt and a 50% discount on all purchases from our website.

Your Visa or Mastercard will be billed once a month, until you tell us to stop. Or until our efforts succeed in bringing the revolution around. Or the financial meltdown of Capital makes plastic redundant. Whichever comes first.

Another War Is Possible: Militant Anarchist Experiences in the Antiglobalization Era

Tomas Rothaus
with a Foreword by CrimethInc.

ISBN: 979-8-88744-105-4
$28.95   416 pages

This is history come to life.

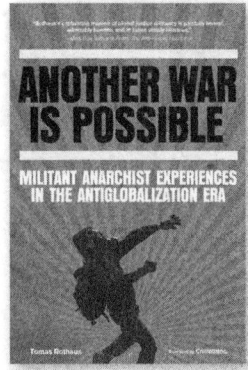

At the turn of the century, the movement against capitalist globalization exploded onto the world stage with mass mobilizations in Quebec City, Washington, Genoa, and other cities. Anarchists faced off against heads of state, captains of industry, and riot police by the thousands. While the authorities sought to bend all living things to the profit imperative, anarchists set out to demonstrate a way of fighting that could open the road to a future beyond capitalism. The twenty-first century was up for grabs. And every time, Tomas Rothaus was there, fighting on the front line.

In *Another War Is Possible*, we follow Tomas from his days as a young militant to his tenure editing the publication *Barricada*. In vivid prose, he recounts the lessons he learned from veterans of the Spanish CNT—his first experience trading blows with police in the streets of Paris—and his adventures slipping across borders to participate in epoch-making riots. With Tomas, we breathe tear gas, we tear down fences, we tour the squats and battlefields of three continents.

Along the way, Tomas shows that the tragedies of the twenty-first century were not inevitable—that another war was possible. His testimony is proof that another world remains possible today.

"**Another War Is Possible** *is a compelling invitation to revolutionaries of the past, present, and future to think critically and historically about their years of struggle. Rothaus's captivating memoir of global justice militancy beyond puppets and platitudes is painfully honest, admirably humble, and at times simply hilarious.*"
—Mark Bray, author of *Antifa: The Anti-Fascist Handbook*

"*In an age where anarchist ideas are being both embraced by a new generation of activists and demonized by the rich and powerful, Rothaus shines a light onto those who were punching Nazis and fighting the police before the rise of Trumpism. Part riot diary and part personal reflection,* **Another War Is Possible** *is a must-read for anyone looking for both an exciting page-turner and an inside look at militant anticapitalist and antifascist resistance.*"
—It's Going Down

From Riot to Insurrection: The G8 Summit of 2001 & The Battle of Genoa

Tomas Rothaus with a Foreword by Mark Bray

ISBN: 979-8-88744-172-6
$23.95   256 pages

"... but in the end, we will win."

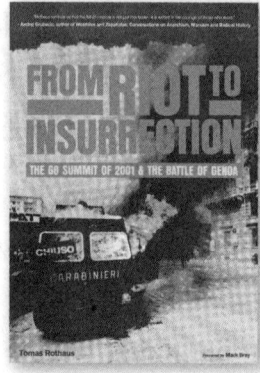

In 1992, following the collapse of the Eastern Bloc, the ruling class declared the end of history and the triumph of capitalism. Less than two years later, the Zapatista uprising in Chiapas galvanized a worldwide movement against capitalist globalization. All around the world, history began to crack and move again, like a frozen river thawing in the spring.

This momentum culminated in July 2001 with the protests against the G8 summit, in what became known as the battle of Genoa. For days, tens of thousands of aspiring revolutionaries clashed with an army of police in a city on fire.

From Riot to Insurrection offers a vivid account of this pivotal moment. In electrifying prose, Tomas Rothaus escorts the reader through those explosive days, recounting the chaotic street battles, the exhilarating sense of possibility, the heart-wrenching moments of triumph and loss. This is an ode to audacity, to what we become capable of when we believe in our collective power.

The real lesson of the end of the Cold War is not that capitalism is inevitable; it is that empires always fall. While "socialism without freedom" had crumbled by 1992, "freedom without socialism" has yet to expire. That revolution remains possible—even today—provided that we fight for it the way people did in Genoa.

"Tomas Rothaus's writing is able to thread the ever-thin needle between lived history, the rush of revolutionary moments, incisive analysis, and humor in his writings on Genoa. I cannot recommend his work highly enough to anyone who wants to understand both radical anarchist politics and the lessons that the antiglobalization movement of the 1990s and early 2000s has to offer us."
—Charlie Allison, author of *No Harmless Power: The Life and Times of the Ukrainian Anarchist Nestor Makhno*

Soccer vs. the State: Tackling Football and Radical Politics

Gabriel Kuhn
with a Foreword by Boff Whalley

ISBN: 978-1-62963-572-9
$20.00   352 pages

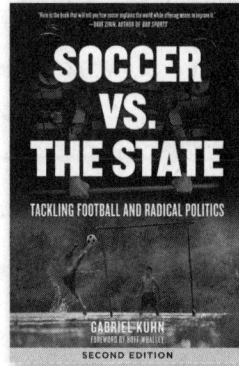

Soccer has turned into a multi-billion-dollar industry. Professionalism and commercialization dominate its global image. Yet the game retains a rebellious side, maybe more so than any other sport co-opted by moneymakers and corrupt politicians. From its roots in working-class England to political protests by players and fans, and a current radical soccer underground, the notion of football as the "people's game" has been kept alive by numerous individuals, teams, and communities.

This book not only traces this history but also reflects on common criticisms— that soccer ferments nationalism, serves right-wing powers, and fosters competitiveness—exploring alternative perspectives and practical examples of egalitarian DIY soccer. *Soccer vs. the State* serves both as an orientation for the politically conscious football supporter and as an inspiration for those who try to pursue the love of the game away from televisions and big stadiums, bringing it to back alleys and muddy pastures.

This second edition has been expanded to cover events of recent years, including the involvement of soccer fans in the Middle Eastern uprisings of 2011–2013, the FIFA scandal of 2015, and the 2017 strike by the Danish women's team.

"Gabriel Kuhn's Soccer vs. the State *is a wondrous reminder of all the times and ways and places where football has slipped its chains and offers what it always promised: new solidarities and identities, a site of resistance, a celebration of spontaneity and play."*
—David Goldblatt, author of *The Ball Is Round* and *The Game of Our Lives*

"There is no sport that reflects the place where sports and politics collide quite like soccer. Athlete-activist Gabriel Kuhn has captured that by going to a place where other sports writers fear to tread. Here is the book that will tell you how soccer explains the world while offering means to improve it."
—Dave Zirin, author of *Game Over* and *Brazil's Dance with the Devil*

"Gabriel Kuhn has written the programme notes for the most important match of all, The People's Game vs. Modern Football."
—Mark Perryman, cofounder of Philosophy Football

The George Floyd Uprising

Edited by Vortex Group

ISBN: 978-1-62963-966-6
$22.95   288 pages

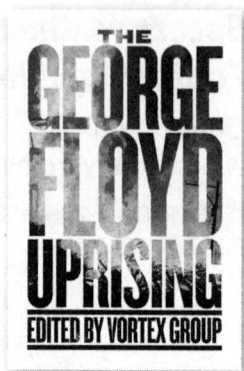

In the summer of 2020, America experienced one of the biggest uprisings in half a century. Waves of enraged citizens took to the streets in Minneapolis to decry the murder of George Floyd at the hands of the police. Battles broke out night after night, with a pandemic-weary populace fighting the police and eventually burning down the Third Precinct. The revolt soon spread to cities large and small across the country, where protesters set police cars on fire, looted luxury shopping districts, and forced the president into hiding in a bunker beneath the White House. As the initial crest receded, localized rebellions continued to erupt throughout the summer and into the fall in Atlanta, Chicago, Kenosha, Louisville, Philadelphia, and elsewhere.

Written during the riots, *The George Floyd Uprising* is a compendium of the most radical writing to come out of that long, hot summer. These incendiary dispatches—from those on the front lines of the struggle—examine the revolt and the obstacles it confronted. It paints a picture of abolition in practice, discusses how the presence of weapons in the uprising and the threat of armed struggle play out in an American context, and shows how the state responds to and pacifies rebellions. *The George Floyd Uprising* poses new social, tactical, and strategic plans for those actively seeking to expand and intensify revolts of the future. This practical, inspiring collection is essential reading for all those hard at work toppling the state and creating a new revolutionary tradition.

"*Exemplary reflections from today's frontline warriors that will disconcert liberals but inspire young people who want to live the struggle in the revolutionary tradition of Robert F. Williams, the Watts 65 rebels, and Deacons for Defense and Justice.*"
—Mike Davis, author of *Planet of Slums* and *Old Gods, New Enigmas*

"*This anthology resists police and vigilante murders. It is not an easy read. We will not all agree on its analyses or advocacy. Yet, its integrity, clarity, vulnerability, love and rage are clear. As a librarian who archives liberators and liberation movements, I recognize essential reading as a reflection of ourselves and our fears. With resolution, this text resonates with narratives of mini-Atticas. The 1971 prison rebellion and murderous repression by government and officialdom reveal the crises that spark radical movements and increasing calls for self-defense. This volume offers our cracked mirrors as an opportunity to scrutinize missteps and possibilities, and hopefully choose wisely even in our sacrifices.*"
—Joy James, author of *Resisting State Violence: Radicalism, Gender, and Race in U.S. Culture*

The Hands That Crafted the Bomb: The Making of a Lifelong Antifascist

Josh Fernandez

ISBN: 979-8-88744-023-1
$22.95   256 pages

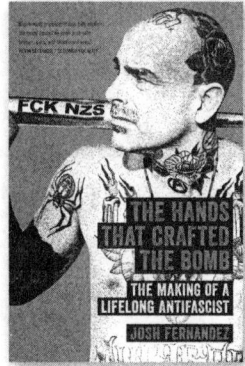

Josh Fernandez is a community college professor in Northern California who finds himself under investigation for "soliciting students for potentially dangerous activities" after starting an antifascist club on campus.

As Fernandez spends the year defending his job, he reflects on a life lived in protest of the status quo, swept up in chaos and rage, from his childhood in Boston dealing with a mentally ill father and a new family to a move to Davis, California, where, in the basement shows of the early '90s, Nazi boneheads proliferated the music scene, looking for heads to crack. His crew's first attempts at an antifascist group fall short when a member dies in a knife fight.

A born antiauthoritarian, filled with an untamable rage, Fernandez rails against the system and aggressively chooses the path of most resistance. This leads to long spates of living in his car, strung out on drugs, and robbing the whiteboys coming home from the clubs at night. He eventually realizes that his rage needs an outlet and finds relief for his existential dread in the form of running. And fighting Nazis. Fernandez cobbles together a life for himself as a writing professor, a facilitator of a self-defense collective, a boots-on-the-ground participant in antifa work, and a proud father of two children he unapologetically raises to question authority.

"Fernandez is scathing on the corporate-minded liberals who talk about equity and diversity, antiracism, and gay rights but can't deal with people actually defending themselves or challenging authority. What he offers instead isn't heroics or militant slogans or even measured analysis—it's the messy story of a 'fucked-up person' trying to 'channel rage into something less destructive,' a guy who tends to run face-first into danger but also has the good sense to run away screaming when confronted with a knife-wielding racist. Fernandez's account of violence, trauma, and loneliness is hard to read in places, but there's an underlying sweetness here, a hopefulness about flawed people helping each other out, a sense that if we can get past the lies, we can remake this world together."
—Matthew N. Lyons, author of *Insurgent Supremacists: The U.S. Far Right's Challenge to State and Empire*

We Go Where They Go: The Story of Anti-Racist Action

Shannon Clay, Lady, Kristin Schwartz, and Michael Staudenmaier with a Foreword by Gord Hill

ISBN: 978-1-62963-972-7 (paperback)
       978-1-62963-977-2 (hardcover)
$24.95/$59.95   320 pages

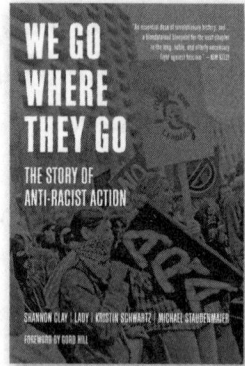

What does it mean to risk all for your beliefs? How do you fight an enemy in your midst? *We Go Where They Go* recounts the thrilling story of a massive forgotten youth movement that set the stage for today's antifascist organizing in North America. When skinheads and punks in the late 1980s found their communities invaded by white supremacists and neo-nazis, they fought back. Influenced by anarchism, feminism, Black liberation, and Indigenous sovereignty, they created Anti-Racist Action. At ARA's height in the 1990s, thousands of dedicated activists in hundreds of chapters joined the fights—political and sometimes physical—against nazis, the Ku Klux Klan, antiabortion fundamentalists, and racist police. Before media pundits, cynical politicians, and your uncle discovered "antifa," Anti-Racist Action was bringing it to the streets.

Based on extensive interviews with dozens of ARA participants, *We Go Where They Go* tells ARA's story from within, giving voice to those who risked their safety in their own defense and in solidarity with others. In reproducing the posters, zines, propaganda, and photos of the movement itself, this essential work of radical history illustrates how cultural scenes can become powerful forces for change. Here at last is the story of an organic yet highly organized movement, exploring both its triumphs and failures, and offering valuable lessons for today's generation of activists and rabble-rousers. *We Go Where They Go* is a page-turning history of grassroots antiracism. More than just inspiration, it's a roadmap.

"I was a big supporter and it was an honor to work with the Anti-Racist Action movement. Their unapologetic and uncompromising opposition to racism and fascism in the streets, in the government, and in the mosh pit continues to be inspiring to this day."
—Tom Morello

It Did Happen Here: An Antifascist People's History

Edited by Moe Bowstern, Mic Crenshaw, Alec Dunn, Celina Flores, Julie Perini, and Erin Yanke

ISBN: 978-1-62963-351-0
$21.95   304 pages

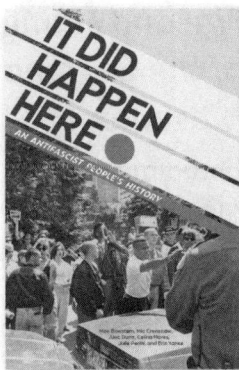

Portland, Oregon, 1988: the brutal murder of Ethiopian immigrant Mulugeta Seraw by racist skinheads shocked the city. In response disparate groups quickly came together to organize against white nationalist violence and right-wing organizing throughout the Rose City and the Pacific Northwest.

It Did Happen Here compiles interviews with dozens of people who worked together during the waning decades of the twentieth century to reveal an inspiring collaboration between groups of immigrants, civil rights activists, militant youth, and queer organizers. This oral history focuses on participants in three core groups: the Portland chapters of Anti-Racist Action, Skinheads Against Racial Prejudice, and the Coalition for Human Dignity.

Using a diversity of tactics—from out-and-out brawls on the streets and at punk shows, to behind-the-scenes intelligence gathering—brave antiracists unified on their home ground over and over, directly attacking right-wing fascists and exposing white nationalist organizations and neo-nazi skinheads. Embattled by police and unsupported by the city, these citizen activists eventually drove the boneheads out of the music scene and off the streets of Portland. This book shares their stories about what worked, what didn't, and ideas on how to continue the fight.

"By the time I moved my queer little family to Portland at the turn of the millennium, the city had a reputation as a homo-friendly bastion of progressive politics, so we were somewhat taken aback when my daughter's racially diverse sports team was met with a burning cross at a suburban game. So much progress had been made yet, at times, it felt like the past hadn't gone anywhere. If only we'd had It Did Happen Here. This documentary project tells the forgotten history of Portland's roots as a haven for white supremacists and recounts the ways antiracists formed coalitions across subcultures to protect the vulnerable and fight the good fight against nazi boneheads and the bigoted right. Through the voices of lived experience, It Did Happen Here illuminates community dynamics and lays out ideas and inspiration for long-term and nonpolice solutions to poverty and hatred."
—Ariel Gore, author of We Were Witches

Fire and Flames: A History of the German Autonomist Movement

Geronimo
with an Introduction by George
Katsiaficas and Afterword by Gabriel
Kuhn

ISBN: 978-1-60486-097-9
$19.95   256 pages

Fire and Flames was the first comprehensive study of the German autonomous movement ever published. Released in 1990, it reached its fifth edition by 1997, with the legendary German *Konkret* journal concluding that "the movement had produced its own classic." The author, writing under the pseudonym of Geronimo, has been an autonomous activist since the movement burst onto the scene in 1980–81. In this book, he traces its origins in the Italian *Autonomia* project and the German social movements of the 1970s, before describing the battles for squats, "free spaces," and alternative forms of living that defined the first decade of the autonomous movement. Tactics of the "Autonome" were militant, including the construction of barricades or throwing molotov cocktails at the police. Because of their outfit (heavy black clothing, ski masks, helmets), the Autonome were dubbed the "Black Bloc" by the German media, and their tactics have been successfully adopted and employed at anti-capitalist protests worldwide.

Fire and Flames is no detached academic study, but a passionate, hands-on, and engaging account of the beginnings of one of Europe's most intriguing protest movements of the last thirty years. An introduction by George Katsiaficas, author of *The Subversion of Politics*, and an afterword by Gabriel Kuhn, a long-time autonomous activist and author, add historical context and an update on the current state of the Autonomen.

"The target audience is not the academic middle-class with passive sympathies for rioting, nor the all-knowing critical critics, but the activists of a young generation."
— Edition I.D. Archiv

"Some years ago, an experienced autonomous activist from Berlin sat down, talked to friends and comrades about the development of the scene, and, with Fire and Flames, *wrote the best book about the movement that we have."*
— Düsseldorfer Stadtzeitung für Politik und Kultur

Mutual Aid: An Illuminated Factor of Evolution

Peter Kropotkin
Illustrated by N.O. Bonzo with an
Introduction by David Graeber &
Andrej Grubačić, Foreword by Ruth
Kinna, Postscript by GATS, and an
Afterword by Allan Antliff

ISBN: 978-1-62963-874-4 (paperback)
     978-1-62963-875-1 (hardcover)
$30.00/$70.00   336 pages

One hundred years after his death, Peter Kropotkin is still one of the most inspirational figures of the anarchist movement. It is often forgotten that Kropotkin was also a world-renowned geographer whose seminal critique of the hypothesis of competition promoted by social Darwinism helped revolutionize modern evolutionary theory. An admirer of Darwin, he used his observations of life in Siberia as the basis for his 1902 collection of essays *Mutual Aid: A Factor of Evolution*. Kropotkin demonstrated that mutually beneficial cooperation and reciprocity—in both individuals and as a species—plays a far more important role in the animal kingdom and human societies than does individualized competitive struggle. Kropotkin carefully crafted his theory making the science accessible. His account of nature rejected Rousseau's romantic depictions and ethical socialist ideas that cooperation was motivated by the notion of "universal love." His understanding of the dynamics of social evolution shows us the power of cooperation—whether it is bison defending themselves against a predator or workers unionizing against their boss. His message is clear: solidarity is strength!

Every page of this new edition of *Mutual Aid* has been beautifully illustrated by one of anarchism's most celebrated current artists, N.O. Bonzo. The reader will also enjoy original artwork by GATS and insightful commentary by David Graeber, Ruth Kinna, Andrej Grubačić, and Allan Antliff.

"N.O. Bonzo has created a rare document, updating Kropotkin's anarchist classic Mutual Aid, *by intertwining compelling imagery with an updated text. Filled with illustrious examples, their art gives the words and histories, past and present, resonance for new generations to seed flowers of cooperation to push through the concrete of resistance to show liberatory possibilities for collective futures."*
—scott crow, author of *Black Flags and Windmills* and *Setting Sights*

Insurgent Supremacists: The U.S. Far Right's Challenge to State and Empire

Matthew N. Lyons

ISBN: 978-162-963-511-8
$24.95   384 pages

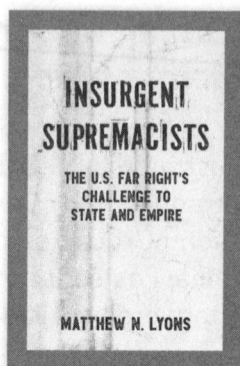

INSURGENT
SUPREMACISTS

THE U.S. FAR RIGHT'S
CHALLENGE TO
STATE AND EMPIRE

MATTHEW N. LYONS

A major study of movements that strive to overthrow the U.S. government, that often claim to be anti-imperialist and sometimes even anti-capitalist yet also consciously promote inequality, hierarchy, and domination, generally along explicitly racist, sexist, and homophobic lines. Revolutionaries of the far right: insurgent supremacists.

In this book, Matthew N. Lyons takes readers on a tour of neo-nazis and Christian theocrats, by way of the patriot movement, the LaRouchites, and the alt-right. Supplementing this, thematic sections explore specific dimensions of far-right politics, regarding gender, decentralism, and anti-imperialism.

Intervening directly in debates within left and antifascist movements, Lyons examines both the widespread use and abuse of the term "fascism," and the relationship between federal security forces and the paramilitary right. His final chapter offers a preliminary analysis of the Trump presidential administration's relationship with far-right politics and the organized far right's shifting responses to it.

Both for its analysis and as a guide to our opponents, *Insurgent Supremacists* promises to be a powerful tool in organizing to resist the forces at the cutting edge of reaction today.

"Drawing on deep expertise and years of experience tracking the shifting constellations of the insurrectionist right, Matthew Lyons guides readers through the history, ideology, and agendas of these seemingly obscure but increasingly powerful political forces in America. If you want to understand them, you need to read this book."
—Mark Rupert, author of *Ideologies of Globalization: Contending Visions of a New World Order*

"A brilliant exploration of the U.S. far right today and its many different strains. In wonderfully clearheaded, deeply researched prose, Matthew N. Lyons provides a cogent and innovative analysis of far-right movements, using historical examination and his own contemporary reporting to expose surprising truths about the far right's base, motivations, and ambivalent relationship to capitalism. A vital resource for anyone who wants to fight the alt-right and other 'insurgent supremacists' in our midst."
—Donna Minkowitz, author of *Ferocious Romance: What My Encounters with the Right Taught Me about Sex, God, and Fury*